THE C BOOK
Featuring the draft
ANSI C Standard

THE C BOOK
Featuring the draft
ANSI C Standard

Mike Banahan
The Instruction Set Ltd

Addison-Wesley Publishing Company
Wokingham, England · Reading, Massachusetts · Menlo Park, California
New York · Don Mills, Ontario · Amsterdam · Bonn · Sydney
Singapore · Tokyo · Madrid · Bogota · Santiago · San Juan

the Instruction set

The Instruction Set Series
Published in collaboration with The Instruction Set Ltd.

© 1988 The Instruction Set Ltd.
© 1988 Addison-Wesley Publishers Ltd.
© 1988 Addison-Wesley Publishing Company, Inc.

Cover design by Crayon Design of Henley-on-Thames.
This book was typeset using the SQtroff typesetting package.
Printed and bound in Great Britain by The Bath Press, Avon.
First printed 1988.

British Library Cataloguing in Publication Data

Banahan, M.F.
   The C Book : featuring the draft ANSI C
   Standard. – (The Instruction set series).
   1. C (Computer program language)
   I. Title   II. Series
   005.13′3   QA76.73.C15

   ISBN 0–201–17370–0

Library of Congress Cataloging in Publication Data

Banahan, Mike.
   The C book, featuring the draft ANSI C standard.

   (The Instruction set)
   Includes index.
   1. C (Computer program language)   I. Title.
II. Series
QA76.73.C15B36 1987 005.13′3 87–1225
ISBN 0–201–17370–0

Trademark notices
UNIX is a trademark of AT&T in the USA and other countries.
DEC, VAX and PDP are trademarks of Digital Equipment Corporation.

Preface

This is a book for two groups of people. It's for those who have never used C before and who want to learn about a language that has become, quietly and without fuss, an important tool for systems and applications programmers alike. It's also for those who already know C, but want to learn more about the language, especially the proposed ANSI standard for C. The language described here is *not* the language in current use (early 1987), but the proposed ANSI Standard C Programming Language as defined by the X3J11 standard committee. It is expected that this standard will rapidly become the version of C that is used by the majority of programmers.

From the beginner's point of view, the book is intended for programmers who already have some experience of using a modern, high level procedural programming language. C isn't really appropriate for complete beginners – though many have managed to use it – so the book will assume that its readers have already done battle with the notions of statements, variables, conditional execution, arrays, procedures (or subroutines) and so on. Instead of wasting your time by ploughing through tedious descriptions of how to add two numbers together and explaining that the symbol for multiplication is *, the book will concentrate on the things that are special to C. In particular, it's the *way* that C is used which will be emphasized.

The second type of reader will already know C, but be interested in the new proposals for the language, and how previously valid programs are affected. For these readers, the difference is that they know the language but want to know what the new stuff means – for the beginner that may not seem to be of very much interest. Oddly enough, the 'old' and new standards *are* an issue for the beginner too. At the time that this book is written, there are no compilers available to try out. It seems a fair bet that for some time to come, programmers will have to exist in a world where they might encounter either the new or the old language depending on the system in use. For that reason, the book will highlight where the old and new features differ seriously. Beginners will be able to understand the peculiar error messages that an old compiler will generate when faced with a program written the new way, and old hands who have been using C previously will be able to spot the changes more easily.

Typographical conventions

The book will try hard to stick to a consistent style in its use of special or technical terms. Words with a special meaning to C, such as **reserved words** or the names of **library functions**, will be printed in a different typeface. Examples are `int` and `printf`. Terms used by the book that have a meaning not to C but in the **language reference manual** or the text of the book, will be **bold** if they have not been introduced recently. They will *not* be bold everywhere, because that rapidly annoys the reader. As you have noticed, italics will also be used for emphasis from time to time, also to introduce loosely defined terms. Occasionally quote marks will be used around 'special terms' if there is a danger of them being understood in their normal English meaning because of surrounding context. Anything else will be at the whim of the author, or simply by accident.

The ANSI standard

The proposed standard is *not* yet a standard, or necessarily close to what any eventual standard will look like. As it stands it is a draft, waiting for public reaction and comment. There is a fair chance that public comment will result in it changing to some extent from the document currently published, although few people would realistically expect that the changes will be profound. Copies are available from the ANSI secretariat, whose address can be found at the end of this preface. Despite all that, this book will refer to the 'Standard' for brevity; readers are expected to understand that it is the 'draft standard' that is meant.

The standard has been written by members of the X3J11 committee, working under the auspices of the American National Standards Institute, usually abbreviated to ANSI. The committee is made up of members from industry, representing suppliers and users of the language, as well as those concerned with teaching the language to new users. The committee has tried to reach a usable definition of the language that allows portable programs to be written, while keeping the spirit of the language as it was in days gone by. C is a language that was designed to allow efficient access to the low level features of many computers but not to display the rudimentary data structures and control of flow that is exhibited by typical assemblers and assembly language programs. Most programmers who have used assembly code in the past have been surprised to find that C can offer the flexibility and power, as well as the efficiency of assembly code, yet still offer the productivity and in most cases the portability of high level language programs. The Committee has tried hard to ensure that the new standard works the same way: in fact a number of improvements have been introduced that allow for even greater efficiency to be achieved in the right circumstances.

In particular, the work that has been done to standardize the libraries will prove to be an enormous benefit to applications programmers.

The original design of C was to allow systems programmers to enjoy the benefits outlined above. Since its popularity has spread with the spread of UNIX, C has become more widely used by programmers who simply want to use it as a language for general-purpose programming. It is in the field of applications programming that C is at its weakest, largely because of its lack of built-in I/O; something that most other languages take pains to describe. In fact, it is probably *because* of this lack of built-in functions that C has been as successful as it has. Pascal has been seriously hampered because of its painful, rudimentary views on I/O, as was Algol before it. Because C has no defined I/O, implementors have been able to provide whatever the customer wanted without having to do violence to the design of C itself.

The lack of a well designed I/O subsystem has, however, caused problems for applications programmers. Without a guaranteed library of I/O functions such as the Standard I/O Library available with UNIX, it is hard to write programs that both perform input or output and are portable. Programmers can end up constrained to one particular implementation of C, with real portability problems if the programs have to be moved to a new environment. One way to get around this is to write your own libraries, but unfortunately a lot of the sort of things that you want from such a library are inherently non-portable – they have to be re-designed in different environments. So the long and the short of it is that C is often thought of coming in two parts: a language that allows you to write programs that can't talk to anyone, and, for most C programmers, a library that is essential if your programs aren't to be some sort of latter day pinball wizard, deaf dumb and blind.

The Standard knows this and provides for it. A large part of the Standard is the definition of the library functions that must be supplied for a hosted environment. A hosted environment is one that provides libraries. The standard permits both hosted and non-hosted environments and goes to some length to differentiate between them. Who would want to go without libraries? Well, anybody writing 'stand alone' programs. Operating systems, embedded systems like washing machine controllers and firmware for instrumentation, unusual library packages: these are all examples of the case where a hosted environment might be inappropriate. Programs written for a hosted environment have to be aware of the fact that the names of *all* the library functions are reserved for use by the implementation. There is no such restriction on the programmer working in a non-hosted environment, although it isn't a good idea to go using names that are used in the standard library, simply because it will mislead readers of the program. Chapter 9 describes the names and uses of the library functions, but you may also wish to refer to the Standard itself.

Order of topics

The order of presentation of topics in this book follows closely the order that is taught in The Instruction Set's introductory course. It starts with an overview of the essential parts of the language that will let you start to write useful programs quite quickly. The introduction is followed by a detailed coverage of the material that was ignored before, then it goes on to discuss the standard libraries in depth. This means that in principle, if you felt so inclined, you could read the book as far as you like and stop, yet still have learnt a reasonably coherent subset of the language. Previous experience of C will render Chapter 1 a bit slow, but it is still worth persevering with it, if only once.

Example programs
The examples given have not been tested by a standard-conforming compiler, although many of them have been checked using a C-like language called C++. The C++ language has provided some of the input to the Standard Committee's work, and some of the ideas in the Standard were taken and put into C++ as the work continued. However, there are significant differences between the languages at the moment, although it is believed that plans for C++ are to make it highly compatible with ANSI C in the long term.

As a result, most of the examples stand a good chance of being correct. None the less, experience warns that despite careful checking, *some* errors are bound to creep in. Please be understanding with any errors that you may find.

Address for the Standard
Copies of the Standard can be obtained from:

X3 Secretariat,
CBEMA,
311 First Street, NW,
Suite 500,
Washington DC 20001-2178,
USA.

Phone (+1) (202) 737 8888

Contents

An Introduction to C

1.1 The form of a C program

If you're used to the block-structured form of, say, Pascal, then at the outer level the layout of a C program may surprise you. If your experience lies in the FORTRAN camp you will find it closer to what you already know, but the inner level will look quite different. C has borrowed shamelessly from both kinds of language, and from a lot of other places too. The input from so many varied sources has spawned a language a bit like a cross-bred terrier: inelegant in places, but a tenacious brute that the family is fond of. Biologists refer to this phenomenon as 'hybrid vigour'. They might also draw your attention to the 'chimera', an artificial crossbreed of creatures such as a sheep and a goat. If it gives wool and milk, fine, but it might equally well just bleat and stink!

At the coarsest level, an obvious feature is the multi-file structure of a program. The language permits **separate compilation**, where the parts of a complete program can be kept in one or more **source files** and compiled independently of each other. The idea is that the compilation process will produce files which can then be **linked** together using whatever link editor or loader that your system provides. The block structure of the Algol-like languages prevents this from being done by insisting that the whole program comes in one chunk.

The reason for C's approach is historical and rather interesting. It is supposed to speed things up: the idea is that compiling a program into relocatable **object code** is slow and expensive in terms of resources; compiling is hard work. Using the loader to bind together a number of object code modules should simply be a matter of sorting out the absolute addresses of each item in the modules when combined into a complete program. This should be relatively inexpensive. The expansion of the idea to arrange for the loader to scan **libraries** of object modules, and select the ones that are needed, is an obvious one. The benefit is that if you change one small part of a program then the expense of recompiling all of it may be avoided; only the module that was affected has to be recompiled.

All, the same, it's true that the more work put on to the loader, the slower it becomes, in fact sometimes it can be the slowest and most resource consuming part of the whole procedure. It is possible that, for some systems, it would be quicker to recompile everything in one go than to have to use the loader: Ada has sometimes

1

been quoted as an example of this effect occurring. For C, the work that has to be done by the loader is not large and the approach is a sensible one. Figure 1.1 shows the way that this works.

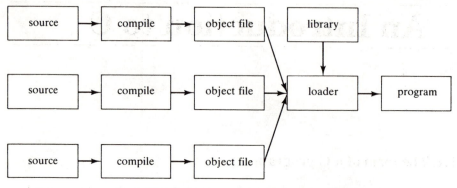

Figure 1.1   Separate compilation

1.2 Functions

A C program is a collection of **external objects**; these are mainly **functions** and what we could loosely call **global variables**. External objects are those that can be used throughout the program; as we will see later there are also **internal objects** whose use is much more restricted. Although this book is going to avoid the use of complicated terms (like those) where it can, sometimes there isn't a plainer way of saying things. The last two are terms that you are going to become familiar with. The only external objects that we will use for a while will be functions.

Functions are C's equivalents of functions and subroutines in FORTRAN, functions and procedures in Pascal/Algol. Neither BASIC in its common mutations, nor COBOL has much like C's functions.

The idea of a function is, of course, to allow you to encapsulate one idea or operation, give it a name, then to call that operation from various parts of the rest of your program simply by using the name. The detail of what is going on is not immediately visible at the point of use, nor should it be. In well designed, properly structured programs, it should be possible to change the way that a function does its job (as long as the job itself doesn't change) with no effect on the rest of the program.

There is one function in C whose name is special; it is the function known as `main`. This function is the first one entered when your program starts running. When the program leaves the main function, the whole program comes to an end. Here's a simple program containing two functions:

```
#include <stdio.h>

/*
 * Warn the compiler that we want
```

```
 * to use a function called show_message.
 * It has no arguments and returns no value
 * This is the ''declaration''.
 */
void show_message(void);


/*
 * Another function, but this includes the body of
 * the function. This is a ''definition''.
 */
main() {
    int count;

    count = 0;
    while (count < 10) {
        show_message();
        count = count + 1;
    }
    return (0);
}


/*
 * The body of the simple function.
 * This is now a ''definition''.
 */
void show_message(void) {
    printf("hello\n");
}
```
                                                              (E1.1)

1.3 A description of Example 1.1

1.3.1 What was in it

There's a lot of explaining to do after that example! It contained two functions, a #include 'statement', and some **comment**. Since comment is the easiest bit to handle, let's look at that first.

1.3.2 Layout and comment

The layout of a C program is not very important to the compiler, although for readability it is most important to use this relative freedom to carry extra information for the human reader. C allows you to put space, tab or newline characters practically anywhere in the program without any special effect on the meaning of the program. All of those three characters are the same as far as the compiler is concerned and are called collectively **white space**, because they just move the printing position without causing any 'visible' printing on an output device. White space can occur practically anywhere in a program except in the middle of **identifiers, strings,** or **character constants.** An identifier is simply the name of a function or some other object; strings and character constants will be discussed later – don't worry about them for the moment.

Apart from the special cases, the only place that white space must be used is to separate things that would otherwise run together and become confused. In the example above, the fragment `void show_message` needs space to separate the two words, whereas `show_message(` could have space in front of the (or not, it would be purely a matter of taste.

Comment is introduced to a C program by the pair of characters /*, which must not have a space between them. From then on, everything found up to and including the pair of characters */ is gobbled up and the whole lot is replaced by a single space. In pre-standard C, this was not the case. The rule used to be that comment could occur anywhere that space could occur: the rule is now that comment *is* space. A consequence of the rule for the end of comment is that you can't put a piece of comment inside another piece, because the *first* */ pair will finish all of it. This is a minor nuisance, but you learn to live with it.

It is common practice to make a comment stand out by making each line of multi-line comment always start with a *, as the example illustrates.

1.3.3 Preprocessor statements

The first statement in the example is a **preprocessor directive.** In days gone by, the C compiler used to have two phases: the **preprocessor,** followed by the real compiler. The preprocessor was a **macro processor,** whose job was to perform simple textual manipulation of the program before passing the modified text on to be compiled. The preprocessor rapidly became an essential aspect of the compiler and so has now been defined as part of the language, although it used to be possible to do without it.

The preprocessor only knows about lines of text; unlike the rest of the language it is sensitive to the end of a line and though it is possible to write multi-line preprocessor directives, they are uncommon and a source of some wonder when they are found. Any line whose first visible character is a # is a line that will be used to communicate with the preprocessor.

In the example that we have, the preprocessor directive `#include` causes the line where it occurs to be replaced completely by the contents of another file. In this case the filename is found between the < and > brackets. This is a widely used technique to incorporate the text of standard **header files** into your program without having to go through the effort of typing it all yourself. The `stdio.h` file is an important one, containing the necessary information that allows you to use the standard library for input and output. If you want to use the I/O library you *must* include `stdio.h`. Old C was more relaxed on this point.

Define statements

Another of the preprocessor's talents which is widely exploited is the #define statement. It is used like this:

```
#define IDENTIFIER   replacement
```

which says that the name represented by IDENTIFIER will be replaced by the text of replacement whenever IDENTIFIER occurs in the program text. Invariably, the identifier is a name in upper-case; this is a stylistic convention that helps the reader to understand what is going on. The replacement part can be any text at all – remember the preprocessor doesn't know C, it just works on text. The most common use of the statement is to declare names for constant numbers:

```
#define PI                3.141592
#define SECS_PER_MIN      60
#define MINS_PER_HOUR     60
#define HOURS_PER_DAY     24
```

and to use them like this

```
circumf = 2*PI*radius;
if(timer >= SECS_PER_MIN){
     mins = mins+1;
     timer = timer - SECS_PER_MIN;
}
```

the output from the preprocessor will be as if you had written this:

```
circumf = 2*3.141592*radius;
if(timer >= 60){
     mins = mins+1;
     timer = timer - 60;
}
```

1.3.4 Function declaration and definition

Declaration

After the stdio.h file is included comes a **function declaration**. This tells the compiler that show_message is a function which takes no arguments and returns no values. This demonstrates one of the changes made by the Standard – it is an example of a **function prototype**, a subject which Chapter 4 discusses in detail. It isn't always necessary to declare functions in advance – C will use some (old) default rules in such cases – but it is now strongly recommended that you *do* declare them in advance. The distinction between a **declaration** and a **definition** is that the former simply describes the type of the function and any arguments that it might take, the latter is where the body of a function is provided. These terms become more important later.

By declaring `show_message` before it is used, the compiler is able to check that it is used correctly. The declaration describes three important things about the function: its name, its type, and the number and type of its arguments. The `void show_message(` part indicates that it is a function and that it returns a value of type `void`, which is discussed in a moment. The second use of `void` is in the declaration of the function's argument list, `(void)`, which indicates that there are *no* arguments to this function.

Definition

Right at the end of the program is the function definition itself; although it is only three lines long, it usefully illustrates a complete function.

In C, functions perform the tasks that some other languages split into two parts. Most languages use a function to return a value of some sort, typical examples being perhaps trigonometric functions like sin, cos, or maybe a square root function; C is the same in this respect. Other similar jobs are done by what look very much like functions but which don't return a value: FORTRAN uses **subroutines**, Pascal and Algol call them **procedures**. C simply uses functions for all of those jobs, with the *type* of the function's return value specified when the function is defined. In the example, the function `show_message` doesn't return a value so we specify that its type is `void`.

The use of `void` in this way is a little on the subtle side. Superficially it is pretty obvious that a function returning `void` doesn't return anything at all. To split hairs, a void function *does* return a value of type `void`, but the `void` type is the type whose set of values is empty. There's only one thing you can do with a value of that type – ignore it – which is exactly what happens.

The type of the function is `void`, its name is `show_message`. The parentheses `()` following the function name are needed to let the compiler know that this is talking about a function and not some other sort of thing. If the function did take any arguments, then their names would be put between the parentheses. This one hasn't got any, which is made explicit by putting `void` between the parentheses.

The body of the function is a **compound statement**, a sequence of other statements surrounded by curly brackets `{}`. There is only one statement in there, but the brackets are still needed. In general, C allows you to put a compound statement anywhere that the language allows the use of a single simple statement; the job of the brackets being to turn several statements in a row into what is effectively a single statement.

It is reasonable to ask whether or not the brackets are strictly needed, if their only job is to bind multiple statements into one and all that we have in the example is a single statement. Oddly, the answer is yes – they *are* strictly needed. The only place in C where you can't put a single statement but *must* have a compound statement is when you are defining a function. The simplest function of all is therefore the empty function, which does nothing at all:

```
void do_nothing(void){}
```

The statement inside `show_message` is a call of the library function `printf`. `Printf` is used to format and print things, this example being one of the simplest of its uses. `Printf` takes one or more arguments, values that are passed forward from the point of the call into the function itself. In this case the argument is a **string**. The contents of the string are interpreted by `printf` and used to control the way the values of the other arguments are printed. It bears a little resemblance to the FORMAT statement in FORTRAN; but not enough to predict how to use it.

1.3.5 Strings

In C, strings are a sequence of characters surrounded by quote marks:

```
"like this"
```

Because a string is a single element, a bit like an identifier, it is not allowed to continue across a line – although space or tab characters are permitted inside a string.

```
"This is a legal string"
"This has a newline in it
and is NOT a legal string"
```

To get a very long string there are two things that you can do. You could take advantage of the fact that absolutely everywhere in a C program, the sequence 'backslash end-of-line' disappears totally.

```
"This would not be legal but doesn't have \
a newline in it as far as the compiler is concerned"
```

The other thing you could do is to to use the string joining feature, which says that two adjacent strings are considered to be just one.

```
"All this " "comes out as "
"just one string"
```

The sequence '\n' in the string is an example of an **escape sequence** which in this case represents 'newline'. `Printf` simply prints the contents of the string on the program's output file, so the output will read 'hello', followed by a new line.

1.3.6 The `main` **function**

In Example 1.1 there are actually two functions, `show_message` and `main`. Although `main` is a bit longer than `show_message` it is obviously built in the same shape: it has a name, the parentheses () are there, followed by the opening bracket { of the compound statement that must follow in a function definition. True, there's a lot more stuff too, but right at the end of the example you'll find the matching closing bracket } that goes with the first one to balance the numbers.

This is a much more realistic function now, because there are several statements inside the function body, not just one. You might also have noticed that the function is *not* declared to be `void`. There is a good reason for this: it returns a proper value.

Don't worry about its arguments yet; that problem is solved in Chapter 9.

The most important thing about `main` is that it is the first function to be called. Your C language system arranges, magically, for a call on the `main` function (hence its name) when the program is first started. When the function is over, so is the program. It's obviously an important function. Equally important is the stuff *inside* `main`'s compound statement. As mentioned before, there can be several statements inside a compound statement, so let's look at them in turn.

1.3.7 Declarations

The first statement is this:

```
int count;
```

not an instruction to do anything, but simply introducing a variable to the program. It declares something whose name is `count`, and whose type is 'integer'; in C the keyword that declares integers is unaccountably shortened to `int`. C has an idiosyncratic approach to these keywords with some having their names spelled in full and some being shortened like `int`. At least `int` has some sort of meaning that is intuitive: wait until we get on to `static` if you want something to complain about!

As a result of that declaration the compiler now knows that there is something that will be used to store integral quantities, and that its name is `count`. In C, all variables must be declared before they are used; there is none of FORTRAN's implicit declarations. In a compound statement, all declarations must come first; they must precede any 'ordinary' statements and are therefore somewhat special.

Moving down the example we find a familiar thing, an **assignment statement**. This is where the first value is assigned to the variable `count`, in this case the value assigned is a constant whose value is zero. Prior to the assignment, the value of `count` was undefined and unsafe to use. You might be a little surprised to find that the assignment symbol (strictly speaking an **assignment operator**) is a single = sign. This is not fashionable in modern languages, but hardly a major blemish.

So far then, we have declared a variable and assigned the value of zero to it. What next?

1.3.8 The `while` statement

Next is one of C's loop control statements, the `while` statement. Look carefully at its form. The formal description of the `while` statement is this:

```
while (expression)
    statement
```

Is that what we have got? Yes it is. The bit that reads

```
count < 10
```

is a **relational expression**, which is an example of a legal expression, and the expression is followed by a compound statement, which is a form of legal statement. As a result, it fits the rules for a properly constructed while statement.

What it does must be obvious to anyone who has written programs before. For as long as the relationship count < 10 holds true, the body of the loop is executed and the comparison repeated. If the program is ever to end, then the body of the loop must do something that will eventually cause the comparison to be false: of course it does.

There are just two statements in the body of the loop. The first one is a function call, where the function show_message is invoked. To do this, all that is needed is the name of the function followed by a list of the arguments that we are going to provide for it. When you call a function, an empty list (exactly what we need, since show_message is a function taking no arguments) is represented by the parentheses (). If there were any arguments, they would be put between the parentheses like this:

```
/* call a function with several arguments */
function_name(first_arg, second_arg, third_arg);
```

and so on. The call of printf is another example. More is explained in Chapter 4.

The last statement in the loop is an assignment containing an ordinary piece of arithmetic. Essentially it adds one to the variable count, which means that the requirement for program completion will eventually be met.

1.3.9 The return statement

The last statement that is left to discuss is the return statement. As it is written, it looks like another function call, but in fact the rule is that the statement is written

```
return expression;
```

where the *expression* is optional. The example has used a common stylistic convention, which is to put the *expression* into parentheses. This has no effect on the value of the expression.

The return causes a value to be returned from the current function to its caller. If the expression is missing, then an unknown value is passed back to the caller – this is almost certainly a mistake unless the function is void. So what type of value does main return? It wasn't declared with any type at all, unlike `show_message`. The answer is `int`, hardly obvious but a widely used feature of C. There are a number of places where the language allows you to declare things by default: the default type of functions is `int`, so it is common to see them used in this way. An equivalent way of writing the relevant line from the example program would have been

```
int main(){
```

and exactly the same results would have occurred.

You can't use the same feature to get a default type for variables because their types must be provided explicitly.

One of the areas of confusion surrounding the `return` statement in the `main` function of a C program is where the value is supposed to go. In Old C, the value was passed back to the operating system or whatever was used to start the program running. In a UNIX-like environment, the value of 0 meant 'success' in some way, any other value (traditionally −1) meant 'failure'. The Standard has enshrined this, stating that 0 stands for correct termination of the program. This *does not* mean that 0 is to be passed back, but instead the appropriate 'success' value for the system that you are using – this may mean that some translation of the returned value occurs. Returning from the `main` function is the same as calling the library function `exit` with the returned value. The difference is that `exit` may be called from *anywhere* in the program, and terminates it at that point, after doing some tidying up activities.

1.3.10 Summary

This example program, although short, has allowed us to introduce several important language features, amongst them:

- Program structure
- Comment
- File inclusion
- Function definition
- Compound statements
- Function calling
- Variable declaration
- Arithmetic
- Looping

although of course none of this has been covered rigorously.

1.4 Some more programs

While we're still in the informal phase, let's look at two more examples. You will have to work out for yourself what some of the code does, but as new or interesting features appear, they will be explained.

1.4.1 A program to find prime numbers

```
/*
 *
 * Dumb program that generates prime numbers.
 */
#include <stdio.h>

main() {
    int this_number, divisor, not_prime;

    this_number = 3;

    while(this_number < 10000){
        divisor = this_number / 2;
        not_prime = 0;
        while(divisor > 1){
            if(this_number % divisor == 0){
                not_prime = 1;
                divisor = 0;
            }
            else
                divisor = divisor-1;
        }

        if(not_prime == 0)
            printf("%d is a prime number\n", this_number);
        this_number = this_number + 1;
    }
    return(0);
}
```

(E1.2)

What was interesting in there? A few new points, perhaps. The program works in a really stupid way: to see if a number is prime, it divides that number by all the numbers between half its value and two – if any divide without remainder, then the number isn't prime. The two operators that you haven't seen before are the remainder operator %, and the equality operator, which is a double equal sign ==. That last one is without doubt the cause of more bugs in C programs than any other single factor.

The problem with the equality test is that wherever it can appear it is also legal to put the single = sign. The first, ==, compares two things to see if they are equal, and is generally what you need in fragments like these:

```
if(a == b)

while (c == d)
```

The assignment operator = is, perhaps surprisingly, also legal in places like those, but of course it assigns the value of the right-hand expression to whatever is on the left. The problem is particularly bad if you are used to the languages where comparison for equality is done with what C uses for assignment. There's nothing that you can do to help, so start getting used to it now.

There is also the introduction for the first time of the if statement. Like the while statement, it tests an expression to see if the expression is true. You might have noticed that also like the while statement, the expression that controls the if statement is in parentheses. That is always the case: all of the conditional control of flow statements require a parenthesized expression after the keyword that introduces them. The formal description of the if statement goes like this:

```
if (expression)
    statement

if (expression)
    statement
else
    statement
```

showing that it comes in two forms. Of course, the effect is that if the expression part is evaluated to be true, then the immediately following statement is executed. If the evaluation is false, then the following statement is not executed. When there is an else part, the statement associated with it is executed only if the evaluation gives a false result.

If statements have a famous problem. In the following piece of code, is the *statement-2* executed or not?

```
if(1 > 0)
    if(1 < 0)
        statement-1
else statement-2
```

The answer is that it *is*. Ignore the indentation (which is misleading). The else could belong to either the first or second if, according to the description of the if statement that has just been given; so an extra rule is needed to make it unambiguous. The rule is simply that an else is associated with the nearest else-less if above it. To make the example work the way that the indentation implied, we have to invoke a compound statement:

```
if(1 > 0){
    if(1 < 0)
        statement-1
}
else
    statement-2
```

Here, at least, C adheres to the same practice used by most other languages. In fact a lot of programmers who are used to languages where the problem exists have never even realized that it is there – they just thought that the disambiguating rule was 'obvious'. Let's hope that everyone feels that way.

1.4.2 The division operators

The division operators are the true division operator /, and the remainder operator %. Division does what you would expect, except that when it is applied to integer operands it give a result that is truncated towards zero. For example, 5/2 gives 2, 5/3 gives 1. The remainder operator is the way to get the truncated remainder. 5%2 gives 1, 5%3 gives 2. The signs of the remainder and quotient depend on the divisor and dividend in a way that is defined in the Standard and shown in Chapter 2.

1.4.3 An example performing input

It's useful to be able to perform input as well as just to write programs that print out more or less interesting lists and tables. The simplest of the library routines (and the only one that we'll look at just now) is called getchar. It reads single characters from the program's input and returns an integer value. The value returned is whatever value the program uses as a representation of that character and can be used to print the same character on the program output. It can also be compared against character constants or other characters that have been read, although the only test that makes sense is to see if both characters are the same. Comparing for greater or less than each other is not portable; there is no guarantee that a is less than b, although on most common systems that would be the case. Here is one example.

```
#include <stdio.h>
main(){
    int ch;

    ch = getchar();
    while(ch != 'a'){
        if(ch != '\n')
            printf("ch was %c, value %d\n", ch, ch);
        ch = getchar();
    }
    return(0);
}
```
(E1.3)

There are two interesting points in there. The first is to notice that at the end of each line of input read, the character represented by

'\n'

(a character constant) will be seen. This just like the way that the same symbol results in a new line when `printf` prints it. Second is the way that `%c` is used to output a character by `printf`, when it appears as itself. Printing it with `%d` prints the same variable, but displays the integer value used by your program to store the character.

If you try that program out, you may find that some systems do not pass characters one by one to a program, but make you type a whole line of input first. Then the whole line is made available as input, one character at a time. Beginners have been known to be confused: the program is started, they type some input, and nothing comes back. This behaviour is nothing to do with C; it depends on the computer and operating system in use.

1.4.4 Simple arrays

The use of **arrays** in C is often a surprise to the beginner. The declaration of arrays isn't too difficult, especially the one-dimensional ones, but a constant source of confusion is the fact that their indices always count from 0. To declare an array of 5 `ints`, the declaration would look like this:

```
int something[5];
```

In array declarations C uses square brackets, as you can see. There is no support for arrays with indices whose ranges do not start at 0 and go up; in the example, the valid array elements are `something[0]` to `something[4]`. Notice very carefully that `something[5]` is *not* a valid array element.

This program reads some characters from its input, sorts them into the order suggested by their representation, then writes them back out. Work out what it does for yourself; the algorithm won't be given much attention in the explanation which follows.

```
#include <stdio.h>
#define ARSIZE   10
main(){
    int ch_arr[ARSIZE],count1;
    int   count2, stop, lastchar;

    lastchar = 0;
    stop = 0;
    /*
     * Read characters into array.
     * Stop if end of line, or array full.
     */
    while(stop != 1){
        ch_arr[lastchar] = getchar();
        if(ch_arr[lastchar] == '\n')
            stop = 1;
```

```
            else
                lastchar = lastchar + 1;
            if(lastchar == ARSIZE)
                stop = 1;
    }
    lastchar = lastchar-1;

    /*
     * Now the traditional bubble sort.
     */
    count1 = 0;
    while(count1 < lastchar){
        count2 = count1 + 1;
        while(count2 <= lastchar){
            if(ch_arr[count1] > ch_arr[count2]){
                /* swap */
                int temp;
                temp = ch_arr[count1];
                ch_arr[count1] = ch_arr[count2];
                ch_arr[count2] = temp;
            }
            count2 = count2 + 1;
        }
        count1 = count1 + 1;
    }

    count1 = 0;
    while(count1 <= lastchar){
        printf("%c\n", ch_arr[count1]);
        count1 = count1 + 1;
    }
    return(0);
}
```
(E1.4)

You might note that the defined constant ARSIZE is used everywhere instead of the actual array size. Because of that, to change the maximum number of characters that can be sorted by this program simply involves a change to one line and then re-compiling. Not so obvious but critical to the safety of the program is the detection of the array becoming full. Look carefully; you'll find that the program stops when element ARSIZE-1 has been filled. That is because in an N element array, only elements 0 through to N-1 are available (giving N in total).

Unlike some other languages it is unlikely that you will be told if you 'run off' the end of an array in C. It results in what is known as **undefined behaviour** on the part of your program, this generally being to produce obscure errors in the future. Most skilled programmers avoid this happening by rigorous testing to make sure either that it can't happen given the particular algorithm in use, or by putting in an explicit test before accessing a particular member of an array. This is a common source of run-time errors in C; you have been warned.

1.5 Summary

This chapter has introduced many of the basics of the language although informally. Functions, in particular, form the basic building block for C. Chapter 4 provides a full description of these fundamental objects, but you should by now understand enough about them to follow their informal use in the intervening material.

Although the idea of library functions has been introduced, it has not been possible to emphasize their importance to the C application programmer. The Standard Library, described in Chapter 9, is *extremely* important, both in the way that it helps to improve the portability of programs intended for general use, and also in the great improvement in productivity that these useful functions can provide.

The use of variables, expressions and arithmetic are soon to be described in great detail. As this chapter has shown, at a simple level, C differs little from most other modern programming languages.

Only the use of structured data types still remains to be introduced, although arrays have had a very brief airing.

Exercises

1.1   Type in and test Example 1.1 on your system.

1.2   Using Example 1.2 as a pattern, write a program that prints prime pairs – a pair of prime numbers that differ by 2, for example 11 and 13, 29 and 31. (If you can detect a pattern between such pairs, congratulations! You are either a genius or just wrong.)

1.3   Write a function that returns an integer: the decimal value of a string of digits that it reads using getchar. For example, if it reads 1 followed by 4 followed by 6, it will return the number 146. You may make the (non-portable) assumption that the digits 0 – 9 are consecutive in the computer's representation and that the function will only have to deal with valid digits and newline, so error checking is not needed.

1.4   Use the function that you just wrote to read a sequence of numbers. Put them into an array declared in main, by repeatedly calling the function. Sort them into ascending numerical order, then print the sorted list.

1.5   Again using the function from Exercise 1.3, write a program that will read numbers from its input, then print them out in binary, decimal and hexadecimal form. You should not use any features of `printf` apart from those mentioned in this chapter (especially the hexadecimal output format!). You are expected to work out what digits to print by calculating each one in turn and making sure that they are printed in the right order. This is not particularly difficult, but it is not trivial either.

CHAPTER 2

Variables and Arithmetic

2.1 Some fundamentals

Here is where we start to look in detail at the bits that the last chapter chose to sweep under the carpet while it did its 'Instant C' introduction. The problem is, of course, the usual one of trying to introduce enough of the language to let you get a feel for what it's all about, without drowning the beginner in a froth of detail that isn't essential at the time.

Because this is a lengthy chapter, and because it deliberately chooses to cover some subtle problems that are often missed out in introductory texts, you should make sure that you are in the right mood and proper frame of mind to read it.

The weary brain may find that the breaks for exercises are useful. I strongly recommend that you do actually attempt the exercises on the way through. They help to balance the weight of information, which otherwise turns into an indigestible lump.

It's time to introduce some of the fundamentals.

2.2 The alphabet of C

This is an interesting area; alphabets are important. Not every computer language has bothered to recognize that the alphabet which it is written in has serious implications for its user. There's an assumption that the English alphabet augmented by a sprinkling of more or less arbitrary punctuation symbols will be available in every environment that is trying to support the language. The assumption is not always borne out by experience. Older languages suffer less from this sort of problem, but try sending C programs by Telex and you'll understand the difficulty.

The Standard requires that an alphabet of 96 symbols is available for C as follows:

```
space, horizontal and vertical tab
form feed, newline
26 upper and lower case letters
```

```
10 digits
! " # % & ' ( ) * + , - . /
: ; < = > ? [ \ ] ^ _ { | } ~
```

It turns out that most of the commonly used computer alphabets contain all the symbols that are needed for C with a few notorious exceptions. The C alphabetic characters shown below are missing from the ISO (International Standards Organization) 646 standard 7-bit character set, which was chosen as a subset of all widely used computer alphabets.

```
# [ \ ] ^ { | } ~
```

To cater for systems that can't provide the full 96 characters needed by C, the Standard specifies a method of using the ISO 646 characters to represent the missing few; the technique is the use of **trigraphs**.

2.2.1 Trigraphs

Trigraphs are a sequence of three ISO 646 characters that get treated as if they were one character in the C alphabet; all of the trigraphs start with two question marks ?? which helps to indicate that 'something funny' is going on. Table 2.1 below shows the trigraphs defined in the Standard.

Table 2.1 Trigraphs

C character	Trigraph
#	??=
[	??(
]	??)
{	??<
}	??>
\	??/
|	??!
~	??-
^	??'

As an example, let's assume that your terminal doesn't have the # symbol. To write the preprocessor line

```
#define MAX 32767
```

is not possible; you must use trigraph notation instead:

```
??=define MAX    32767
```

Of course trigraphs will work even if you do have a # symbol; they are there to help in difficult circumstances more than to be used for routine programming.

To remove any ambiguity, the Standard states that ? followed by two more ??s stands for itself, the trailing two queries possibly being part of a trigraph, depending on what follows them.

It would be a mistake to assume that programs written to be highly portable would use trigraphs 'in case they had to be moved to systems that only support ISO 646'. If your system can handle all 96 characters in the C alphabet, then that is what you should be using. Trigraphs will only be seen in restricted environments, and it is extremely simple to write a character-by-character translator between the two representations. However, all compilers that conform to the Standard will recognize trigraphs when they are seen.

Trigraph substitution is the very first operation that a compiler performs on its input text.

2.2.2 Program layout

The examples so far have used the sort of indentation and line layout that is common in languages belonging to the same family as C. They are 'free format' languages and you are free to lay the program out in a way that enhances its readability and highlights the logical structure of the program. Space (including horizontal tab) characters can be used for indentation anywhere except in identifiers or keywords without any effect on the meaning of the program. New lines work in the same way as space and tab *except* on preprocessor command lines, which have a line-by-line structure.

If a line is getting too long for comfort there are two things you can do. Generally it will be possible to replace one of the spaces by a newline and use simply two lines instead, as this example shows.

```
/* a long line */
a = fred+bill*((this/that)*sqrt(3.14159));
/* the same line */
a = fred+bill*
    ((this/that)*
    sqrt(3.14159));
```

If you're unlucky it may not be possible to break the lines like that; this problem is almost invariably confined to long preprocessor command lines. There, it's useful to know that the sequence 'backslash newline' becomes invisible to the C translation system. As a result, the sequence is legal even in unusual places such as the middle of identifiers, keywords, strings and so on. Only trigraphs are processed before this step.

The only time that you might want to use this way of breaking lines (outside of preprocessor control lines) is to prevent long strings from disappearing off the right-hand side of a program listing. New lines are *not* permitted inside strings and character constants, so you might think that the following is a good idea.

```
/* not a good way of folding a string */
printf("This is a very very very\
long string\n");
```

It is much preferable to make use of a new feature introduced by the Standard: two adjacent strings are joined together.

```
/* This string joining will not work in Old C */
printf("This is a very very very"
       "long string\n");
```

The second example allows you to indent the continuation portion of the string without changing its meaning; adding indentation in the first example would have put the indentation into the string.

Incidentally, both examples contain what is probably a mistake. There is no space in front of the 'long' in the continuation string, which will contain the sequence 'verylong' as a result. Did you notice?

2.2.3 Comment

Comment , as has been said already, is introduced by the character pair /* and terminated by */. It is translated into a single space wherever it occurs and so it follows exactly the same rules that spaces do. It's important to realize that it doesn't simply disappear, which it used to do in Old C, and that it is not possible to put comment into strings or character constants. Comment in such a place becomes part of the string or constant:

```
/*"This is comment"*/
"/*The quotes mean that this is a string*/"
```

2.2.4 Translation phases

The various character translation, line splicing, comment recognition and other early phases of translation are specified to occur in a certain order. If this is not defined properly, it is impossible to predict the way that a given system will work. The Standard says that the translation is to proceed as if the phases occurred in this order (there are more phases, but these are the important ones):

1.   Trigraph translation.
2.   Line joining.
3.   Translate comment to space (but not in strings or character constants).
4.   Translate the program.

Each stage is completed before the next is started.

2.3 Keywords and identifiers

Now that the alphabet of C is defined, we can look at how it is used to write programs. The most obvious of the language elements are **keywords** and **identifiers**; their forms are identical (although their meanings are different). They will be considered first.

2.3.1 Keywords

C keeps a small set of **keywords** for its own use. These keywords cannot be used as identifiers in the program – a common restriction with modern languages. Where users of Old C may be surprised is in the introduction of some new keywords; if those names were used as identifiers in previous programs, then the programs will have to be changed. At least it is an easy error to spot. Here is the list of keywords used in Standard C; you will notice that none of them use upper-case letters.

auto	double	int	struct
break	else	long	switch
case	enum	register	typedef
char	extern	return	union
const	float	short	unsigned
continue	for	signed	void
default	goto	sizeof	volatile
do	if	static	while

The new keywords that are likely to surprise old programmers are: `const`, `signed`, `void` and `volatile` (although `void` has been around for a while). Eagle eyed readers may have noticed that some implementations of C used to use the keywords `entry`, `asm`, and `fortran`. These are not part of the Standard, and few will mourn them.

2.3.2 Identifiers

Identifier is the fancy term used to mean 'name'. In C, identifiers are used to refer to a number of things: we've already seen them used to name variables and functions. They are also used to give names to some things we haven't seen yet, in particular **labels** and the 'tags' of **structures**, **unions**, and **enums**. Those new things will be discussed when the time is appropriate.

The rules for the construction of identifiers are simple: you may use the 52 upper and lower case alphabetic characters, the 10 digits and finally the underscore '_', which is considered to be an alphabetic character for this purpose. The only restriction is the usual one; identifiers *must* start with an alphabetic character.

Although there is no restriction on the length of identifiers in the Standard, this is a point that needs a bit of explanation. In Old C, as in Standard C, there has never been any restriction on the length of identifiers; this sounds very nice. The problem is that there was never any guarantee that more than a certain number of characters would be checked when names were compared for equality – in Old C this was eight characters, in Standard C this has changed to 31.

So, practically speaking, the new limit is 31 characters – although identifiers *may* be longer, they must differ in the first 31 characters if you want to be sure that your programs are portable. The Standard allows for implementations to support longer names if they wish to, so if you do use longer names, make sure that you don't rely on the checking stopping at 31!

One of the most controversial parts of the Standard is the length of **external identifiers**. External identifiers are the ones that have to be visible outside the current source code file. Typical examples of these would be library routines or functions which have to be called from several different source files.

The Standard chose to stay with the old restrictions on these external names: they are not guaranteed to be different unless they differ from each other in the first *six* characters. Worse than that, upper and lower case letters may be treated the same!

The reason for this is a pragmatic one: the way that most C compilation systems work is to use operating system specific tools to bind library functions into a C program. These tools are outside the control of the C compiler writer, so the Standard has to impose realistic limits that are likely to be possible to meet. There is nothing to prevent any specific implementation from giving better limits than these, but for maximum portability the six monocase characters must be all that you expect.

2.4 Declaration of variables

Well, those were the rules about forming names, but of course it's much more interesting to see what the names are used for. So far we have only found out about functions and variables and it's time now to look at what it actually means to give names to variables. Functions have a whole chapter to themselves, so they can wait.

Variables are declared in **declarations**; the syntax of these can be very complicated in certain cases. C has tried to make the declaration of variables resemble their use in what the original designer of the language, Dennis Ritchie, has been reported to describe as an 'experiment'. Whether it worked or not is for you to judge, but fortunately it will be some time before the really complicated ones are seen.

2.4.1 Declarations and definitions

You will probably remember from Chapter 1 that C insists on knowing in advance the name of everything used in a function, the only exception to this rule being the names of integer functions and labels. The place where names are introduced is a **declaration**. In the examples that we have seen so far, most of the declarations have also been **definitions**. The crucial difference between them is that a declaration introduces a name and a type for an object, but does not reserve any memory to store the thing. A definition is also a declaration but has the added feature that it *does* reserve storage.

The distinction between declaration and definition is an important one, and it is a shame that the two words sound alike enough to cause confusion. From now on they will have to be used for their formal meaning, so if you are in doubt about the differences between them, refer back to this point.

The rules about what makes a declaration into a definition are rather complicated, so they will be deferred for a while. In the meantime, here are some examples and rule-of-thumb guidelines which will work for the examples that we have seen so far, and will do for a while to come.

```
/*
 * A function is only defined if its body is given
 * This is a declaration only
 */

int func_dec(void);


/*
 * Because this has a body, it is also
 * a definition.
 * Any variables declared inside will be definitions,
 * unless the keyword `extern' is used.
 * Don't use `extern' until you understand it!
 */

int def_func(void){
      float f_var;       /* a definition */
      int rand_num(void); /* declare another function */
      int counter;       /* another definition */

      return(0);
}
```

Exercises

2.1   Why are trigraphs used?

2.2   When would you expect to find them in use, and when not?

2.3   When is a newline not equivalent to a space or tab?

2.4   When would you see the sequence of 'backslash newline' in use?

2.5   What happens when two strings are put side by side?

2.6   Why can't you put one piece of comment inside another one? (This prevents the technique of 'commenting out' unused bits of program, unless you are careful.)

2.7   What are the longest names that may safely be used for variables?

2.8   What is a *declaration*?

2.9   What is a *definition*?

2.4.2 Real types

It's easier to deal with the realtypes first because there is less to say about them and they don't get as complicated as the integer types. This is even more true now than with Old C. As is the spirit of C, there are no rules laid down for the precision or range of the real numbers supported in any given implementation, although the implementation is supposed to tell you what it provides.

The varieties of real numbers are these:

```
float
double
long double
```

Each of the types gives access to a particular way of representing real numbers in the target computer. If it only has one way of doing things, they might all turn out to be the same; if it has more than three, then C has no way of specifying the extra ones. The type `float` is intended to be the small, fast representation corresponding to what FORTRAN would call REAL. You would use `double` for extra precision, and `long double` for even more.

Because C is supposed to be a language that sticks close to the underlying hardware, it gives no guarantees about the behaviour of floating point numbers. Instead, it is the responsibility of the implementors to tell you what you are getting. For some users this is extremely important information, but it is of a highly technical nature and is likely only to be fully understood by numerical analysts. It can be found in the standard header file `float.h` if you are interested; the contents are derived from the standard for FORTRAN.

The main points of interest are that in the increasing 'lengths' of `float`, `double` and `long double`, each type must give at least the same range and precision as the previous type. For example, taking the value in a `double` and putting it into a `long double` must result in the same value.

There is no requirement for the three types of 'real' variables to differ in their properties, so if a machine only has one type of real arithmetic, all of C's three types could be implemented in the same way. None the less, the three types would be considered to be different from the point of view of type checking; it would be 'as if' they really were different. That helps when you move the program to a system where the three types really are different – there won't suddenly be a set of warnings coming out of your compiler about type mismatches that you didn't get on the first system.

In contrast to more 'strongly typed' languages, C permits expressions to mix all of the arithmetic types: the various flavours of integers, the real numbers and also the pointer types. When an expression contains a mixture of types there are implicit conversions invoked which can be used to work out what the overall type of the result will be. These rules are quite important and are known as the **usual arithmetic conversions**; it will be worth committing them to memory later. The full set of rules is described in Section 2.6; for the moment, we will investigate only the ones that involve mixing float, double and long double to see if they make sense.

The only time that the conversions are needed is when two different types are mixed in an expression, as in the example below:

```
int  f(void){
    float  f_var;
    double  d_var;
    double  l_d_var;

    f_var = 1; d_var = 1; l_d_var = 1;
    d_var = d_var + f_var;
    l_d_var = d_var + f_var;
    return(l_d_var);
}
```
(E2.1)

In fact there are a lot of forced conversions in that example. Getting the easiest of them out of the way first, let's look at the assignments of the constant value 1 to each of the variables. As the section on constants will point out, that 1 has type int, i.e. it is an integer, not a 'real' constant. The assignment converts the integer value to the appropriate real type, which is easy to cope with.

The interesting conversions come next. The first of them is on the line

```
d_var = d_var+f_var;
```

What is the type of the expression involving the + operator? The answer is easy when you know the rules. Whenever two different real types are involved in an expression, the lower precision type is first implicitly converted to the higher precision type and then the arithmetic is performed at that precision. The example involves both a double and a float, so the value of f_var is converted to type double and is then added to the value of the double d_var. The result of the expression is naturally of type double too, so it is clearly of the correct type to assign to d_var.

The second of the additions is a little bit more complicated, but still perfectly O.K. Again, the value of f_var is converted and the arithmetic performed with the precision of double, forming the sum of the two variables. Now there's a problem. The result (the sum) is double, but the assignment is to a long double. Once again the obvious procedure is to convert the lower precision value to the higher one, which is done, and then make the assignment.

So we've taken the easy ones. The difficult thing to see is what to do when forced to assign a higher precision result to a lower precision destination. In those cases it may be necessary to lose precision, in a way specified by the implementation. Basically, the implementation must specify whether and in what way it rounds or truncates. Even worse, the destination may be unable to hold the value at all. The Standard says that in these cases loss of precision may occur; if the destination is unable to hold the necessary value – say by attempting to add the largest representable number to itself – then the behaviour is undefined, your program is faulty and you can make no predictions whatsoever about any subsequent behaviour.

It is no mistake to re-emphasize that last statement. What the Standard means by **undefined behaviour** is exactly what it says. Once a program's behaviour has entered the undefined region, absolutely anything can happen. The program might be stopped by the operating system with an appropriate message, or just as likely nothing observable would happen and the program be allowed to continue with an erroneous value stored in the variable in question. It is your responsibility to prevent your program from exhibiting undefined behaviour. Beware!

2.4.3 Summary of real arithmetic

Arithmetic with any two real types is done at the highest precision of the members involved. Assignment involves loss of precision if the receiving type has a lower precision than the value being assigned to it.

Further conversions are often implied when expressions mix other types, but they have not been described yet.

2.4.4 Printing real numbers

The usual output function, printf, can be used to format real numbers and print them. There are a number of ways to format these numbers, but we'll stick to just one for now. Table 2.2 below shows the appropriate format description for each of the real types.

Table 2.2   Format codes for real numbers

Type	Format
float	%f
double	%f
long double	%lf

Here's an example to try:

```
#include <stdio.h>
#include <stdlib.h>

#define BOILING 212 /* degrees Fahrenheit */

main(){
    float f_var; double d_var; long double l_d_var;
    int i;

    i = 0;
    printf("Fahrenheit to Centigrade\n");
    while(i <= BOILING){
        l_d_var = 5*(i-32);
        l_d_var = l_d_var/9;
        d_var = l_d_var;
        f_var = l_d_var;
        printf("%d %f %f %lf\n", i,
                f_var, d_var, l_d_var);
        i = i+1;
    }
    exit(0);
}
```
                                                                        (E2.2)

Try that example on your own computer to see what results you get.

Exercises

2.10 Which type of variable can hold the largest range of values?

2.11 Which type of variable can store values to the greatest precision?

2.12 Are there any problems possible when assigning a float or double to a double or long double?

2.13 What could go wrong when assigning, say, a long double to a double?

2.14 What predictions can you make about a program showing 'undefined behaviour'?

2.5 Integral types

The real types were the easy ones. The integral types are a lot more complicated, but still tolerable, and these rules really should be learnt. Fortunately, the only types used in C for routine data storage are the real and integer types, or **structures** and **arrays** built up from them. C definitely doesn't have special types for character manipulation or the handling of logical (boolean) quantities. They are both done with integral types.

We will start by looking at the various types and then the conversion rules.

2.5.1 Plain integers

There are two types (often called 'flavours') of integer variables. Other types can be built from these, as we'll see, but the plain undecorated `int`s are the base. The most obvious of the pair is the 'signed' `int`, the less obvious is its close relative, the `unsigned int`. These variables are supposed to be stored in whatever is the most convenient unit for the machine running your program. The `int` is the natural choice for undemanding requirements when you just need a simple integral variable, say as a counter in a short loop. There isn't any guarantee about the number of bits that an `int` can hold, except that it will *always* be 16 or more. The standard header file `limits.h` details the actual number of bits available in a given implementation.

Curiously, Old C had no guarantee whatsoever about the length of an `int`, but consensus and common practice has always assumed at least 16 bits.

Actually, `limits.h` doesn't quite specify a number of bits, but gives maximum and minimum values for an `int` instead. The values it gives are 32767 and −32767 which implies 16 bits or more. Those of you who ask why the minimum isn't −32768 are assuming that the numbers will be stored using two's complement notation, which is not the view that C takes. On a one's complement machine, 16 bits gives exactly the range in `limits.h`, though of course there is nothing to stop a given implementation from providing a greater range in either direction.

The range specified in the Standard for an `unsigned int` is 0 to at least 65535, meaning that it cannot be negative. More about these shortly.

If you aren't used to thinking about the number of bits in a given variable, and are beginning to get worried about the portability implications of this apparently machine-dependent concern for the number of bits, then you're doing the right thing. C takes portability seriously and actually bothers to tell you what values and ranges are guaranteed to be safe. The bitwise operators encourage you to think about the number of bits in a variable too, because they actually give direct access to the bits, which you manipulate one by one or in groups. Almost paradoxically, the overall result is that C programmers have a healthy awareness of portability issues which leads to more portable programs. This is *not* to say that you can't write C programs that are horribly non-portable!

2.5.2 Character variables

A bit less obvious than int is the other of the plain integral types, the char. It's basically just another sort of int, but has a different application. Because so many C programs do a lot of character handling, it's a good idea to provide a special type to help, especially if the range provided by an int uses up much more storage than is needed by characters. The limits file tells us that three things are guaranteed about char variables: they have at least 8 bits, they can store a value of at least +127, and the minimum value of a char is zero or lower. This means that the only guaranteed range is 0–127.

There's an extra guarantee too, but it isn't in the limits file. A char variable will *always* be positive if it is holding a bona fide character from the character set of the machine running your program. Because chars are integral types, there may be ways of getting negative values into them, but assigning a genuine character isn't one of them.

In short, a character variable will probably take less storage than an int and will most likely be used for character manipulation. It's still an integer type though, and can be used for arithmetic, as this example shows.

```
#include <limits.h>
#include <stdio.h>
#include <stdlib.h>

main () {
    char c;

    c = CHAR_MIN;
    while(c != CHAR_MAX){
        printf("%d\n", c);
        c = c+1;
    }

    exit(0);
}                                                    (E2.3)
```

Running that program is left as an exercise for the easily amused. If you are bothered about where CHAR_MIN and CHAR_MAX come from, find limits.h and read it.

Here's a more enlightening example. It uses character constants, which are formed by placing a character in single quotes:

```
'x'
```

Because of the rules of arithmetic, the type of this sort of constant turns out to be int, but that doesn't matter since their value is always small enough to assign them to char variables without danger of overflow. (Unfortunately, there is a multi-character version where that guarantee does not hold. Ignore it for the moment.) When a character variable is printed using the %c format with printf, the appropriate character is output. You can use %d, if you like, to see what integer value is used to represent the character. Why %d? Because a char is just another integral type.

It's also useful to be able to read characters into a program. The library function getchar is used for the job. It reads characters from the program's normal input and returns an int value suitable for storing into a char. The int value is for one reason only: not only does getchar return all possible character values, but it also returns an *extra* value to indicate that end-of-input has been seen. The range of a char might not be enough to hold this extra value, so the int has to be used.

The following program reads its input and counts the number of commas and full stops that it sees. On end of input, it prints the totals.

```
#include <stdio.h>
#include <stdlib.h>
main(){
    int this_char, comma_count, stop_count;

    comma_count = stop_count = 0;
    this_char = getchar();
    while(this_char != EOF){
        if(this_char == '.')
            stop_count = stop_count+1;
        if(this_char == ',')
            comma_count = comma_count+1;
        this_char = getchar();
    }
    printf("%d commas, %d stops\n", comma_count,
            stop_count);
    exit(0);
}                                                       (E2.4)
```

The two features of note in that example were the multiple assignment to the two counters and the use of the defined constant EOF. EOF is the value returned by getchar on end of input (it stands for End Of File), and is defined in stdio.h. The multiple assignment is a fairly common feature of C programs but has its own little surprises for the unwary. It works the way you expect it to provided all of the variables are of the same type, or you are assigning zero (as this example is).

Another example, I think. This will either print out the whole lower case alphabet, if your implementation has its characters stored consecutively, or something even more interesting if they aren't. C doesn't make any guarantees about the ordering of characters in internal form, so this program produces *non-portable* results!

```
#include <stdio.h>
#include <stdlib.h>
main(){
    char c;

    c = 'a';
    while(c <= 'z'){
        printf("value %d char %c\n", c, c);
        c = c+1;
    }

    exit(0);
}
```
                                                                    (E2.5)

Yet again this example emphasizes that a char is only another form of integer variable and can be used just like any other form of variable. It is *not* a 'special' type with its own rules.

The space saving that a char offers when compared to an int only becomes worthwhile if a lot of them are being used. Most character-processing operations involve the use of not just one or two character variables, but large arrays of them. That's when the saving can become noticeable: imagine an array of 1024 ints. On a lot of common machines that would eat up 4096 8-bit bytes of storage, assuming the common length of 4 bytes per int. If the computer architecture allows it to be done in a reasonably efficient way, the C implementor will probably have arranged for char variables to be packed one per byte, so the array would only use 1024 bytes and the space saving would be 3072 bytes.

Sometimes it doesn't matter whether or not a program tries to save space; sometimes it does. At least C gives you the option of choosing an appropriate type.

2.5.3 More complicated types

The last two types were easy to come to terms with, in both their declaration and subsequent use. For serious systems programming they just aren't adequate in the precision of control over main store that they provide and the behaviour that they follow. To correct this problem, C provides extra forms of integral types, split into the categories of signed and unsigned. (Although both these terms are reserved words, they will also be used as adjectives.) The difference between the two types is obvious. Signed types are those that are capable of being negative, the unsigned types cannot be negative at any time. Unsigned types are usually used for one of two reasons: to get an extra bit of precision, or when the concept of being negative is simply not present in the data that is being represented.

Unsigned types also have the special property of never overflowing in arithmetic. Adding 1 to a signed variable that already contains the maximum possible positive number for its type will result in overflow, and the program's behaviour becomes undefined. That can never happen with unsigned types, because they are defined to work modulo one greater than the maximum number that they can hold. What this means is best illustrated by example:

```
#include <stdio.h>
#include <stdlib.h>
main() {
    unsigned int x;
    x = 0;
    while (x >= 0) {
        printf("%u\n", x);
        x = x+1;
    }

    exit(0);
}
```
(E2.6)

Assuming that the variable x is stored in 16 bits, then its range of values will be 0–65535 and that sequence will be printed endlessly. The program can't terminate: the test

```
x >= 0
```

can never be false for an unsigned variable.

For both the signed and unsigned integral types there are three subtypes: short, ordinary and long. Taking those into account, here is a list of all of the possible integral types in C, except for the character types:

```
unsigned short int
unsigned int
unsigned long int
signed short int
signed int
signed long int
```

In the last three, the signed keyword is unnecessary because the int types are signed types anyway: you *have* to say unsigned to get anything different. It's also permissible, but not recommended, to drop the int keyword from any of those declarations provided that there is at least one other keyword present – the int will be 'understood' to be present. For example long is equivalent to signed long int. The long and short forms give you more control over the amount of space used to store variables. Each has its own minimum range specified in limits.h which in practice means at least 16 bits in a short and an int, and at least 32 bits in a long, whether signed or unsigned. As always, an implementation can choose to give you more bits than the minimum if it wants to. The only restriction is that the limits must be equalled or bettered, and that you don't get more bits in a shorter type than a longer one (not an unreasonable rule).

The only character types are these: `signed char` and `unsigned char`. The difference between `char` and `int` variables is that, unless otherwise stated, all `int`s are signed. The same is not true for `char`s, which are signed or unsigned depending on the implementor's choice; the choice is presumably taken on efficiency grounds. You can of course explicitly force signed or unsignedness with the right keyword. The only time that it is likely to matter is if you are using character variables as extra short `short`s to save more space.

To summarize the integral types, we have `short`, `long`, `signed`, `unsigned` and plain `int`s. The commonest is the ordinary `int`, which is signed unless declared not to be. The `char` variables *can* be made signed or unsigned, as you prefer, but in the absence of indications to the contrary, they will be allocated the most efficient type.

2.5.4 Printing the integral types

Once again you can use `printf` to print these various types. Character variables work exactly the same way that the other integral variables do, so you can use the standard format letters to print their contents – although the actual numbers stored in them are not likely to be very interesting. To see their contents interpreted as characters, use `%c` as was done earlier. All of the integral types can be printed as if they were signed decimal numbers by using the `%d` format, or `%ld` for long types. Other useful formats are shown in Table 2.3; notice that in every case a letter 'l' is put in front of the normal format letter if a `long` is to be printed. That's not just there to get the right result printed: the behaviour of `printf` is undefined if the wrong format is given.

Table 2.3   More format codes

Format	Use with
`%c`	`char` (in character form)
`%d`	decimal `signed int, short, char`
`%u`	decimal `unsigned int, short, char`
`%x`	hexadecimal `int, short, char`
`%o`	octal `int, short, char`
`%ld`	decimal `signed long`
`%lu  %lx  %lo`	as above, but for `long`s

A full description of the format codes that you can use with `printf` is given in Chapter 9.

2.6 Expressions and arithmetic

Expressions in C can get rather complicated, because of the number of different types and operators that can be mixed together. This section explains what happens, but can get deep at times. You may need to re-read it once or twice to make sure that you have understood all of the points.

First, a bit of terminology. Expressions in C are built from combinations of **operators** and **operands**, so for example in this expression

```
x = a+b*(-c)
```

we have the operators =, +, * and -. The operands are the variables x, a, b and c. You will also have noticed that parentheses can be used for grouping sub-expressions such as the -c. Most of C's unusually rich set of operators are either **binary operators**, which take two operands, or **unary operators**, which take only one. In the example, the - was being used as a unary operator, and is performing a different task from the binary subtraction operator which uses the same - symbol. It may seem like hair-splitting to argue that they are different operators when the job that they do seems conceptually the same, or at least similar. It's worth doing though, because, as you will find later, some of the operators have both a binary and a unary form where the two meanings bear no relation to each other; a good example would be the binary multiplication operator *, which in its unary form means indirection via a pointer variable!

A peculiarity of C is that operators may appear consecutively in expressions without the need for parentheses to separate them. The previous example could have been written as

```
x = a+b*-c;
```

and still have been a legal expression. Because of the number of operators that C has, and because of the strange way that assignment works, the **precedence** of the operators (and their **associativity**) is of much greater importance to the C programmer than in most other languages. It will be discussed fully after the introduction of the important arithmetic operators.

First, we must look at the type conversions which may occur.

2.6.1 Conversions

C allows types to be mixed in expressions, and permits operations that result in type conversions happening implicitly. This section describes the way that the conversions must occur. Any conversions that happen *must* follow these rules.

There are the **integral promotions** which occur even in the absence of any operators. One effect of this is that all integral arithmetic is done with at least the range of an int, even if you try to reduce it by specifying short variables.

There are also the **usual arithmetic conversions**, which occur in most ordinary expressions. For example, in the following fragment

```
double x;
unsigned long y;

x = 1;
```

```
y = -(3*x);
```

a number of type conversions are demanded. The **usual arithmetic conversions** in conjunction with the **integral promotions** allow us to predict the conversions and values that will result. You will need to learn them by heart if you ever intend to program seriously in C.

You should also note that the rules are *not* the same as Old C. The Standard has, among some controversy, introduced what are known as **value preserving** rules, where a knowledge of the target computer is required to work out what the type of an expression will be. Previously, whenever an unsigned type occurred in an expression, you knew that the result had to be unsigned too. Now, the result will only be unsigned if the conversions demand it; in many cases the result will be an ordinary signed type.

For example, it used to be the case that an expression involving an unsigned int and a long had the result of unsigned long. Now, the result will be simply long, with the proviso that in converting the unsigned int to long its value is unchanged.

The reason for the change was to reduce some of the surprises possible when you mix signed and unsigned quantities together; it isn't always obvious when this has happened and the intention is to produce the 'more commonly required' result.

Characters and integers

These are known as the *integral promotions* and will be referred to several times later.

No arithmetic is done by C at a precision shorter than int. Whenever a short or a char (or a **bitfield**, which we haven't met yet) occurs in an expression, the type is first converted to int, if an int can hold all of the values of the original type. Otherwise, the conversion will be to unsigned int. This preserves both the value and the sign of the original type. Note that whether a plain char is treated as signed or unsigned is implementation dependent.

Whenever an integer is converted into a shorter unsigned type, there can be no 'overflow', so the result is defined to be 'the non-negative remainder on division by the number one greater than the largest unsigned number that can be represented in the shorter type'. That simply means that in a two's complement environment the low-order bits are copied into the destination and the high-order ones discarded.

Converting to a shorter signed type, there may not be enough room to hold the value. In that case, the result is implementation defined.

Signed and unsigned integers

The Standard says that when an unsigned integer is promoted to a longer signed integer, its value is unchanged.

When converting a signed integer to an unsigned integer, either of the same or of greater length, if the signed integer is positive the value is unchanged. If the value was negative, then if the destination is longer than the original type, the value is first converted to a signed type of the longer length (this equalizes the lengths, without any value change yet). Then the signed quantity is converted to unsigned by adding it to the largest number that the unsigned can hold plus one.

The overall effect is to give the same result that you would get working in two's complement with sign extension.

Floating and integral

Converting a floating to an integral type simply throws away any fractional part. If the integral type can't hold the value that is left, then the behaviour is undefined – this is a sort of overflow.

As has already been said, going up the scale from float to double to long double, there is no problem with conversions – each higher one in the list can hold all the values of the lower ones, so the conversion occurs with no loss of information.

Converting in the opposite direction, if the value is outside the range that can be held, the behaviour is undefined. If the value *is* in range, but can't be held exactly, then the result is one of the two nearest values that *can* be held, chosen in a way that the implementation defines. This means that there will be a loss of precision.

The usual arithmetic conversions

A lot of expressions involve the use of subexpressions of mixed types together with operators such as +, * and so on. For example, adding *type-1* to *type-2* means that both types will be converted to the type of the result, then the addition will be done. Here are the rules specifying what conversions are to be done. Where both operands in an expression are already of the same type these rules will result in unnecessary (and harmless) conversions being specified; obviously converting a long into another long has no effect.

1. If either operand is a long double, then the other one is converted to long double and that is the type of the result.

2. Otherwise, if either operand is a double, then the other one is converted to double, and that is the type of the result.

3. Otherwise, if either operand is a float, then the other one is converted to float, and that is the type of the result.

4. Otherwise, if either operand is an unsigned long int, then the other one is converted to unsigned long int, and that is the type of the result.

5. Otherwise, if either operand is a long int, then the other one is converted to long int, and that is the type of the result.

6. Otherwise the *integral promotions* (see above) are performed. Then, if either operand is an unsigned int, then the other one is converted to unsigned int, and that is the type of the result.

7. Otherwise, both operands must be of type int, so that is the type of the result.

The Standard contains a strange phrase: 'operands may be converted to other types provided that neither range nor precision is lost ... the type of the result is not changed thereby'. This is in fact to allow the Old C treatment of floats. In Old C, float variables were automatically promoted to double, the way that the integral promotions promote char to int. So, an expression involving purely float variables may be done as if they were double, but the type of the result must appear to be float. The only effect is likely to be on performance and is not particularly important to most users.

In general, the type conversions and type mixing rules don't cause a lot of trouble, but there is one pitfall to watch out for. Mixing signed and unsigned quantities is fine until the signed number is negative; then its value can't be represented in an unsigned variable and something has to happen. The standard says that to convert a negative number to unsigned, the largest possible number that can be held in the unsigned plus one is added to the negative number; that is the result. Because there can be no overflow in an unsigned type, the result always has a defined value. Taking a 16-bit int for an example, the unsigned version has a range of 0–65535. Converting a signed value of –7 to this type involves adding 65536, resulting in 65529. What is happening is that the Standard is enshrining previous practice, where the bit pattern in the signed number is simply assigned to the unsigned number; the description in the standard is exactly what would happen if you did perform the bit pattern assignment on a two's complement computer. The one's complement implementations are going to have to do some real work to get the same result.

Putting it plainly, a small magnitude negative number will result in a large positive number when converted to unsigned. If you don't like it, suggest a better solution – it is plainly a mistake to try to assign a negative number to an unsigned variable, so it's your own fault.

Well, it's easy to say 'don't do it', but it can happen by accident and the results can be *very* surprising. Look at this example.

```
#include <stdio.h>
#include <stdlib.h>
main(){
    int i;
    unsigned int stop_val;

    stop_val = 0;
    i = -10;

    while(i <= stop_val){
        printf("%d\n", i);
        i = i + 1;
    }
    exit(0);
}
```

(E2.7)

You might expect that to print out the list of values from −10 to 0, but it won't. The problem is in the comparison. The variable i, with a value of −10, is being compared against an unsigned 0. By the rules of arithmetic (check them) we must convert both types to `unsigned int` first, then make the comparison. The −10 becomes at least 65526 (see `limits.h`) when it's converted, and is plainly somewhat larger than 0, so the loop is never executed. The moral is to steer clear of unsigned numbers unless you really have to use them, and to be perpetually on guard when they are mixed with signed numbers.

Exercises

2.15 Assuming that chars, ints and longs are respectively 8, 16 and 32 bits long, and that char defaults to unsigned char on a given system, what is the resulting type of expressions involving the following combinations of variables?

  a)   Simply `signed char`.
  b)   Simply `unsigned char`.
  c)   `int, unsigned int`.
  d)   `unsigned int, long`.
  e)   `int, unsigned long`.
  f)   `char, long`.
  g)   `char, float`.
  h)   `float, float`.
  i)   `float, long double`.

Casts
From time to time you will find that an expression turns out not to have the type that you wanted it to have and you would like to force it to have a different type. That is what **casts** are for. By putting a type name in parentheses, for example

    (int)

you create a unary operator known as a **cast**. A cast turns the value of the expression on its right into the indicated type. If, for example, you were dividing two integers a/b then the expression would use integer division and discard any remainder. To force the fractional part to be retained, you could either use some intermediate float variables, or a cast. This example does it both ways.

```
#include <stdio.h>
#include <stdlib.h>
```

```
    /*
     * Illustrates casts.
     * For each of the numbers between 2 and 20,
     * print the percentage difference between it and the c
     * before
     */

main(){
        int   curr_val;
        float temp, pcnt_diff;

        curr_val = 2;
        while(curr_val <= 20){
            /*
             * % difference is
             * 1/(curr_val)*100
             */
            temp = curr_val;
            pcnt_diff = 100/temp;
            printf("Percent difference at %d is %f\n",
                curr_val, pcnt_diff);
            /*
             * Or, using a cast:
             */
            pcnt_diff = 100/(float)curr_val;
            printf("Percent difference at %d is %f\n",
                curr_val, pcnt_diff);
            curr_val = curr_val + 1;
        }
        exit(0);
}
```

(E2.8)

The easiest way to remember how to write a cast is to write down exactly what you would use to declare a variable of the type that you want. Put parentheses around the entire declaration, then delete the variable name; that gives you the cast. Table 2.4 shows a few simple examples – some of the types shown will be new to you, but it's the complicated ones that illustrate best how casts are written. Ignore the ones that you don't understand yet, because you will be able to use the table as a reference later.

Table 2.4 Casts

Declaration	Cast	Type
`int x;`	`(int)`	`int`
`float f;`	`(float)`	`float`
`char x[30];`	`(char [30])`	array of `char`
`int *ip;`	`(int *)`	pointer to `int`
`int (*f)();`	`(int (*)())`	pointer to function returning `int`

2.6.2 Operators

The multiplicative operators
Or, put another way, multiplication $*$, division / and the remainder operator %.
Multiplication and division do what is expected of them for both real and integral
types, with integral division producing a truncated result. The truncation is
towards zero. The remainder operator is only defined to work with integral types,
because the division of real numbers doesn't produce a remainder.

If the division is not exact and neither operand is negative, the result of / is
positive and rounded toward zero – to get the remainder, use %. For example,

```
9/2 == 4
9%2 == 1
```

If either operand is negative, the result of / may be the nearest integer to the
true result on either side, and the sign of the result of % may be positive or
negative. Both of these features are implementation defined.

It is always true that the following expression is equal to zero:

```
(a/b)*b + a%b - a
```

unless b is zero.

Additive operators
Addition + and subtraction – also follow the rules that you expect. The binary
operators and the unary operators both have the same symbols, but rather different
meanings. For example, the expressions a+b and a−b both use a binary operator
(+ or −), and result in addition or subtraction. The unary operators with the same
symbols would be written +b or −b. The unary minus has an obvious function – it
takes the negative value of its operand; what does the unary plus do? In fact the
answer is almost nothing: the unary plus is a new addition to the language. It does
have its uses, as we'll see later on when we look into the order of evaluation of
expressions, but the unary plus has no effect on the *value* of its operand, only on
when its operand is evaluated.

The bitwise operators

One of the great strengths of C is the way that it allows systems programmers to do what had, before the advent of C, always been regarded as the province of the assembly code programmer. That sort of code was by definition highly non-portable. As C demonstrates, there isn't any magic about that sort of thing, and into the bargain it turns out to be surprisingly portable. What is it? It's what is often referred to as 'bit-twiddling' – the manipulation of individual bits in integer variables. None of the bitwise operators may be used on real operands because they aren't considered to have individual or accessible bits.

There are six bitwise operators, listed in Table 2.5.

Table 2.5 Bitwise operators

Operator	Effect
&	bitwise AND
|	bitwise OR
^	bitwise XOR
<<	left shift
>>	right shift
~	one's complement

Only the last, the one's complement, is a unary operator. It inverts the state of every bit in its operand and has the same effect as the unary minus on a one's complement computer. Most modern computers work with two's complement, so it isn't a waste of time having it there.

Illustrating the use of these operators is easier if we can use hexadecimal notation rather than decimal, so now is the time to see hexadecimal constants. Any number written with 0x at its beginning is interpreted as hexadecimal; both 15 and 0xf (or 0XF) mean the same thing. Try running this or, better still, try to predict what it does first and then try running it.

```
#include <stdio.h>
#include <stdlib.h>

main(){
    int x,y;
    x = 0; y = ~0;

    while(x != y){
        printf("%x & %x = %x\n",x,0xff, x&0xff);
        printf("%x | %x = %x\n",x,0x10f, x|0x10f);
        printf("%x ^ %x = %x\n",x,0xf00f, x^0xf00f);
        printf("%x >> 2 = %x\n",x,x >> 2);
        printf("%x << 2 = %x\n",x,x << 2);
```

```
            x = (x << 1) | 1;
      }
      exit(0);
}
```
(E2.9)

The way that the loop works in that example is the first thing to study. The controlling variable is x, which is initialized to zero. Every time round the loop it is compared against y, which has been set to a word-length independent pattern of all 1's by taking the one's complement of zero. At the bottom of the loop, x is shifted left once and has 1 ORed into it, giving rise to a sequence that starts 0, 1, 11, 111, ... in binary.

For each of the AND, OR, and XOR (exclusive OR) operators, x is operated on by the operator and some other interesting operand, then the result printed.

The left and right shift operators are in there too, giving a result which is the value of their left-hand operand shifted in the required direction a number of places specified by their right-hand operand. Shifting by more bits than there are in a word gives an implementation dependent result. Shifting left guarantees to shift zeros into the low-order bits.

Right shift is fussier. Your implementation is allowed to choose whether, when shifting signed operands, it performs a logical or arithmetic right shift. This means that a logical shift shifts zeros into the most significant bit positions; an arithmetic shift copies the current contents of the most significant bit back into itself. The position is clearer if an unsigned operand is right shifted, because there is no choice: it must be a logical shift. For that reason, whenever right shift is being used, you would expect to find that the thing being shifted had been declared to be unsigned, or cast to unsigned for the shift, as in the example:

```
int i, j;
i = (unsigned)j >> 4;
```

The second (right-hand) operand of a shift operator does not have to be a constant; any expression is legal. It is always converted to int and then the shift of the appropriate number of bits is made. Importantly, the rules involving mixed types of operands do not apply to the shift operators. The result of the shift has the same type as the thing that got shifted, and depends on nothing else.

Now something different; one of those little tricks that C programmers find helps to write better programs. If for any reason you want to form a value that has 1's in all but its least significant so-many bits, which are to have some other pattern in them, you don't have to know the word length of the machine. For example, to set the low order bits of an int to 0x0f0 and all the other bits to 1, this is the way to do it:

```
int some_variable;
some_variable = ~0xf0f;
```

The one's complement of the desired low-order bit pattern has been one's complemented. That gives exactly the required result and is completely independent of word length; it is a very common sight in C code.

There isn't a lot more to say about the bit-twiddling operators, and my experience of teaching C has been that most people find them easy to learn. Let's move on.

The assignment operators

No, that isn't a mistake, 'operators' was meant to be plural. C has several assignment operators, even though we have only seen the plain = so far. An interesting thing about them is that they are all like the other binary operators; they take two operands and produce a result, the result being usable as part of an expression. In this statement

```
x = 4;
```

the value 4 is assigned to x. The result has the type of x and the value that was assigned. It can be used like this

```
a = (x = 4);
```

where a will now have the value 4 assigned to it, after x has been assigned to. All of the simpler assignments that we have seen until now (except for one example) have simply discarded the resulting value of the assignment, even though it is produced.

It's because assignment has a result that an expression like

```
a = b = c = d;
```

works. The value of d is assigned to c, the result of that is assigned to b and so on. It makes use of the fact that expressions involving only assignment operators are evaluated from right to left, but is otherwise like any other expression. (The rules explaining what groups right to left and vice versa are given in Table 2.7.)

As a previous example pointed out, surprises can result. For example, when the following program was run on a DEC Vax machine, the value assigned to 11 turned out to be 0xffffffff, c1 printed as 0xffffffff and 12 was 0xff;

```
#include <stdio.h>
#include <stdlib.h>

main(){
      long l1, l2;
      char c1;
      l1 = c1 = l2 = 0xff;
      printf("l1 %lx l2 %lx c1 %x\n", l1, l2, c1);
      exit(0);
}
```

                                                          (E2.10)

Why? Because the assignment to 12 worked correctly, resulting in 0xff. That value was assigned to c1, which was an 8-bit byte on the machine. What's more, it was stored as a signed char, and on that two's complement machine it was the right bit pattern to represent -1. Both when printed and when assigned to l1, c1 was expanded to an int value of -1, as the integral promotions said it should be. Printed in hexadecimal, that has a value of 0xffffffff because the Vax ints are 32 bits long. That is the same value that l1 came out with, because long variables have the same size as int variables in that particular implementation. Be careful! To repeat the warning in the previous example: it is only safe to use multiple assignments with variables whose types are all the same, or when assigning 0.

If you look back to the section describing 'conversions', there is a description of what happens if you convert longer types to shorter types: that is what happens when the left-hand operand of an assignment is shorter than the right-hand one.

The remaining assignment operators are the compound assignment operators. They allow a useful shorthand, where an assignment containing the same left- and right-hand sides can be compressed; for example

```
x = x + 1;
```

can be written as

```
x += 1;
```

using one of the compound assignment operators. The result is the same in each case. It is a useful thing to do when the left-hand side of the operator is a complicated expression, not just a variable; such things occur when you start to use arrays and pointers. Most experienced C programmers tend to use the form given in the second example because somehow it 'feels better', a sentiment that no beginner has ever been known to agree with. Table 2.6 lists the compound assignment operators; you will see them used a lot from now on.

Table 2.6 Compound assignment operators

*=	/=	%=
+=	-=	
&=	|=	^=
>>=	<<=	

Reiterating: the result of an assignment operator has both the value and the type of the object that was assigned to.

Increment and decrement operators

It is so common to simply add or subtract 1 in an expression that C has two special unary operators to do the job. The increment operator ++ adds 1, the decrement -- subtracts 1. They are used like this:

```
x++;
++x;
x--;
--x;
```

where the operator can come either before or after its operand. In the cases shown it doesn't matter where the operator comes, but in more complicated cases the difference has a definite meaning and must be used properly.

Here is the difference being used.

```
#include <stdio.h>
#include <stdlib.h>
main(){
      int a,b;
      a = b = 5;

      printf("%d\n", ++a+5);
      printf("%d\n", a);
      printf("%d\n", b++ +5);
      printf("%d\n", b);
      exit(0);
}
```

(E2.11)

The results printed were

```
11
6
10
6
```

The difference is caused by the different positions of the operators. If the inc/decrement operator appears in front of the variable, then its value is changed by one and the *new* value is used in the expression. If the operator comes after the variable, then the *old* value is used in the expression and the variable's value is changed afterwards.

C programmers never add or subtract one with statements like this

```
x += 1;
```

they invariably use one of

```
x++; /* or */ ++x;
```

as a matter of course. A warning is in order though: it is not safe to use a variable more than once in an expression if it has one of these operators attached to it. There is no guarantee of when, within an expression, the affected variable will actually change value. The compiler might choose to 'save up' all of the changes and apply them at once, so an expression like this

```
y = x++ + --x;
```

does not guarantee to assign twice the original value of x to y. It might be evaluated as if it expanded to this instead:

```
y = x + (x-1);
```

because the compiler notices that the overall effect on the value of x is zero.

Exercises

2.16 Given the following variable definitions

```
int i1, i2;
float f1, f2;
```

a)   How would you find the remainder when i1 is divided by i2?

b)   How would you find the remainder when i1 is divided by the value of f1, treating f1 as an integer?

c)   What can you predict about the sign of the remainders calculated in the previous two questions?

d)   What meanings can the – operator have?

e)   How would you turn off all but the low-order four bits in i1?

f)   How would you turn on all the low-order four bits in i1?

g)   How would you turn off only the low-order four bits in i1?

h)   How would you put into i1 the low-order 8 bits in i2, but swapping the significance of the lowest four with the next four up?

i)   What is wrong with the following expression?

```
f2 = ++f1 + ++f1;
```

2.6.3 Precedence and grouping

After looking at the operators we have to consider the way that they work together. For things like addition it may not seem important; it hardly matters whether

```
a + b + c
```

is done as

```
(a + b) + c
```

or

```
a + (b + c)
```

does it? Well, yes in fact it does. If a+b would overflow and c held a value very close to -b, then the second grouping might give the correct answer where the first would cause undefined behaviour. The problem is much more obvious with integer division:

```
a/b/c
```

gives very different results when grouped as

```
a/(b/c)
```

or

```
(a/b)/c
```

If you don't believe that, try it with a=10, b=2, c=3. The first gives 10/(2/3); 2/3 in integer division gives 0, so we get 10/0 which immediately overflows. The second grouping gives (10/2), obviously 5, which divided by 3 gives 1.

The grouping of operators like that is known as **associativity**. The other question is one of **precedence**, where some operators have a higher priority than others and force evaluation of sub-expressions involving them to be performed before those with lower precedence operators. This is almost universal practice in high-level languages, so we 'know' that

```
a + b * c + d
```

groups as

```
a + (b * c) + d
```

indicating that multiplication has higher precedence than addition.

The large set of operators in C gives rise to 15 levels of precedence! Nobody bothers to remember them all. The complete list is given in Table 2.7, which indicates both precedence and associativity. Not all of the operators have been mentioned yet. Beware of the use of the same symbol for both unary and binary operators: the table indicates which are which.

Table 2.7   Operator precedence and associativity

Operator	Direction	Notes
() [] -> .	left to right	1
! ˜ ++ -- - + (cast) * & sizeof	right to left	all unary
* / %	left to right	binary
+ -	left to right	binary
<< >>	left to right	binary
< <= > >=	left to right	binary
== !=	left to right	binary
&	left to right	binary
^	left to right	binary
|	left to right	binary
&&	left to right	binary
||	left to right	binary
?:	right to left	2
= += and all combined assignment	right to left	binary
,	left to right	binary

1. Parentheses are for expression grouping, *not* function call.

2. This is unusual. See Section 3.4.1.

The question is, what can you do with that information, now that it's there? Obviously it's important to be able to work out both how to write expressions that evaluate in the proper order, and also how to read other people's. The technique is this: first, identify the unary operators and the operands that they refer to. This isn't such a difficult task but it takes some practice, especially when you discover that operators such as unary * can be applied an arbitrary number of times to their operands; this expression

a*****b

means a multiplied by *something*, where the something is an expression involving b and several unary * operators.

It's not too difficult to work out which are the unary operators; here are the rules.

1.   ++ and -- are always unary operators.

2.   The operator immediately to the right of an operand is a binary operator unless (1) applies, when the operator to *its* right is binary.

3.   All operators to the left of an operand are unary unless (2) applies.

Because the unary operators have very high precedence, you can work out what they do before worrying about the other operators. One thing to watch out for is the way that ++ and -- can be before or after their operands; the expression

```
a + -b++ + c
```

has two unary operators applied to b. The unary operators all associate right to left, so although the - comes first when you read the expression, it really parenthesizes (for clarity) like this:

```
a + -(b++) + c
```

The case is a little clearer if the prefix, rather than the postfix, form of the inc/decrement operators is being used. Again the order is right to left, but at least the operators come all in a row.

After sorting out what to do with the unary operators, it's easy to read the expression from left to right. Every time you see a binary operator, remember it. Look to the right: if the next binary operator is of a lower precedence, then the operator you just remembered is part of a subexpression to evaluate before anything else is seen. If the next operator is of the same precedence, keep repeating the procedure as long as equal precedence operators are seen. When you eventually find a lower precedence operator, evaluate the subexpression on the left according to the associativity rules. If a higher precedence operator is found on the right, forget the previous stuff: the operand to the left of the higher precedence operator is part of a subexpression separate from anything on the left so far. It belongs to the new operator instead.

If that lot isn't clear don't worry. A lot of C programmers have trouble with this area and eventually learn to parenthesize these expressions 'by eye', without ever using formal rules.

What *does* matter is what happens when you have fully parenthesized these expressions. Remember the 'usual rules of arithmetic'? They explained how you could predict the type of an expression from the operands involved. Now, even if you mix all sorts of types in a complicated expression, the types of the subexpressions are determined only from the the types of the operands in the subexpression. Look at this.

```
#include <stdio.h>

main(){
    int i,j;
    float f;
```

```
i = 5; j = 2;
f = 3.0;

f = f + j / i;
printf("value of f is %f\n", f);
return(0);
}
```
                                                                    (E2.12)

The value printed is 3.0000, not 5.0000 – which might surprise some, who thought that because a float was involved the whole statement involving the division would be done in that real type.

Of course, the division operator had only int types on either side, so the arithmetic was done as integer division and resulted in zero. The addition had a float and an int on either side, so the rules meant that the int was converted to float for the arithmetic, and that was the correct type for the assignment.

The previous section on casts showed one way of changing the type of an expression from its natural one to the one that you want. Be careful though:

```
(float)(j/i)
```

would still use integer division, *then* convert the result to float. To keep the remainder, you should use

```
(float)j/i
```

which would force real division to be used.

2.6.4 Parentheses and unary plus

C allows you to override the normal effects of precedence and associativity by the use of parentheses as the examples have illustrated. *Do not make the mistake* of thinking that the parentheses mean anything else. In some languages the parentheses force a particular order of evaluation. In C, the following four statements are identical in effect:

```
int a, b, c;
a+b+c;
(a+b)+c;
a+(b+c);
```

The parentheses will be ignored by the compiler where they are unnecessary. What's more, expressions involving more than one occurrence of the same commutative and associative binary operator, one of *, +, &, ^, |, can be regrouped arbitrarily provided that a regrouping does not change the type of the expression. If you want to *force* a particular order of evaluation – perhaps because you know that you can avoid overflow that way, or are taking the difference of two very close real numbers – then you can do one of two things.

You can either use an assignment to an explicit temporary variable to force a particular order:

```
float f1, f2, f3;
float temp;

temp = f1 - f2;
f3 = f3 + temp;
```

or you can use the unary +, which forces the evaluation of its operand *without* rearrangement:

```
float f1, f2, f3;

f3 = f3 + +(f1-f2);
```

In the absence of the unary + above, the compiler would have been entirely free to rearrange the expression to add f1 to f3 then subtract f2, which might give a different answer.

2.6.5 Side effects

To repeat and expand the warning given for the increment operators: it is unsafe to use the same variable more than once in an expression if evaluating the expression changes the variable and the new value could affect the result of the expression. This is because the change(s) may be 'saved up' and only applied at the end of the statement. So f = f+1; is safe even though f appears twice in a value-changing expression, f++; is also safe, but f = f++; is unsafe.

The problem can be caused by using an assignment, use of the increment or decrement operators, or by calling a function that changes the value of an external variable that is also used in the expression. These are generally known as 'side effects'. C makes almost no promise that side effects will occur in a predictable order within a single expression. (The discussion of 'sequence points' in Chapter 8 will be of interest if you care about this.)

2.7 Constants

2.7.1 Integer constants

The normal integer constants are obvious: things like 1, 1034 and so on. You can put l or L at the end of an integer constant to force it to be long. To make the constant unsigned, one of u or U can be used to do the job.

Integer constants can be written in hexadecimal by preceding the constant with 0x or 0X and using the upper or lower case letters a, b, c, d, e, f in the usual way.

Be careful about octal constants. They are indicated by starting the number with 0 and only using the digits 0, 1, 2, 3, 4, 5, 6, 7. It is easy to write 015 by accident, or out of habit, and not to realize that it is *not* in decimal. The mistake is most common with beginners, because experienced C programmers are forever alert to the danger.

The Standard has now invented a new way of working out what type an integer constant is. In the old days, if the constant was too big for an `int`, it got promoted to a `long` (without warning). Now, the rule is that a plain decimal constant will be fitted into the first in this list

```
int      long      unsigned long
```

that can hold the value.

Plain octal or hexadecimal constants will use this list

```
int      unsigned int      long      unsigned long
```

If the constant is suffixed by u or U:

```
unsigned int      unsigned long
```

If it is suffixed by l or L:

```
long      unsigned long
```

and finally, if it suffixed by both u or U and l or L, it can only be an `unsigned long`.

All that was done to try to give you 'what you meant'; what it does mean is that it is hard to work out exactly what the type of a constant expression is if you don't know something about the hardware. Hopefully, good compilers will warn when a constant is promoted up to another length and the U or L etc. is not specified.

A nasty bug hides here:

```
printf("value of 32768 is %d\n", 32768);
```

On a 16-bit two's complement machine, 32768 will be a `long` by the rules given above. But `printf` is only expecting an `int` as an argument (the `%d` indicates that). The type of the argument is just wrong. For the ultimate in safety-conscious programming, you should cast such cases to the right type:

```
printf("value of 32768 is %d\n", (int)32768);
```

It might interest you to note that there are no negative constants; writing −23 is an expression involving a positive constant and an operator.

Character constants are written by placing a sequence of characters between single quote marks:

```
'a'
'b'
'like this'
```

Although it is legal to have more than one character in the sequence, it gives a machine-dependent result. Single characters are the best from the portability point of view, resulting in an ordinary integer constant whose value is the machine representation of the single character.

To ease the way of representing some special characters that would otherwise be hard to get into a character constant (or hard to read; does ' ' contain a space or a tab?), there is what is called an **escape sequence** which can be used instead. Table 2.8 shows the escape sequences defined in the Standard.

Table 2.8 C escape sequences

Sequence	Represents
\a	audible alarm
\b	backspace
\f	form feed
\n	newline
\r	carriage return
\t	tab
\v	vertical tab
\\	backslash
\'	quote
\"	double quote
\?	question mark

It is also possible to use a sequence of either \0ooo or \0xddd, where the ooo and ddd are octal or hexadecimal digits respectively. That notation allows a specific value to be stated – it assumes that you know the internal representation that you want to specify. A common version of that is '\033', which is used by those who know that on an ASCII based machine, octal 33 is the ESC (escape) code.

Some of them aren't too obvious, so a brief explanation is needed. To get a single quote as a character constant you type '\'', to get a question mark you may have to use '\?'; not that it matters in that example, but to get two of them in there you can't use '??', because the sequence ??' is a trigraph! You would have to use '\?\?'. The escape \" is only necessary in strings, which will come later.

There are two distinct purposes behind the escape sequences. It's obviously necessary to be able to represent characters such as single quote and backslash unambiguously: that is one purpose. The second purpose applies to the following sequences which control the motions of a printing device when they are sent to it, as follows:

\a   Ring the bell if there is one. Do not move.

\b   Backspace.

\f   Go to the first position on the 'next page', whatever that may mean for the output device.

\n   Go to the start of the next line.

\r   Go back to the start of the current line.

\t   Go to the next horizontal tab position.

\v   Go to the start of the line at the next vertical tab position.

For \b, \t, \v, if there is no such position, the behaviour is unspecified. The Standard carefully avoids mentioning the physical directions of movement of the output device which are not necessarily the top to bottom, left to right movements common in Western cultural environments.

It is guaranteed that each escape sequence has a unique integral value which can be stored in a char.

2.7.2 Real constants

These follow the usual format:

```
1.0
2.
2.634
2.e5
2.e+5
2.5e5
3.1E-6
```

and so on. For readability, even if part of the number is zero, it is a good idea to show it:

```
1.0
0.1
```

The exponent part shows the number of powers of ten that the rest of the number should be raised to, so

```
3.0e3
```

is equivalent in value to the integer constant

```
3000
```

As you can see, the e can also be E. These constants all have type double unless they are suffixed with f or F to mean float or l or L to mean long double.

For completeness, here is the formal description of a real constant:

A real constant is one of:

* A **fractional constant** followed by an optional **exponent**.
* A **digit sequence** followed by an **exponent**.

In either case followed by an optional one of f, l, F, L, where:

* A **fractional constant** is one of:

    — An optional **digit sequence** followed by a decimal point followed by a **digit sequence**.
    — A **digit sequence** followed by a decimal point.

* An **exponent** is one of

    — e or E followed by an optional + or – followed by a **digit sequence**.

* A **digit sequence** is an arbitrary combination of one or more digits.

2.8 Summary

This has been a lengthy, and perhaps disconcerting chapter.

The alphabet of C, although of relevance, is not normally a day-to-day consideration of practising programmers, so it has been discussed but can now be largely ignored.

Much the same can be said regarding keywords and identifiers, since the topic is not complicated and simply becomes committed to memory.

The declaration of variables is rarely a problem, although it is worth re-emphasizing the distinction between a declaration and a definition. If that still remains unclear, you might find it of benefit to go back and re-read the description.

Beyond any question, the real complexity lies in what happens when the integral promotions and the arithmetic conversions occur. For beginners, it is often worthwhile to remember that here is a difficult and arduous piece of terrain. Nothing else in the language requires so much attention or is so important to the production of correct, reliable programs. Beginners should *not* try to remember it all, but to go on now and to gain confidence with the rest of the language. After two or three months' practice at using the easier parts of the language, the time really does come when you can no longer afford to ignore Section 2.6 .

Many highly experienced C programmers never bother to learn the different precedences of operators, except for a few important cases. A precedence table is always pinned just above my desk, for easy reference.

The Standard has substantially affected parts of the language described in this chapter. In particular, the change from 'unsignedness preserving' to 'value preserving' rules of arithmetic may cause some surprises to experienced C programmers. Even they have some real re-learning to do.

Exercises

2.17 First, fully parenthesize the following expressions according to the precedence and associativity rules. Then, replacing the variables and constants with the appropriate type names, show how the type of the expression is derived by replacing the highest precedence expressions with its resulting type.

The variables are:

```
char c;
int i;
unsigned u;
float f;
```

For example: `i = u+1;` parenthesizes as `(i = (u + 1));`
The types are

```
(int = (unsigned + int));
```

then

```
(int = (unsigned)); /* usual arithmetic conversions */
```

then

```
(int); /* assignment */
```

```
a)   c = u * f + 2.6L;
b)   u += --f / u % 3;
c)   i <<= u * - ++f;
d)   u = i + 3 + 4 + 3.1;
e)   u = 3.1 + i + 3 + 4;
f)   c = (i << - --f) & 0xf;
```

CHAPTER 3

Control of Flow and Logical Expressions

3.1 But I have to start from here ...

In this chapter we do two main jobs. We look at the various ways that the control of flow statements can be used in a C program, including some statements that haven't been introduced so far. They are almost always used in conjunction with **logical expressions** to select the next action. Examples of logical expressions that have been seen already are some simple ones used in `if` or `while` statements. As you might have expected, you can use expressions more complicated than simple comparison (>, <= == etc.); what may surprise you is the *type* of the result.

3.1.1 Logical expressions

All of the examples used so far in this book have deliberately avoided using complicated logical expressions in the control of flow statements. We have seen expressions like this

```
if(a != 100){...
```

and presumably you have formed the idea that C supports the concept of 'true' and 'false' for these relationships. In a way, it does, but in a way that differs from what is often expected.

All of the relational operators shown in Table 3.1 are used to compare two operands in the way indicated.

Be extra careful of the test for equality, ==. As has already been pointed out, it is often legal to use assignment = where you might have meant == and C can't tell you about your mistake. The results are normally different and it takes a long time for beginners to get used to using == and =.

Now, that usefully introduces the question 'why?'. Why are both legal? The answer is simple. C's concept of 'true' and 'false' boils down to simply 'non-zero' and 'zero', respectively. Anywhere that the relational operators appear, so may any other expression. If the expression evaluates to non-zero, then the result is effectively true. If the reverse is the case, then of course the result is false. The relational operators themselves have to perform comparison of their operands, and

58

Table 3.1 Relational operators

Operator	Operation
<	less than
<=	less than or equal to
>	greater than
>=	greater than or equal to
==	equal to
!=	not equal to

they give zero for false and (remember this) 1 for true. The result is of type `int`. This example shows how they work.

```
#include <stdio.h>
#include <stdlib.h>

main() {
    int i;

    i = -10;
    while(i <= 5){
        printf("value of i is %d, ", i);
        printf("i == 0 = %d, ", i==0 );
        printf("i > -5 = %d\n", i > -5);
        i++;
    }
    exit(0);
}                                                     (E3.1)
```

Which produces this on its standard output:

```
value of i is -10, i == 0 = 0, i > -5 = 0
value of i is -9, i == 0 = 0, i > -5 = 0
value of i is -8, i == 0 = 0, i > -5 = 0
value of i is -7, i == 0 = 0, i > -5 = 0
value of i is -6, i == 0 = 0, i > -5 = 0
value of i is -5, i == 0 = 0, i > -5 = 0
value of i is -4, i == 0 = 0, i > -5 = 1
value of i is -3, i == 0 = 0, i > -5 = 1
value of i is -2, i == 0 = 0, i > -5 = 1
value of i is -1, i == 0 = 0, i > -5 = 1
value of i is 0, i == 0 = 1, i > -5 = 1
value of i is 1, i == 0 = 0, i > -5 = 1
value of i is 2, i == 0 = 0, i > -5 = 1
value of i is 3, i == 0 = 0, i > -5 = 1
```

```
value of i is 4, i == 0 = 0, i > -5 = 1
value of i is 5, i == 0 = 0, i > -5 = 1
```

In this probably mistaken piece of code, work out what happens.

```
if(a = b)...
```

The value of b is assigned to a. As you know, the result has the type of a and whatever value was assigned to a. The if will execute the next statement if the value assigned is not zero. If zero is assigned, the next statement is ignored.

Now you will understand the problem with assignment! In all of the statements that test the value of an expression, the if, while, do, and for statements, the expression is simply tested to see if its result is zero or not.

We will look at each one in turn.

3.2 Control of flow

3.2.1 The if statement

The if statement has two forms:

>   if (*expression*) *statement*

>   if (*expression*) *statement1*
>   else *statement2*

In the first form, if (and only if) the *expression* is non-zero, the *statement* is executed. If the *expression* is zero, the *statement* is ignored. Remember that the *statement* can be compound; that is the way to put several statements under the control of a single if.

The second form is like the first except that if the statement shown as *statement1* is selected then *statement2* will not be, and vice versa.

Either form is considered to be a single statement in the syntax of C, so the following is completely legal.

>   if (*expression*)
>   if (*expression*) *statement*

The first if (*expression*) is followed by a properly formed, complete if statement. Since that is legally a statement, the first if can be considered to read

>   if (*expression*) *statement*

and is therefore itself properly formed. The argument can be extended as far as you like, but it's a bad habit to get into. It is better style to make the *statement* compound even if it isn't necessary. That makes it a lot easier to add extra statements if they are needed and generally improves readability.

The form involving `else` works the same way, so we can also write this.

```
if (expression)
      if (expression)
            statement
      else
            statement
```

As Chapter 1 has said already, this is now ambiguous. It is not clear, except as indicated by the indentation, which of the `if`s is responsible for the `else`. If we follow the rules that the previous example suggests, then the second `if` is followed by a statement, and is therefore itself a statement, so the `else` belongs to the first `if`.

That is *not* the way that C views it. The rule is that an `else` belongs to the first `if` above that hasn't already got an `else`. In the example we're discussing, the `else` goes with the second `if`.

The territory associated with an `if` does not extend outside any compound statement that contains it, so to prevent any unwanted association between an `else` and an `if` just above it, the `if` can be hidden away by using a compound statement. To repeat the example in Chapter 1, here it is.

```
if (expression) {
      if (expression)
            statement
}else
      statement
```

Putting in all the compound statement brackets, it becomes this:

```
if (expression) {
      if (expression) {
            statement
      }
}else{
      statement
}
```

If you happen not to like the placing of the brackets, it is up to you to put them where you think they look better; just be consistent about it.

3.2.2 The `while` and `do` statements

The `while` is ludicrously simple. Here, as with the `if`, is the form of a `while`.

```
while (expression)
      statement
```

The *statement* is only executed if the *expression* is non-zero. After every execution of the *statement*, the *expression* is evaluated again and the process repeats if it is non-zero. What could be plainer than that? The only point to watch out for is that the *statement* may never be executed, and that if nothing in the *statement* affects the value of the *expression* then the while will either do nothing or loop for ever, depending on the initial value of the *expression*.

It is occasionally desirable to guarantee at least one execution of the statement following the while, so an alternative form exists known as the do statement. It looks like this:

```
do
      statement
while (expression) ;
```

and you should pay close attention to that semicolon – it is not optional! The effect is that the statement part is executed before the controlling expression is evaluated, so this guarantees at least one trip around the loop. It was an unfortunate decision to use the keyword while for both purposes, but it doesn't seem to cause too many problems in practice.

If you feel the urge to use a do, think carefully. It is undoubtedly essential in certain cases, but experience has shown that the use of the do statement is often associated with poorly constructed code. Not every time, obviously, but as a general rule you should stop and ask yourself if you have made the right choice. Their use often indicates a hangover of thinking methods learnt with other languages, or just sloppy mental practices. When you *do* convince yourself that nothing else will give you just what is wanted, then you'll have learnt something.

Handy hints

A *very* common trick in C programs is to use the result of an assignment to control while and do loops. It is so commonplace that, even if you look at it the first time and blench, you've got no alternative but to learn it. It falls into the category of 'idiomatic' C and eventually becomes second nature to anybody who really uses the language. Here is the most common example of all:

```
#include <stdio.h>

main(){
    int input_c;

    /* The Classic Bit */
    while( (input_c = getchar()) != EOF){
        printf("%c was read\n", input_c);
    }
    return(0);
}
```
                                                                    (E3.2)

The clever bit is the expression assigning to `input_c`. It is assigned to, compared with EOF (End Of File), and used to control the loop all in one go. Embedding the assignment like that is a very useful thing to be able to do. Admittedly it only saves one line of code, but the benefit in terms of readability (once you have got used to seeing it) is quite large. Learn where the parentheses are, too. They're necessary for precedence reasons – work out why!

Note that `input_c` is an `int`. This is because `getchar` has to be able to return not only every possible value of a `char`, but also an extra value, EOF. To do that, a type longer than a `char` is necessary.

Both the `while` and the `do` statements are themselves syntactically a single statement, just like an `if` statement. They occur anywhere that any other single statement is permitted. If you want them to control *several* statements, then you will have to use a compound statement, as the examples for `if` illustrated.

3.2.3 The `for` statement

It's very common to see a loop that is controlled by some variable used as a counter, which is generally called 'the loop control variable'. The counter doesn't always have to count consecutive values, but the normal arrangement is for it to be initialized outside the loop, for it to be checked every time around the loop to see when to finish and for it to be updated each time around the loop. There are three important places, then, where the loop control is concentrated: initialize, check, update. This example shows them.

```
#include <stdio.h>
#include <stdlib.h>
main(){
    int i;

    /* initialise */
    i = 0;
    /* check */
    while(i <= 10){
        printf("%d\n", i);
        /* update */
        i++;
    }
    exit(0);
}                                                    (E3.3)
```

As you will have noticed, the initialization and check parts of the loop are close together and their location is obvious because of the presence of the `while` keyword. What is harder to spot is the place where the update occurs, especially if the value of the controlling variable is used within the loop. In that case, which is by far the most common, the update has to be at the very end of the loop, far away from the initialize and check. Readability suffers; it is now hard to work out how the loop is going to perform unless you read the whole body of the loop carefully. What is needed is some way of bringing the initialize, check and update parts into one place so that they can be read quickly and conveniently. That is exactly what the for statement is designed to do. Here it is.

for (*initialize; check; update*) *statement*

The *initialize* part is an expression; nearly always an assignment expression which is used to initialize the control variable. After the initialization, the *check* expression is evaluated: if it is non-zero, the *statement* is executed, followed by evaluation of the *update* expression which generally increments the control variable, then the sequence restarts at the *check*. The loop terminates as soon as the *check* evaluates to zero.

There are two important things to realize about that last description: one, that each of the three parts of the for statement between the parentheses are just expressions; two, that the description has carefully explained what they are intended to be used for without insisting that they should be used for nothing else – that was done deliberately. You can use the expressions to do whatever you like, but at the expense of readability if they aren't used for their intended purpose.

Here is a program that does the same thing twice, the first time using a while loop, the second time with a for. The use of the increment operator is exactly the sort of use that you will see in everyday practice.

```
#include <stdio.h>
#include <stdlib.h>
main(){
    int i;

    i = 0;
    while(i <= 10){
        printf("%d\n", i);
        i++;
    }

    /* the same done using ''for'' */
    for(i = 0; i <= 10; i++){
        printf("%d\n", i);
    }
    exit(0);
}                                                          (E3.4)
```

There isn't any difference betweeen the two, so you only have to remember that in this case the for loop is more convenient and maintainable than the while statement. You should always use the for when it's appropriate; when a loop is being controlled by some sort of counter. The while is more at home when an indeterminate number of cycles of the loop are part of the problem. As always, it needs a degree of judgement on behalf of the author of the program; an understanding of form, style, elegance and the poetry of a well written program. These qualities are, sadly, not common.

Any of the three expressions (initialize, check, update) in the for statement can be omitted, although the semicolons must stay. This can happen if the counter is already initialized, or gets updated in the body of the loop. If the check is omitted, it is assumed to result in a 'true' value and the loop never terminates. A common way of writing never-ending loops is either

```
for(;;)
```

or

```
while(1)
```

and both can be seen in existing programs.

3.2.4 A brief pause

The control of flow statements that we've just seen are quite adequate to write programs of any degree of complexity. They lie at the core of C and even a quick reading of everyday C programs will illustrate their importance, both in the provision of essential functionality and in the structure that they emphasize. The remaining statements are used to give programmers finer control or to make it easier to deal with exceptional conditions. Only the switch statement is enough of a heavyweight to need no justification for its use; yes, it can be replaced with lots of ifs, but it adds a lot of readability. The others, break, continue and goto, are like the spices in your program's soup. Used carefully they can turn something commonplace into a treat, but use too heavy a hand and they will drown the flavour of everything else.

3.2.5 The switch statement

This is not an essential part of C. You could do without it, but the language would have become significantly less expressive and pleasant to use.

It is used to select one of a number of alternative actions depending on the value of an expression, and nearly always makes use of another of the lesser statements: the break. It looks like this.

```
switch (expression) {
         case const1:    statements
         case const2:    statements
         default:        statements
}
```

The *expression* is evaluated and its value compared with all of the *const1* etc. expressions, which must all evaluate to different constant values. If any of them has the same value as the *expression* then the statement following the case label is selected for execution. If the default is present, it will be selected when there is no matching value found. If there is no default and no matching value, the entire switch statement will do nothing and execution will continue at the following statement.

One curious feature is that the cases are *not* exclusive, as this example shows.

```
#include <stdio.h>
#include <stdlib.h>
main(){
    int i;
    for(i = 0; i <= 10; i++){
        switch(i){
            case 1:
            case 2:
                printf("1 or 2\n");
            case 7:
                printf("7\n");
            default:
                printf("default\n");
        }
    }
    exit(0);
}
```
(E3.5)

The loop cycles with i having values 0-10. A value of 1 or 2 will cause the printing of the message 1 or 2 by selecting the first of the printf statements. What you might not expect is the way that the remaining messages would also appear! It's because the switch only selects one entry point to the body of the statement; after starting at a given point all of the following statements are also executed. The case and default prefixes simply allow you to indicate *which* of the statements is to be selected. When i has the value of 7, only the last two messages will be printed. Any value other than 1, 2, or 7 will find only the last message.

The prefixes can occur in any order, but no two values may be the same and you are allowed either one or no default (which doesn't have to be the last prefix). Several prefixes can be put in front of one statement and several statements can be put after one prefix.

The expression controlling the switch can be of any of the integral types. Old C used to insist on *only* int here, and some compilers would forcibly truncate any longer types used!

The major restriction
The biggest problem with the switch statement is obviously that it doesn't allow you to select mutually exclusive courses of action; once the body of the statement

has been entered any subsequent statements within the body will all be executed. What is needed is the break statement. Here is the previous example, but amended to make sure that the messages printed come out in a more sensible order. The break statements cause execution to leave the switch statement immediately and prevent any further statements in the body of the switch from being executed.

```
#include <stdio.h>
#include <stdlib.h>
main(){
    int i;
    for(i = 0; i <= 10; i++){
        switch(i){
            case 1:
            case 2:
                printf("1 or 2\n");
                break;
            case 7:
                printf("7\n");
                break;
            default:
                printf("default\n");
        }
    }
    exit(0);
}                                                    (E3.6)
```

The break has further uses. Its own section follows.

3.2.6 The break statement

This is a simple statement. It only makes sense if it occurs in the body of a switch, do, while or for statement. When it is executed the control of flow jumps to the statement immediately following the body of the statement containing the break. Its use is widespread in switch statements, where it is more or less essential to get the control that most people want.

The use of the break within loops is of dubious legitimacy. It has its moments, but is really only justifiable when exceptional circumstances have happened and the loop has to be abandoned. It would be nice if more than one loop could be abandoned with a single break but that isn't how it works. Here is an example.

```
#include <stdio.h>
#include <stdlib.h>
main(){
    int i;
```

```
for(i = 0; i < 10000; i++){
    if(getchar() == 's')
        break;
    printf("%d\n", i);
}
exit(0);
}
```
(E3.7)

It reads a single character from the program's input before printing the next in a sequence of numbers. If an 's' is typed, the break causes an exit from the loop.

If you want to exit from more than one level of loop, the break is the wrong thing to use. The goto is the only easy way, but since it can't be mentioned in polite company, we'll leave it till last.

3.2.7 The continue statement

This statement has only a limited number of uses. The rules for its use are the same as for break, with the exception that it doesn't apply to switch statements. Executing a continue starts the next iteration of the smallest enclosing do, while or for statement immediately. The use of continue is largely restricted to the top of loops, where a decision has to be made whether or not to execute the rest of the body of the loop. In this example it ensures that division by zero (which gives undefined behaviour) doesn't happen.

```
#include <stdio.h>
#include <stdlib.h>
main(){
    int i;

    for(i = -10; i < 10; i++){
        if(i == 0)
            continue;
        printf("%f\n", 15.0/i);
    }
    exit(0);
}
```
(E3.8)

You could justifiably argue that, instead of a conditional continue, the body of the loop should be made conditional instead. It is a valid argument, but is too puritanical for my taste. I'd rather have the continue than the extra level of indentation, particularly if the body of the loop is large.

Of course the continue can be used in other parts of a loop, too, where it may occasionally help to simplify the logic of the code and improve readability. It deserves to be used sparingly.

Do remember that continue has no special meaning to a switch statement, where break does have. Inside a switch, continue is only legal if there is a loop that encloses the `switch`, in which case the next iteration of the loop will be started.

There is an important difference between loops written with `while` and `for`. In a `while`, a `continue` will go immediately to the test of the controlling expression. The same thing in a `for` will do two things: first the update expression is evaluated, *then* the controlling expresion is evaluated.

3.2.8 `goto` and labels

Everybody knows that the `goto` statement is a 'bad thing'. Used without care it is a great way of making programs hard to follow and of obscuring any structure in their flow. Dijkstra wrote a famous paper in 1968 called 'Goto Statement Considered Harmful', which everybody refers to and almost nobody has read.

What's especially annoying is that there are times when it is the most appropriate thing to use in the circumstances! In C, it is used to escape from multiple nested loops, or to go to an error handling exit at the end of a function. You will need a **label** when you use a `goto`; this example shows both.

```
goto L1;
/* whatever you like here */
L1: /* anything else */
```

A label is an identifier followed by a colon. Labels have their own 'name space' so they can't clash with the names of variables or functions. The name space only exists for the function containing the label, so label names can be re-used in different functions. The label can be used before it is declared, too, simply by mentioning it in a `goto` statement.

Labels *must* be part of a full statement, even if it's an empty one. This usually only matters when you're trying to put a label at the end of a compound statement – like this.

```
label_at_end: ; /* empty statement */
}
```

The `goto` works in an obvious way, jumping to the labelled statements. It is only possible to jump to a label in the same function as the `goto`. The names of any labels used in a function are forgotten at the end of it, so you only have to worry about using the same name twice in a single function.

It's hard to give rigid rules about the use of `goto`s but, as with the `do`, `continue` and the `break` (except in `switch` statements), over-use should be avoided. Think carefully every time you feel like using one, and convince yourself that the structure of the program demands it. More than one `goto` per 3–5 functions is a symptom that should be viewed with deep suspicion.

3.2.9 Summary

Now we've seen all of the control of flow statements and examples of their use. Some should be used whenever possible, some are not for use line by line but for special purposes where their particular job is called for. It is possible to write elegant and beautiful programs in C if you are prepared to take the extra bit of care necessary; the specialized control of flow statements give you the chance to add the extra polish that some other languages lack.

All that remains to be done to complete the picture of flow of control in C is to finish off the logical operators.

3.3 Logical expressions

This chapter has already shown how C makes no distinction between 'logical' and other values. The relational operators all give a result of 0 or 1 for false and true, respectively. Whenever the control of flow statements demand it, an expression is evaluated to determine what to do next. A 0 means 'don't do it'; anything else means 'do'. It means that the fragments below are all quite reasonable.

```
while (a<b)...
while (a)....
if ( (c=getchar()) != EOF)...
```

No experienced C programmer would be surprised by any of them. The second of them, `while (a)`, is a common abbreviation for `while (a != 0)`, as you should be able to work out.

What we need now is a way of combining expressions that are only being used in the true or false sense. So far, it has to be done like this, when we wanted to say `if(a<b AND c<d)`

```
if (a < b){
    if (c < d)...
}
```

It will not be a source of great amazement to find that there is a way of expressing such a statement.

There are three operators involved in this sort of operation: the logical AND `&&`, the logical OR `||` and the NOT `!`. The last is unary, the other two are binary. All of them take expressions as their operands and give as results either 1 or 0. The `&&` gives 1 only when both of its operands are non-zero. The `||` gives 0 only when both operands are zero. The `!` gives 0 if its operand is non-zero and vice versa. Easy really. The results are of type `int` for all three.

Do not confuse `&` and `|` (the bitwise operators) with their logical counterparts. They will give different results.

One special feature of the logical operators, found in very few of the other operators, is their effect on the sequence of evaluation of an expression. C generally makes no guarantee about when the various parts of an expression will be evaluated; the precedence and associativity rules only serve to show how things 'bind together' in the absence of parentheses. Subexpressions with side effects, say assignment, cannot be forced to evaluate in any special order. This rather nasty piece of code illustrates the problem:

```
b + (b=c)
```

Whether that assigns c to b and then adds the new value to the new value or the old value of b depends on when the assignment is considered to have been completed. C explicitly makes no promises – it doesn't even have to be done consistently the same way (but see the discussion of 'sequence points' in Chapter 8). The problem is your own; you shouldn't have written code that depends on such sequencing. Even the unary plus doesn't help here.

The logical operators are the only ones that do give a guarantee: they evaluate left to right (after precedence is taken into account) and every logical expression ceases evaluation as soon as the overall result can be determined. For example, a sequence of | |s can stop as soon as one operand is found to be non-zero. This next fragment guarantees never to divide by zero.

```
if (a!=0 && b/a > 5)...
/* alternative */
if (a && b/a > 5)
```

In either version a must be non-zero to make the next expression a candidate for evaluation. If a were zero, the overall result would already have been decided, so the evaluation must stop to conform with C's rules for the logical operators.

The unary NOT is simple. It isn't all that common to see it in use largely because most expresssions can be rearranged to do without it. The example shows why.

```
if (!a)...
/* alternative */
if (a==0)...

if(!(a>b))
/* alternative */
if(a <= b)
```

Now, I wouldn't argue that either example is more readable (but I understand C). Most beginners are already a bit unhappy about if (a) being the same as if (a!=0), so it would be the last straw to write an expression involving ! as well. It seems to be an attitude that carries over into code written by mature programmers. In the next example, the reason is more obvious.

```
if (!(a>b && c<d))...
```

```
/* or */
if (a<=b || c>=d)...
```

Once again the result is the same in each case and the ! is not essential. You might find that one or the other feels more right in terms of the problem being solved. If that is the case, use the most natural one, because it is likely to be more readable.

Most expressions using these logical operators work out just about right in terms of the precedence rules, but you can get a few nasty surprises. If you look back to the precedence tables, you will find that there are some operators with lower precedence than the logical ones. In particular, this is a very common mistake:

```
if(a&b == c){...
```

What happens is that b is compared for equality with c, then the 1 or 0 result is anded with a! Some very unexpected behaviour has been caused by that sort of error.

3.4 Strange operators

There are two operators left to mention which look decidedly odd. They aren't 'essential', but from time to time do have their uses. Don't ignore them completely.

3.4.1 The ?: operator

Like playing the accordion, this is easier to demonstrate than to describe.

expression1 ? *expression2* : *expression3*

If *expression1* is true, then the result of the whole expression is *expression2*, otherwise it is *expression3*. Both *expression2* and *expression3* must have the same type, or be convertible to the same type by the usual rules. Further, one may be a pointer and the other a null pointer constant, or one a pointer to an object and the other a pointer to void.

Depending on the value of *expression1*, only one of them will be evaluated when the result is calculated.

The shortest useful example that I can think of is this one, where the string to be printed by printf is selected using this magical operator.

```
#include <stdio.h>
#include <stdlib.h>

main(){
    int i;
```

```
for(i=0; i <= 10; i++){
    printf((i&1) ? "odd\n" : "even\n");
}
exit(0);
}
```

(E3.9)

It's cute when you need it, but the first time that most people see it they look very uncomfortable.

After evaluating the first operand there is one of the **sequence points** described in Chapter 8.

3.4.2 The comma operator

This wins the prize for 'most obscure operator'. It allows a list of expressions to be separated by commas:

expression-1 , expression-2 , expression-3 , . . . , expression-n

and it goes on as long as you like. The *expressions* are evaluated strictly left to right and their values discarded, except for the last one, whose type and value determine the result of the overall expression. Don't confuse this version of the comma with any of the other uses C finds for it, especially the one that separates function arguments. Here are a couple of examples of it in use.

```
#include <stdio.h>
#include <stdlib.h>

main(){
    int i, j;

    /* comma used - this loop has two counters */
    for(i=0, j=0; i <= 10; i++, j = i*i){
        printf("i %d j %d\n", i, j);
    }

    /*
     * In this futile example, all but the last
     * constant value is discarded.
     * Note use of parentheses to force a comma
     * expression in a function call.
     */
    printf("Overall: %d\n", ("abc", 1.2e6, 4*3+2));
    exit(0);
}
```

(E3.10)

Unless you are feeling very adventurous, the comma operator is just as well ignored. Be prepared to see it only on special occasions.

After evaluating each operand there is one of the **sequence points** described in Chapter 8.

3.5 Summary

This chapter has completely described the entire range of control of flow available in C. The only areas that cause even moderate surprise are the way in which cases in a `switch` statement are not mutually exclusive, and the fact that `goto` cannot transfer control to any function except the one that is currently active. None of this is intellectually deep and it has never been known to cause problems to either beginners, or programmers experienced in other languages.

The logical expressions all give integral results. This is perhaps slightly unusual, but once again takes very little time to learn.

Probably the most surprising part about the whole chapter will have been to learn of the conditional and comma operators. A strong case could be made for the abolition of the conditional operator, were it not for compatibility with existing code, but the comma operator does have important uses, especially for automatic generators of C programs.

The Standard has had almost no effect on the contents of this chapter. Prospective users of C should ensure that they are completely familiar with all of the topics discussed here. They are essential to the practical use of the language, and none of the material is hard.

Exercises

3.1   What is the type and value of the result of the relational operators?

3.2   What is the type and value of the result of the logical operators (`&&`, `||`, and `!`)?

3.3   What is unusual about the logical operators?

3.4   Why is `break` useful in `switch` statements?

3.5   Why is `continue` not very useful in `switch` statements?

3.6   What is a possible problem using `continue` in `while` statements?

3.7   How can you jump from one function to another?

## CHAPTER 4

Functions

4.1 Changes

Old C was pretty successful despite a defect which even admirers of the language would admit was bad. The defect was that you could declare neither the number nor the type of arguments to functions. This lead to numerous portability and reliability problems, and to so much general confusion that it has to be the worst single point of Old C by a mile.

The Standard has changed that state of affairs. It is now possible to declare the number and type of arguments and have the compiler check the use of functions for consistency. Another useful feature is a portable way of using functions with a variable number of arguments, like `printf`, which used to be non-portable; the only way to implement it relied upon intimate knowledge of the hardware involved.

There was a while when some of the doom-sayers, the circling vultures around the Standard, were voicing doubts about this. They have been effectively silenced by C++, which uses almost identical syntax to the one proposed in the Standard and has been met with rapture on this issue.

The Standard still retains compatibility with Old C function declarations, but that is purely for the benefit of existing programs. Any new programs should make full use of the much tighter checking that the Standard permits and strenuously avoid the old syntax (which may disappear one day).

4.2 The type of functions

All functions have a type: they all return a value of that type whenever they are used. The reason that C doesn't have 'procedures', which in most other languages are simply functions without a value, is that in C it is permissible (in fact well-nigh mandatory) to discard the eventual value of most expressions. If that surprises you, think of an assignment

```
a = 1;
```

That's a perfectly legal assignment, but don't forget that it has a value too. The value is discarded. If you want a bigger surprise, try this one:

```
1;
```

That is an expression followed by a semicolon. It is a well formed statement according to the rules of the language; nothing wrong with it, it is just useless. A function used as a procedure is used in the same way – a value is *always* returned, but you don't use it:

```
f(argument);
```

is also an expression with a discarded value.

It's all very well saying that the value returned by a function can be ignored, but the fact remains that if the function really *does* return a value then it's probably a programming error not to do something with it. Conversely, if no useful value is returned then it's a good idea to be able to spot anywhere that it is used by mistake. For both of those reasons functions that don't return a useful value should be declared to be `void`.

Functions can return any type supported by C, including the pointers, structures and unions which are described in later chapters.

All functions can be called recursively (except `main`, which the Standard specifically excludes).

4.2.1 Declaring functions

Unfortunately, we are going to have to use some jargon now. This is one of the times that the use of an appropriate technical term really does reduce the amount of repetitive descriptive text that would be needed. The result is a shorter, more accurate and less confusing explanation (I hope). Here are the terms.

declaration
> The point at which a name has a type associated with it.

definition
> Also a declaration, but at this point some storage is reserved for the named object. The rules for what makes a declaration into a definition can be complicated, but are easy for functions: You turn a function declaration into a definition by providing a body for the function in the form of a compound statement.

formal parameter
formal argument
> I will use these terms interchangeably. They are the names used inside a function to refer to its arguments.

actual parameter
actual argument
> Again, interchangeable. These are the names or values used as arguments when the function is actually called. In other words, the values that the

formal parameters will have on entry to the function.

If you use a function before you declare it, it is implicitly declared to be 'function returning int'. Although this will work, and was widely used in Old C, it is dangerous and very bad practice. All functions should be fully declared before they are used. For example, you might be intending to use a function in a private library called, say, aax1. You know that it takes no arguments and returns a double. Here is how it should be declared:

```
double aax1(void);
```

and here is how it might be used:

```
main () {
    double return_v, aax1(void);
    return_v = aax1();
    exit(0);
}
```
                                                                    (E4.1)

The declaration was an interesting one. It defined return_v, actually causing a variable to come into existence. It also declared aax1 without defining it; functions only become *defined* when a body is provided for them. Without a declaration in force, the default rules mean that aax1 would have been assumed to be int when its use was finally found. The presence of void in the argument list in the declaration shows that the function really takes no arguments. If it had been missing, the declaration would have been taken to give no information about the function's arguments. That way, compatibility with Old C is maintained.

To **define** a function you also have to provide a body for it, in the form of a compound statement. Since no function can itself contain the definition of a function, all functions are separate from each other and fall into the category of **external objects**. Here is a possible definition for the function aax1.

```
double
aax1(void) {
    /* code for function body */
    return (1.0);
}
```

It is unusual for a block-structured language to prohibit you from defining functions inside other functions, but this is one of the characteristics of C. Although it isn't obvious, this helps to improve the run-time performance of C by reducing the complexity of function calls.

4.2.2 The return statement

The return statement is very important. Every function except those returning void should have at least one, each return showing what value is supposed to be returned at that point. Although it is possible to return from a function by falling through the last }, unless the function returns void an unknown value will be returned, resulting in undefined behaviour.

Here is another example function. It uses getchar to read characters from the program input and returns whatever it sees except for space, tab or newline, which it throws away.

```
#include <stdio.h>

int
non_space(void){
    int c;
    while ( (c=getchar ())=='\t' || c== '\n'
        || c==' ')
        ; /* empty statement */
    return (c);
}
```

Look at the way that all of the work is done by the test in the while statement, whose body was an empty statement. It is not an uncommon sight to see the semicolon of the empty statement sitting there alone and forlorn, with only a piece of comment for company and readability. Please, please, never write it like this:

```
while (something);
```

with the semicolon hidden away at the end like that. It's too easy to miss it when you read the code, and to assume that the following statement is under the control of the while.

The type of expression returned must match the type of the function, or be capable of being converted to it as if an assignment statement were in use. For example, a function declared to return double could contain

```
return (1);
```

and the integral value will be converted to double. If the function returns one of the more complicated types described later, such as a **structure**, it may not be possible to convert the type of expression to the type of the function. The compiler will let you know!

4.2.3 Arguments to functions

Before the Standard, it was not possible to give any information about a function's arguments except in the definition of the function itself. The information was only used in the body of the function and was forgotten at the end. In those bad old days, it was quite possible to define a function that had three double arguments and only to pass it one int when it was called. The program would compile normally, but simply not work properly. It was considered to be the programmer's job to check that the number and the type of arguments to a function matched correctly. As you would expect, this turned out to be a first-rate source of bugs and portability problems. Here is an example of the definition and use of a function with arguments, but omitting for the moment to declare the function fully.

```c
#include <stdio.h>
#include <stdlib.h>
main(){
    void pmax();                    /* declaration */
    int i,j;
    for(i = -10; i <= 10; i++){
        for(j = -10; j <= 10; j++){
            pmax(i,j);
        }
    }
    exit(0);
}
/*
 * Function pmax.
 * Returns: void
 * Prints larger of its two arguments.
 */
void
pmax(int a1, int a2){               /* definition */
    int biggest;

    if(a1 > a2){
        biggest = a1;
    }else{
        biggest = a2;
    }

    printf("larger of %d and %d is %d\n",
        a1, a2, biggest);
}                                               (E4.2)
```

What can we learn from this? To start with, notice the careful declaration that pmax returns void. In the function definition, the matching void occurs on the line before the function name. The reason for writing it like that is purely one of style; it makes it easier to find function definitions if their names are always at the beginning of a line.

The function declaration (in main) gave no indication of any arguments to the function, yet the use of the function a couple of lines later involved two arguments. That is permitted by both the old and Standard versions of C, but *must nowadays be considered to be bad practice*. It is much better to include information about the arguments in the declaration too, as we will see.

Now on to the function definition, where the body is supplied. The definition shows that the function takes two arguments, which will be known as a1 and a2 throughout the body of the function. The types of the arguments are specified too, as can be seen.

It is permitted, if you want, not to give any explicit type information for a function's formal arguments; they take the type int by default, but it is not good style to rely on this. If you adopt the practice of always declaring arguments, even if they do happen to be int, it adds to a reader's confidence. It indicates that you meant to use that type, instead of getting it by accident: it wasn't simply forgotten. The definition of pmax *could* have been this:

```
/* BAD STYLE OF FUNCTION DEFINITION */

void
pmax(a1, a2){
    /* and so on */
```

4.2.4 Function prototypes

The introduction of **function prototypes** is the biggest change of all in the Standard.

A function prototype is a function declaration or definition which includes information about the number and types of the arguments that the function takes.

Although you are allowed not to specify any information about a function's arguments in a declaration, it is purely because of backwards compatibility with Old C and is to be avoided.

A declaration without any information about the arguments is not a prototype.

Here's the previous example 'done right'.

```
#include <stdio.h>
#include <stdlib.h>
main(){
    void pmax(int first, int second);/*declaration*/
    int i,j;
    for(i = -10; i <= 10; i++){
        for(j = -10; j <= 10; j++){
            pmax(i,j);
        }
    }
    exit(0);
}

void
pmax(int a1, int a2){                    /*definition*/
```

```
        int biggest;

        if(a1 > a2){
            biggest = a1;
        }
        else{
            biggest = a2;
        }

        printf("largest of %d and %d is %d\n",
            a1, a2, biggest);
}                                                    (E4.3)
```

This time, the declaration provides information about the function arguments, so it's a prototype. The names first and second are not an essential part of the declaration, but they are allowed to be there because it makes it easier to refer to named arguments when you're documenting the use of the function. Using them, we can describe the function simply by giving its declaration

```
void pmax (int xx, int yy );
```

and then say that pmax prints whichever of the arguments xx or yy is the larger. Referring to arguments by their position, which is the alternative (e.g. the fifth argument), is tedious and prone to miscounting.

All the same, you can miss out the names if you want to. This declaration is entirely equivalent to the one above.

```
void pmax (int,int);
```

All that is needed is the type names.

For a function that has no arguments the declaration is

```
void f_name (void);
```

and a function that has one int, one double and an unspecified number of other arguments is declared this way:

```
void f_name (int,double,...);
```

The ellipsis (...) shows that other arguments follow. That's useful because it allows functions like printf to be written. Its declaration is this:

```
int printf (const char *format_string,...)
```

where the type of the first argument is 'pointer to const char'; we'll discuss what that means later.

Once the compiler knows the types of a function's arguments, having seen them in a prototype, it's able to check that the use of the function conforms to the declaration.

If a function is called with arguments of the wrong type, the presence of a prototype means that the actual argument is converted to the type of the formal argument 'as if by assignment'. Here's an example: a function is used to evaluate a square root using Newton's method of successive approximations. This is not recommended for everyday use because it doesn't always converge.

```
#include <stdio.h>
#include <stdlib.h>
#define DELTA 0.0001
main(){
    double sq_root(double); /* prototype */
    int i;

    for(i = 1; i < 100; i++){
        printf("root of %d is %f\n", i, sq_root(i));
    }
    exit(0);
}


double
sq_root(double x){   /* definition */
    double curr_appx, last_appx, diff;

    last_appx = x;
    diff = DELTA+1;

    while(diff > DELTA){
        curr_appx = 0.5*(last_appx
            + x/last_appx);
        diff = curr_appx - last_appx;
        if(diff < 0)
            diff = -diff;
        last_appx = curr_appx;
    }
    return(curr_appx);
}
```
(E4.4)

The prototype tells everyone that sq_root takes a single argument of type double. The argument actually passed in the main function is an int, so it has to be converted to double; the conversion is done as if the int were being assigned to a double. The critical point is that if no prototype had been seen, C would assume that the programmer had meant to pass an int and an int is what would be passed. The Standard simply notes that this results in undefined behaviour, which is as understated as saying that catching rabies is unfortunate. This is a *very serious error* and has led to many, many problems in Old C programs.

In the UNIX world, there's a famous tool called `lint`, which checks things for you. It knows quite a lot about the silly things that frail humanity finds hard in C, and it's particularly careful about function arguments. It's just like a C compiler, but it performs a lot of consistency checks and looks for common programming errors that a compiler is not expected to worry about. `Lint`, or something like it, used to be a very useful thing to have.

With the new Standard, it's likely that `lint` will become less important as compilers take upon themselves the burden of doing more checking. The introduction of function prototypes will help considerably, as anyone who has had the chance to try them will testify.

Warning

You must take care to make sure that function prototypes are always visible wherever their associated functions are called. Although function prototypes are not mandatory, once one has been used, it should be thought of as being almost mandatory. The reason for this is that it allows the compiler to do unusual optimizations of argument passing – the lack of a prototype constrains the compiler to pass arguments in what may be an inefficient way.

The easiest, and best, way to do this is *always* to use function prototypes, and to put them at the head of each source code file in the program.

The full set of rules on argument passing is complicated. First, you need to know about the **default argument promotions**. When these apply, as described below, it means that any `char` or `short` arguments undergo the integral promotions (see Chapter 2). It also means that `float` arguments are converted to `double`.

1. At the point of calling a function, if no prototype is in scope, the arguments all undergo the default argument promotions. For this case:

    *   If the number of arguments does not agree with the number of formal parameters to the function, the behaviour is undefined.
    *   If, at the point of defining the function, no prototype was in scope, then the type of the actual arguments after promotion must agree with the types of the formal parameters in the definition after they have been promoted. Otherwise the behaviour is undefined.
    *   If, at the point of defining the function, a prototype was in scope, and any of the formal parameters is of a type affected by the promotions, the behaviour is undefined.

2. At the point of calling a function, if a prototype *is* in scope, the arguments are converted, as if by assignment, to the types specified in the prototype. Any arguments which fall under the variable argument list category (specified by the `...` in the prototype) still undergo the default argument conversions. For this case, if any of the types in the prototype is one which is affected by the

default conversions, then the prototype must be in scope when the function is defined, otherwise the behaviour is undefined.

3. There are no other conversions performed implicitly.

4.2.5 Function definitions

Function prototypes allow the same text to be used for both the declaration and definition of a function. To turn a declaration:

```
double
some_func(int a1, float a2, long double a3);
```

into a definition, we provide a body for the function:

```
double
some_func(int a1, float a2, long double a3){
    /* body of function */
    return(1.0);
}
```

by replacing the semicolon at the end of the declaration with a compound statement.

In either a definition or a declaration of a function, it serves as a prototype if the parameter types are specified; both of the examples above are prototypes.

The Old C syntax for the declaration of a function's formal arguments is still supported by the Standard, although it should not be used by new programs. It looks like this, for the example above:

```
double
some_func(a1, a2, a3)
    int a1;
    float a2;
    long double a3;{

    /* body of function */
    return(1.0);
}
```

Because no type information is provided for the parameters at the point where they are named, this form of definition does *not* act as a prototype.

The Standard warns that support for this syntax may disappear in a later version. It will not be discussed further.

4.2.6 Summary

1. Always use function prototypes.

2. Undefined behaviour results if you call or define a function anywhere in a program unless either

   - a prototype is *always* in scope for *every* call or definition, or
   - you are very, very careful.

3. Functions taking no arguments should have a prototype with (void) as its argument specification.

4. Functions taking a variable number of arguments must take at least one named argument; the variable arguments are indicated by . . . as shown:

```
int
vfunc(int x, float y, ...);
```

Chapter 9 describes how to write this sort of function.

4.2.7 Compound statements

As we have seen, functions always have a compound statement as their body. It is possible to declare new variables inside any compound statement; if any variables of the same name already exist, then the old ones are hidden by the new ones within the new compound statement. This is the same as in every other block-structured language.

However, the Standard has changed things a little with respect to a function's formal arguments. They are now considered to have been declared inside the first compound statement, even though textually they aren't: this goes for both the new and old ways of function definition. So, if a function has a formal argument with the same name as something declared in the outermost compound statement, this causes an error which will be detected by the compiler.

In Old C, accidental redefinition of a function's formal arguments was a horrible and particularly difficult mistake to track down. Here is what it would look like:

```
/* erroneous redeclaration of arguments */

func(a, b, c){
    int a;   /* AAAAgh! */
}
```

4.3 Recursion and argument passing

So far, we've seen how to give functions a type, how to declare both the function and the type of any arguments it takes, and finally how the definition is used to give the body of the function. Next we need to see what the arguments can be used for.

4.3.1 Call by value

The way that C treats arguments to functions is both simple and consistent, with no exceptions to the single rule.

When a function is called, any arguments that are provided by the caller are simply treated as expressions. The value of each expression is used to initialize the corresponding formal parameters in the called function, which then behave in the same way as any other local variables in the function. It's illustrated here:

```
void called_func(int, float);

main(){
    called_func(1, 2*3.5);
    exit(0);
}

void
called_func(int iarg, float farg){
    float tmp;

    tmp = iarg * farg;
}
```
(E4.5)

The call of called_func in main has two expressions, which are evaluated. The value of each expression is used to initialize the parameters iarg and farg in called_func, and the parameters are indistinguishable from the other local variable declared in called_func: tmp.

The initialization of the formal parameters is the last time that any communication occurs between the caller and the called function, except for the return value.

For those who are used to FORTRAN and var arguments in Pascal: forget it. You cannot affect the values of a function's actual arguments by anything that you try. Here is an example to show what I mean.

```
#include <stdio.h>
#include <stdlib.h>
main(){
    void changer(int);
    int i;

    i = 5;
    printf("before i=%d\n", i);
    changer(i);
    printf("after i=%d\n", i);
    exit(0);
}

void
```

```
changer(int x){
    while(x){
        printf("changer: x=%d\n", x);
        x--;
    }
}                                              (E4.6)
```

The result of running that is:

```
before i=5
changer: x=5
changer: x=4
changer: x=3
changer: x=2
changer: x=1
after i=5
```

The function changer uses its formal argument x as an ordinary variable – which is exactly what it is. Although the value of x is changed, the variable i (in main) is unaffected. That is the whole point – the arguments in C are passed into a function by their value only, no changes made by the function are passed back.

4.3.2 Call by reference

It is possible to write functions that take **pointers** as their arguments, giving a form of call by reference. This is described in Chapter 5.

4.3.3 Recursion

With argument passing safely out of the way we can look at recursion. Recursion is a topic that often provokes lengthy and unenlightening arguments from opposing camps. Some think it is wonderful, and the only technique that any sane person would use; some others take exactly the opposite view. Let's just say that when you need it, you really *do* need it, and since it doesn't cost much to put into a language, as you would expect, C supports recursion.

Every function in C, except main, may be called from any other or itself. Each invocation of a function causes a new allocation of the variables declared inside it. In fact, the declarations that we have been using until now have had something missing: the keyword auto, meaning 'automatically allocated'.

```
/* Example of auto */
main(){
    auto int var_name;
    .
    .
    .
}
```

The storage for `auto` variables is automatically allocated and freed on function entry and return; the space used is shared among all the program's functions. If two functions both declare large automatic arrays, the program will only have to find room for both arrays if both functions are active at the same time. Although `auto` is a keyword, it is never used in practice because it is the default for internal declarations. If an explicit initial value (see 'initialization') isn't given for an automatic variable, then its value will be unknown when it is declared. In that state, any use of its value will cause undefined behaviour.

The real problem with illustrating recursion is in the selection of examples. Too often, simple examples are used which don't really get much out of recursion. The problems where it really helps are almost always well out of the grasp of a beginner who is having enough trouble trying to sort out the difference between, say, definition and declaration without wanting the extra burden of having to wrap his or her mind around a new concept as well. The chapter on data structures will show examples of recursion where it is a genuinely useful technique.

The following example uses recursive functions to evaluate expressions involving single digit numbers, the operators *, %, /, +, – and parentheses in the same way that C does. (I was fascinated to note that Stroustrop, in his book about C++, uses almost an identical example to illustrate recursion. This happened purely by chance.) The whole expression is evaluated and its value printed when a character not in the 'language' is read. For simplicity no error checking is performed. Extensive use is made of the `ungetc` library function, which allows the last character read by `getchar` to be 'unread' and become once again the next character to be read. Its second argument is one of the things declared in `stdio.h`.

The grammar used is the following BNF-like one.

```
<primary>  ::= digit| (<exp>)
<unary>    ::=<primary>|-<unary>|+<unary>
<mult>     ::=<unary>|<mult> * <unary>|
             <mult>/<unary> | <mult> % <unary>
<exp>      ::=<exp> + <mult> | <exp>-<mult>|<mult>
```

The main places where recursion occurs are in the function `unary_exp`, which calls itself, and at the bottom level where `primary` calls the top level all over again to evaluate parenthesized expressions.

If you don't understand what it does, try running it. Trace its actions by hand on inputs such as

```
1
1+2
1+2 * 3+4
1+--4
1+(2*3)+4
```

That should keep you busy for a while!

```
/*
 * Recursive descent parser for simple C expressions.
 * Very little error checking.
 */

#include <stdio.h>
#include <stdlib.h>

int expr(void);
int mul_exp(void);
int unary_exp(void);
int primary(void);

main(){
    int val;

    for(;;){
        printf("expression: ");
        val = expr();
        if(getchar() != '\n'){
            printf("error\n");
            while(getchar() != '\n')
                ; /* NULL */
        } else{
            printf("result is %d\n", val);
        }
    }
}

int
expr(void){
    int val, ch_in;

    val = mul_exp();
    for(;;){
        switch(ch_in = getchar()){
        default:
            ungetc(ch_in,stdin);
            return(val);
        case '+':
            val = val + mul_exp();
            break;
        case '-':
            val = val - mul_exp();
            break;
        }
```

```
        }
}

int
mul_exp(void){
    int val, ch_in;

    val = unary_exp();
    for(;;){
        switch(ch_in = getchar()){
        default:
            ungetc(ch_in, stdin);
            return(val);
        case '*':
            val = val * unary_exp();
            break;
        case '/':
            val = val / unary_exp();
            break;
        case '%':
            val = val % unary_exp();
            break;
        }
    }
}

int
unary_exp(void){
    int val, ch_in;

    switch(ch_in = getchar()){
    default:
        ungetc(ch_in, stdin);
        val = primary();
        break;
    case '+':
        val = unary_exp();
        break;
    case '-':
        val = -unary_exp();
        break;
    }
    return(val);
}

int
```

```
primary(void){
    int val, ch_in;

    ch_in = getchar();
    if(ch_in >= '0' && ch_in <= '9'){
        val = ch_in - '0';
        goto out;
    }
    if(ch_in == '('){
        val = expr();
        getchar();   /* skip closing ')' */
        goto out;
    }

    printf("error: primary read %d\n", ch_in);
    exit(-1);
out:
    return(val);
}                                                    (E4.7)
```

4.4 Scope

While the simple examples have carefully avoided the topic, we now have to look into scope, the general term used to describe the accessibility of various objects in a C program. Chapter 1 mentioned that there are essentially two types of object in the language: the internal and external classes. The whole topic is revisited in Chapter 8.

A C program is a collection of **external objects**. The distinction between external and internal is to do with functions: anything declared outside a function is external, anything inside one, including its formal arguments, is internal. Since no function can be defined inside another, functions themselves are always external.

There is a further distinction made when objects are declared in separate files. The term used by the Standard to describe the accessibility from one file of something defined in the same, or another, file is **linkage**. The whole topic is simple in principle, but is not all that easy to explain. Let's start by thinking of a program that is complete with just one file.

The single-file program is processed by C in the same way that each individual file is handled in multi-file programs. The file is considered to be read once only, from beginning to end. From the point where an external declaration is first seen, it is remembered to the end of the file. In this example (the function bodies are empty because we don't care about their contents) the variable i is declared externally. It is accessible from all of the functions, because its declaration is in front of them.

```
int i;
main () {}
f () {}
```

Any reference to i in main or f will be to the same object. Of course, within a compound statement, it is possible to re-declare a name that was declared at an outer level and temporarily to hide the outer name. In this next example, a new i is declared in f, hiding the first one. Function f2 will still be able to access the outer i because the declaration in f finishes its effect at the end of f.

```
int i,
main () {}
f () {int i;}
f2 () {}
```

It is possible to play silly tricks like this one:

```
main () {}
int i;
f () {}
f2 () {}
```

Now f and f2 can use i, but main can't, because the declaration of the variable comes later than that of main. This is not an aspect that is used very much, but it is implicit in the way that C processes declarations. It is a source of confusion for anyone reading the file (external declarations are generally expected to precede any function definitions in a file) and should be avoided.

All externally declared objects are placed into storage which is allocated once, at the time when the program modules (separate files, library routines and so on) are combined by the loader.

To be able to do something with an external variable at a given point in a program, its name must have been made visible somehow. Even external objects from other files can be manipulated from functions in the current file, but only if we have some way of introducing their names. That can be done using the keyword extern, which really means 'not here'. Any declaration prefixed by extern simply means that the actual place where the object is brought into existence is not this one. The name becomes known, though, and can now be mentioned. If the keyword is not present, the declaration becomes a definition: this is the place where the object has storage allocated to it. In the following example, we show how the variable i is defined in one file, declared in another and used in both. Comment is used to indicate file boundaries.

```
/* first file */

int i; /* definition */
main () {
```

```
            void f_in_other_place (void);
            i = 0
}
/* end of first file */


/* start of second file */

extern int i; /* declaration */
void f_in_other_place (void){
                    i++;
}
/* end of second file */
```

(E4.8)

In the case where there is no definition of an external variable (as opposed to functions, which must have a definition somewhere), a definition is assumed to have been given and the variable is initialized to zero, as it is if no explicit initializer is given in its definition.

It isn't possible for C to check that external declarations and definitions are consistent when they occur in different files; it is the program author's responsibility. If they don't match, results are undefined.

Another keyword crops up now: static. Prefixing a declaration or definition with that word has the effect of restricting its visibility. An external static, that is one declared outside a function, has its visibility restricted to that file only. No way of getting at it by name can exist in any other file, no matter what declarations you try to make: it is local to its own file, and that's that. Even functions can be made static. The technique is useful. You can write library modules and guarantee no clash between its own external variables and supporting functions, and those of the module's user. Simply put everything into one file and make sure that only the public parts are declared without static.

```
/* example library module */
/* only 'callable' is visible outside */
static buf [100];
static length;
static void fillup(void);

int
callable (){
    if (length ==0){
        fillup ();
    }
    return (buf [length--]);
}

static void
```

```
fillup (void) {
    while (length <100) {
        buf [length++] = 0;
    }
}
```
(E4.9)

A user of this module can safely use the names declared here, length, buf, and fillup, without any danger of surprising effects. Only the name callable is accessible outside this module.

It is also quite reasonable to declare internal (inside functions) objects as static. Because the declaration is internal, if it is not the declaration of a function then the name that it introduces disappears at the end of the compound statement containing it. This class of variable has interesting properties: it is initialized to zero when the program starts; it retains its value between entry to and exit from the statement containing its declaration; there is only one copy of it, which is shared between all recursive calls of the function containing it.

Internal statics can be used for a number of things. One is to count the number of times that a function has been called; unlike ordinary internal variables whose value is lost after leaving their function, statics are convenient for this. Here's a function that always returns a number between 0 and 15, but remembers how often it was called.

```
int
small_val (void) {
    static unsigned count;
    count ++;
    return (count % 16);
}
```
(E4.10)

They can help detect excessive recursion:

```
void
r_func (void) {
    static int depth;
    depth++;
    if (depth > 200) {
        printf ("excessive recursion\n");
        exit (1);
    }
    else {
        /* do usual thing,
         * not shown here.
         * This last action
         * occasionally results in another
         * call on r_func()
         */
```

```
        x_func();
    }
    depth--;
}                                                        (E4.11)
```

To summarize, we have this position: external objects can be accessed throughout the program, except for `static` external objects which can only be accessed from one file. To bring the name of an external object into scope an `extern` declaration is necessary. Internal `static` is like external, but the scope is limited to the compound statement containing the declaration. For all of the above objects, they are initialized once only, at program start-up. The absence of explicit initialization is taken to be a default initialization of zero.

Now the messy bit. What happens if you do this:

```
func() {
    extern i;
}
```

An internal declaration of an external object? The answer is that the compiler now knows that such an external object exists, but the name goes out of scope at the end of `func` and another declaration will be needed later to bring it back into scope if it is needed elsewhere. Another tricky bit is this:

```
static int i;
func () {
    extern int i;
}
```

Are they the same `i`? The answer to that one is 'yes'. In any file an external name can only refer to one object. For it to be `static`, the very first declaration must have the `static` keyword present.

Finally, since every external object must have, as well as possible declarations, a definition, here are the rules laying down what constitutes a definition of a data object:

- A declaration without `extern` or `static` is a definition.
- A declaration containing an initializer is a definition.
- A declaration containing `static` without an initializer is a 'tentative definition'. If no later absolute definition is found in the file, the first tentative definition becomes a definition.

It's easier for functions. They are defined only where their body is given; anything else is a declaration.

There are a few golden rules for the use of functions that are worth re-stating too.

- To use a function returning non-`int`, a declaration or definition must be in scope.

• Do not return from a function by falling through its body unless its type is void.

A declaration of the types of arguments that a function takes is not mandatory, but it is mandatory that, if such a declaration exists anywhere in a program within scope of the use or definition of the function, an equivalent declaration must be in scope for every reference to the function. (This allows the compiler to optimize argument passing in ways that are not otherwise possible.) If there isn't a declaration giving the types of arguments to a function, you have to be careful when calling it. The right number and types of arguments become your responsibility.

Functions taking a variable number of arguments can be written portably if you use the methods described in Section 9.9.

4.5 Summary

As has been said before, functions are the cornerstone of C. In terms of changes to the language, the Standard has by far its most obvious effect by introducing function prototypes. This change has won widespread approval throughout the user community and should help to produce a substantial improvement in reliability of C programs, as well as opening the possibility of optimization by compilers in areas previously closed to them.

The use of call-by-value is sometimes surprising to people who have used languages that prefer a different mechanism, but at least the C approach is the 'safest' most of the time.

The attempts by the Standard to remove ambiguity in the scope and meaning of declarations are interesting, but frankly have explored an obscure region which rarely caused any difficulties in practice.

From the beginner's point of view, it is important to learn thoroughly everything discussed in this chapter, with the exception of the scope rules. They can be deferred for a more leisurely inspection at some later time.

Exercises

Write a function and the appropriate declaration for the following tasks:

4.1 A function called abs_val that returns int and takes an int argument. It returns the absolute value of its argument, by negating it if it is negative.

4.2 A function called output that takes a single character argument and sends it to the program output with putchar. It will count the current line number and column number reached on the output device – the only values passed to the function are guaranteed to be alphanumeric, punctuation, space and newline characters.

4.3   Construct a program to test `output`, where that function is in a separate file from the functions that are used to test it. In the same file as `output` will be two functions called `current_line` and `current_column` which return the values of the line and column counters. Ensure that those counters are made accessible only from the file that contains them.

4.4   Write and test a recursive function that performs the admittedly dull task of printing a list of numbers from 100 down to 1. On entry to the function it increments a static variable. If the variable has a value below 100, it calls itself again. Then it prints the value of the variable, decrements it and returns. Check that it works.

4.5   Write functions to calculate the sine and cosine of their input. Choose appropriate types for both argument and return value. The series (given below) can be used to approximate the answer. The function should return when the value of the final term is less than 0.000001 of the current value of the function.

```
sin x = x - pow(x,3)/fact(3) + pow(x,5)/fact(5)...
cos x = 1 - pow(x,2)/fact(2) + pow(x,5)/fact(5)...
```

Note the fact that the sign in front of each term alternates (−+−+−+...). `pow   (x,n)` returns x to the *n*th power, `fact(n)` factorial of n (1*2*3*....*n). You will have to write such functions. Check the results against published tables.

CHAPTER 5

Arrays and Pointers

5.1 Effect of the Standard

The arithmetic data types and operators of C are interesting but hardly rivetting. They show, collectively, a certain imagination and spirit that has stamped C with a special flavour, but they form the sauce, not the meat, of this particular dish. For most users, it's the parts of the language covered in this chapter that provide the real feel of C.

The new Standard has left very little mark on the contents of this chapter; it would be nearly word for word the same even if it only talked about Old C. The inference to be drawn is that nothing was wrong with the old version of the language, and that there was nothing to be gained by fixing what wasn't broken. This may be received with some relief by those readers who already knew this part of the old language and who, like the Committee, felt that it was good enough to leave alone.

For the new reader, this is the part of the language that causes the biggest problems. Most beginners with C are at least familiar with the use of arithmetic, functions and arrays; those are not the problem areas. The difficulties arise when we get on to the structured types (structures and unions), and the way that C just wouldn't be C without the use of pointers.

Pointers aren't a feature that you can choose to ignore. They're used everywhere; their influence affects the whole language and must be the single most noticeable feature of all but the simplest C programs. If you think that this is one of the bits you can skip because it's hard and doesn't look too important, you are wrong! Most of the examples used so far in this book have had pointers used in them (although not obviously), so you might as well accept the inevitable and learn how to use them properly.

The most natural way to introduce the use of pointers is by looking into arrays first. C intertwines arrays and pointers so closely that they are hard to separate. Since you are supposed to be familiar with the use of arrays, their treatment will be brief and aimed at using them to illustrate the use of pointers when they are seen later.

5.2 Arrays

Like other languages, C uses arrays as a way of describing a collection of variables with identical properties. The group has a single name for all of the members, with the individual members being selected by a number. Here's an array being declared:

```
double ar[100];
```

The name of the array is `ar` and its members are accessed as `ar[0]` through to `ar[99]` inclusive, as Figure 5.1 shows.

| ar [0] | ar [1] | . . . | ar [99] |

Figure 5.1   100 element array

Each of the hundred members is a separate variable whose type is `double`. Without exception, all arrays in C are numbered from 0 up to one less than the bound given in the declaration. This is a prime cause of surprise to beginners – watch out for it. For simple examples of the use of arrays, look back at earlier chapters where several problems are solved with their help.

One important point about array declarations is that they don't permit the use of varying subscripts. The numbers given must be constant expressions which can be evaluated at compile time, not run time. For example, this function illegally tries to use its argument in the size of an array declaration:

```
f(int x){
      char var_sized_array[x];     /* FORBIDDEN */
}
```

It's forbidden because the value of `x` is unknown when the program is compiled; it's a run-time, not a compile-time, value.

To tell the truth, it would be easy to support arrays whose *first* dimension is variable, but neither Old C nor the Standard permits it, although I do know of one Very Old C compiler that used to do it.

5.2.1 Multidimensional arrays

Multidimensional arrays can be declared like this:

```
int three_dee[5][4][2];
int t_d[2][3]
```

The use of the brackets gives a clue to what is going on. If you refer to the precedence table given on page 49, you'll see that `[]` associates left to right and that, as a result, the first declaration gives us a five-element array called three_dee. The members of that array are each a four element array whose members are an array of two ints. We have declared arrays of arrays, as Figure 5.2 shows for two dimensions.

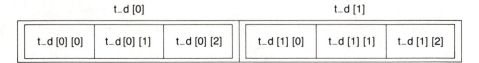

t_d [0]	t_d [1]
t_d [0] [0]	t_d [0] [1]	t_d [0] [2]	t_d [1] [0]	t_d [1] [1]	t_d [1] [2]

Figure 5.2   Two-dimensional array, showing layout

In the diagram, you will notice that t_d[0] is one element, immediately followed by t_d[1] (there is no break). It so happens that both of those elements are themselves arrays of three integers. Because of C's storage layout rules, t_d[1][0] is immediately after t_d[0][2]. It would be possible (but very poor practice) to access t_d[1][0] by making use of the lack of array-bound checking in C, and to use the expression t_d[0][3]. That is not recommended – apart from anything else, if the declaration of t_d ever changes, then the results will be likely to surprise you.

That's all very well, but does it really matter in practice? Not much it's true; but it is interesting to note that in terms of actual machine storage layout the rightmost subscript 'varies fastest'. This has an impact when arrays are accessed via pointers. Otherwise, they can be used just as would be expected; expressions like these are quite in order:

```
three_dee[1][3][1] = 0;
three_dee[4][3][1] += 2;
```

The second of those is interesting for two reasons. First, it accesses the very last member of the entire array – although the subscripts were declared to be [5][4][2], the highest usable subscript is always one less than the one used in the declaration. Second, it shows where the combined assignment operators are a real blessing. For the experienced C programmer it is much easier to tell that only one array member is being accessed, and that it is being incremented by two. Other languages would have to express it like this:

```
three_dee[4][3][1] = three_dee[4][3][1] + 2;
```

It takes a conscious effort to check that the same array member is being referenced on both sides of the assignment. It makes thing easier for the compiler too: there is only one array indexing calculation to do, and this is likely to result in shorter, faster code. (Of course a clever compiler would notice that the left- and right-hand sides look alike and would be able to generate equally efficient code – but not all compilers are clever and there are lots of special cases where even clever compilers are unable to make use of the information.)

It may be of interest to know that although C offers support for multidimensional arrays, they aren't particularly common to see in practice. One-dimensional arrays are present in most programs, if for no other reason than that's what strings are. Two dimensional arrays are seen occasionally, and arrays of higher order than that are most uncommon. One of the reasons is that the array is a rather inflexible data structure, and the ease of building and manipulating other types of data structures in C means that they tend to replace arrays in the more advanced programs. We will see more of this when we look at pointers.

5.3 Pointers

Using pointers is a bit like riding a bicycle. Just when you think that you'll never understand them – suddenly you do! Once learned the trick is hard to forget. There's no real magic to pointers, and a lot of readers will already be familiar with their use. The only peculiarity of C is how heavily it relies on the use of pointers, compared with other languages, and the relatively permissive view of what you can do with them.

5.3.1 Declaring pointers

Of course, just like other variables, you have to declare pointers before you can use them. Pointer declarations look much like other declarations: but don't be misled. When pointers are declared, the keyword at the beginning (int, char and so on) declares the type of variable that the pointer will point to. The pointer itself is *not* of that type, it is of type *pointer to that type*. A given pointer only points to one particular type, not to all possible types. Here's the declaration of an array and a pointer:

```
int ar[5], *ip;
```

We now have an array and a pointer (see Figure 5.3):

Figure 5.3 An array and a pointer

The * in front of ip in the declaration shows that it is a pointer, not an ordinary variable. It is of type pointer to int, and can only be used to refer to variables of type int. It's still uninitialized, so to do anything useful with it, it has to be made to point to something. You can't just stick some integer value into it, because integer values have the type int, not pointer to int, which is what we want. (In any case, what would it mean if this fragment were legal:

```
ip = 6;
```

What would ip be pointing to? In fact it could be construed to have a number of meanings, but the simple fact is that, in C, that sort of thing is just wrong.)

Here is the right way to initialize a pointer:

```
int ar[5], *ip;
ip = &ar[3];
```

In that example, the pointer is made to point to the member of the array ar whose index is 3, i.e. the fourth member. This is important. You can assign values to pointers just like ordinary variables; the difference is simply in what the value means. The values of the variables that we have now are shown in Figure 5.4 (?? means uninitialized).

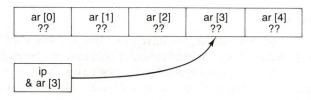

Figure 5.4   Array and initialized pointer

You can see that the variable ip has the value of the expression &ar[3]. The arrow indicates that, when used as a pointer, ip points to the variable ar[3].

What is this new unary &? It is usually described as the 'address-of' operator, a relic of the days on the DEC PDP-11 computer when pointers held the store address of the thing that they pointed to. It's a bit unfortunate that the terminology remains, because it confuses those who don't know what addresses are about, and misleads those who do: thinking about pointers as if they were addresses generally leads to grief. What seems a perfectly reasonable address manipulation on processor X can almost always be shown to be impossible on manufacturer Y's washing machine controller which uses 17-bit addressing when it's on the spin cycle, and reverses the order of odd and even bits when it's out of bleach. (I admit that it is unlikely that *anyone* could get C to work on an architecture like that. But you should see some of the ones it *does* work on; they aren't much better.)

I will continue to use the term 'address of' though, because to invent a different one would be even worse.

Applying the & operator to an operand returns a pointer to the operand:

```
int i;
float f;
    /* ``&i'' would be of type pointer to int */
    /* ``&f'' would be of type pointer to float */
```

In each case the pointer would point to the object named in the expression.

A pointer is only useful if there's some way of getting at the thing that it points to; C uses the unary * operator for this job. If p is of type 'pointer to something', then *p refers to the thing that is being pointed to. For example, to access the variable x via the pointer p, this would work:

```
#include <stdio.h>
#include <stdlib.h>
main(){
    int x, *p;

    p = &x;        /* initialise pointer */
    *p = 0;        /* set x to zero */
    printf("x is %d\n", x);
    printf("*p is %d\n", *p);

    *p += 1;       /* increment what p points to */
    printf("x is %d\n", x);

    (*p)++;        /* increment what p points to */
    printf("x is %d\n", x);

    exit(0);
}                                                    (E5.1)
```

You might be interested to note that, since & takes the address of an object, returning a pointer to it, and since * means 'the thing pointed to by the pointer', the & and * in the combination *& effectively cancel each other out. (But be careful. Some things, constants for example, don't have addresses and the & operator cannot be applied to them.) It's also interesting to see that C is one of the few languages that allows an expression on the left-hand side of an assignment operator. Look back at the example: the expression *p occurs twice in that position, and then the amazing (*p)++; statement. That last one is a great puzzle to most beginners – even if you've managed to wrap your mind around the concept that *p = 0 writes zero into the thing pointed to by p, and that *p += 1 adds one to where p points, it still seems a bit much to apply the ++ operator to *p.

The precedence of (*p)++ deserves some thought. It will be given more later, but for the moment let's work out what happens. The brackets ensure that the * applies to p, so what we have is 'post-increment the thing pointed to by p'.

Looking at Table 2.7, it turns out that ++ and * have equal precedence, but they associate *right to left*; in other words, without the brackets, the implied operation would have been *(p++), whatever that would mean. Later on you'll be more used to it – for the moment, I'll be careful with brackets to show the way that those expressions work.

So, provided that a pointer holds the address of something, the notation *pointer is equivalent to giving the name of the something directly. What benefit do we get from all this? Well, straight away it gets round the call-by-value restriction of functions. Imagine a function that has to return, say, two integers representing a month and a day within that month. The function has some (unspecified) way of determining these values; the hard thing to do is to return two separate values. Here's a skeleton of the way that it can be done:

```
#include <stdio.h>
void
date(int *, int *); /* declare the function */

main() {
        int month, day;
        date (&day, &month);
        printf("day is %d, month is %d\n", day, month);
        exit(0);
}

void
date(int *day_p, int *month_p) {
        int day_ret, month_ret;
        /*
         * At this point, calculate the day and month
         * values in day_ret and month_ret respectively.
         */
        *day_p = day_ret;
        *month_p = month_ret;
}                                                          (E5.2)
```

Notice carefully the advance declaration of date showing that it takes two arguments of type 'pointer to int'. It returns void, because the values are passed back via the pointers, not the usual return value. The main function is careful to pass pointers as arguments to date, which first uses the internal variables day_ret and month_ret for its calculations, then takes those values and assigns them to the places pointed to by its arguments.

When date is called, the situation looks like Figure 5.5.

The arguments have been passed to date, but in main, day and month are uninitialized. When date reaches the return statement, the situation is as shown in Figure 5.6 (assuming that the values for day and month are 12 and 5 respectively).

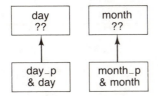

Figure 5.5   Just as 'date' is called

Figure 5.6   Just as 'date' is about to return

One of the great benefits introduced by the new Standard is that it allows the types of the arguments to date to be declared in advance. A great favourite (and disastrous) mistake in C is to forget that a function expects pointers as its arguments, and to pass something else instead. Imagine what would have happened if the call of date above had read

```
date(day, month);
```

and no previous declaration of date had been visible. The compiler would not have known that date expects pointers as arguments, so it would pass the int values of day and month as the arguments. On a large number of computers, pointers and integers can be passed in the same way, so the function would execute, then pass back its return values by putting them into wherever day and month would point if their contents were pointers. This is very unlikely to give any sensible results, and in general causes unexpected corruption of data elsewhere in the computer's store. It can be extremely hard to track down!

Fortunately, by declaring date in advance, the compiler has enough information to warn that a mistake has almost certainly been made.

Perhaps surprisingly, it isn't all that common to see pointers used to give this call-by-reference functionality. In the majority of cases, call-by-value and a single return value are adequate. What is *much* more common is to use pointers to 'walk' along arrays.

5.3.2 Arrays and pointers

Array elements are just like other variables: they have addresses.

```
int ar[20], *ip;

ip = &ar[5];
*ip = 0;     /* equivalent to ar[5] = 0; */
```

Ip is given the address of ar[5], then the place pointed to has zero assigned to it. By itself, this isn't particularly exciting. What *is* interesting is the way that pointer arithmetic works. Although it's simple, it's one of the cornerstones of C.

Adding an integral value to a pointer results in another pointer of the same type. Adding *n* gives a pointer which points *n* elements further along an array than the original pointer did. (Since *n* can be negative, subtraction is obviously possible too.) In the example above, a statement of the form

```
*(ip+1) = 0;
```

would set ar[6] to zero, and so on. Again, this is not obviously any improvement on 'ordinary' ways of accessing an array, but the following is.

```
int ar[20], *ip;

for(ip = &ar[0]; ip < &ar[20]; ip++)
    *ip = 0;
```

That example is a classic fragment of C. A pointer is set to point to the start of an array, then, while it still points inside the array, array elements are accessed one by one, the pointer incrementing between each one. The Standard endorses existing practice by guaranteeing that it's permissible to use the *address* of ar[20] even though no such element exists. This allows you to use it for checks in loops like the one above. The guarantee only extends to one element beyond the end of an array and no further.

Why is the example better than indexing? Well, most arrays are accessed sequentially. Very few programming examples actually make use of the 'random access' feature of arrays. If you do just want sequential access, using a pointer can give a worthwhile improvement in speed. In terms of the underlying address arithmetic, on most architectures it takes one multiplication and one addition to access a one-dimensional array through a subscript. Pointers require no arithmetic at all – they nearly always hold the store address of the object that they refer to. In the example above, the only arithmetic that has to be done is in the for loop, where one comparison and one addition are done each time round the loop. The equivalent, using indexes, would be this:

```
int ar[20], i;
for(i = 0; i < 20; i++)
    ar[i] = 0;
```

The same amount of arithmetic occurs in the loop statement, but an extra address calculation has to be performed for every array access.

Efficiency is not normally an important issue, but here it can be. Loops often get traversed a substantial number of times, and every microsecond saved in a big loop can matter. It isn't always easy for even a smart compiler to recognize that this is the sort of code that could be 'pointerized' behind the scenes, and to convert from indexing (what the programmer wrote) to actually use a pointer in the generated code.

If you have found things easy so far, read on. If not, it's a good idea to skip to Section 5.3.3. What follows, while interesting, isn't essential. It has been known to frighten even experienced C programmers.

To be honest, C doesn't really 'understand' array indexing, except in declarations. As far as the compiler is concerned, an expression like x[n] is translated into *(x+n) and use made of the fact that an array name is converted into a pointer to the array's first element whenever the name occurs in an expression. That's why, amongst other things, array elements count from zero: if x is an array name, then in an expression, x is equivalent to &x[0], i.e. a pointer to the first element of the array. So, since *(&x[0]) uses the pointer to get to x[0], *(&x[0] + 5) is the same as *(x + 5) which is the same as x[5]. A curiosity springs out of all this. If x[5] is translated into *(x + 5), and the expression x + 5 gives the same result as 5 + x (it does), then 5[x] should give the identical result to x[5]! If you don't believe that, here is a program that compiles and runs successfully:

```c
#include <stdio.h>
#include <stdlib.h>
#define ARSZ 20
main(){
    int ar[ARSZ], i;
    for(i = 0; i < ARSZ; i++){
        ar[i] = i;
        i[ar]++;
        printf("ar[%d] now = %d\n", i, ar[i]);
    }

    printf("15[ar] = %d\n", 15[ar]);
    exit(0);
}
```
(E5.3)

5.3.3 Pointer arithmetic

Not only can you add an integral value to a pointer, but you can also compare or subtract two pointers of the same type. They must both point into the same array, or the result is undefined. The difference between two pointers is defined to be the number of array elements separating them; the type of this difference is implementation defined and will be one of short, int, or long. This next example shows how the difference can be calculated and used, but before you read it, you need to know an important point.

In an expression the name of an array is converted to a pointer to the first element of the array. There are only two places where that is not true; when an array name is used in conjunction with sizeof, or when a string is used to initialize an array. We haven't seen either of those cases yet, they will be discussed later. Here's the example.

```
#include <stdio.h>
#define ARSZ 10

main(){
    float fa[ARSZ], *fp1, *fp2;

    fp1 = fp2 = fa; /* address of first element */
    while(fp2 != &fa[ARSZ]){
        printf("Difference: %d\n", (int)(fp2-fp1));
        fp2++;
    }
    return(0);
}                                                          (E5.4)
```

The pointer fp2 is stepped along the array, and the difference between its current and original values is printed. To make sure that printf isn't handed the wrong type of argument, the difference between the two pointers is forced to be of type int by using the cast (int). That allows for machines where the difference between two pointers is specified to be long.

Unfortunately, if the difference does happen to be long and the array is enormous, the last example may give the wrong answers. This is a safe version, using a cast to force a long value to be passed:

```
#include <stdio.h>
#define ARSZ 10

main(){
    float fa[ARSZ], *fp1, *fp2;

    fp1 = fp2 = fa; /* address of first element */
    while(fp2 != &fa[ARSZ]){
        printf("Difference: %ld\n", (long)(fp2-fp1));
        fp2++;
    }
    return(0);
}                                                          (E5.5)
```

There is one other thing that you can do safely with pointers: assign the integer value of zero to them, and compare them to it. A constant of 0 is special in this respect, and is the only integer value that can legally be assigned to a pointer. This value in a pointer is guaranteed to be the value that points nowhere, and is used to indicate a 'null' pointer.

It's common practice in C to write routines that return pointers. If, for some reason, they can't return a valid pointer (perhaps in case of an error), then they will indicate failure by returning 0 instead. An example could be a table lookup routine, which returns a pointer to the object searched for if it is in the table, or 0 if it is not.

The only values that can be assigned to pointers apart from 0 are the values of other pointers of the same type. Pointers to, say, float, are of an entirely different type from pointer to int (or any other type) and cannot be mixed. However, one of the things that makes C a useful replacement for assembly language is that it allows you to do the sort of things that most other languages prevent. Try this:

```
int *ip;
ip = (int *)6;
*ip = 0xFF;
```

What does that do? The pointer has been initialized to the value of 6 (notice the cast to turn an integer 6 into a pointer). This is a highly machine-specific operation, and the bit pattern that ends up in the pointer is quite possibly nothing like the machine representation of 6. After the initialization, hexadecimal FF is written into wherever the pointer is pointing. The int at location 6 has had 0xFF written into it – subject to whatever 'location 6' means on this particular machine.

It may or may not make sense to do that sort of thing; C gives you the power to express it, it's up to you to get it right. As always, it's possible to do things like this by accident, too, and to be *very* surprised by the results.

5.4 Character handling

C is widely used for character and string handling applications. This is odd, in some ways, because the language doesn't really have any built-in string handling features. If you're used to languages that know about string handling, you will almost certainly find C tedious to begin with. And probably to finish with too.

The standard library contains lots of functions to help with string processing but the fact remains that it still feels like hard work. To compare two strings you have to call a function instead of using an equality operator. There is a bright side to this, though. It means that the language isn't burdened by having to support string processing directly, which helps to keep it small and less cluttered. What's more, once you get your string handling programs working in C, they do tend to run very quickly.

Character handling in C is done by declaring arrays (or allocating them dynamically) and moving characters in and out of them 'by hand'. Here is an example of a program which reads text a line at a time from its standard input. If the line consists of the string of characters stop, it stops; otherwise it prints the length of the line. It uses a technique which is invariably used in C programs; it reads the characters into an array and indicates the end of them with an extra character whose value is explicitly 0 (zero). It uses the library strcmp function to compare two strings.

```
#include <stdio.h>
#include <stdlib.h>
#include <string.h>

#define LINELNG 100 /* max. length of input line */

main(){
    char in_line[LINELNG];
    char *cp;
    int c;

    cp = in_line;
    while((c = getc(stdin)) != EOF){
        if(cp == &in_line[LINELNG-1] || c == '\n'){
            /*
             * Insert end-of-line marker
             */
            *cp = 0;
            if(strcmp(in_line, "stop") == 0 )
                exit(0);
            else
                printf("line was %d characters long\n",
                    cp-in_line);
            cp = in_line;
        }
        else
            *cp++ = c;
    }
    exit(0);
}
```
(E5.6)

Once more, the example illustrates some interesting methods used widely in C programs. By far the most important is the way that strings are represented and manipulated.

Here is a possible implementation of strcmp, which compares two strings for equality and returns zero if they are the same. The library function actually does a bit more than that, but the added complication can be ignored for the moment. One thing that should be mentioned, though, is what the const means in the argument declarations. Chapter 8 discusses it further; for the moment, just note that it shows that the pointers point to objects of type const char. This indicates to the compiler that there will not be any attempt to modify the contents of the strings, but just to inspect them.

```
/*
 * Compare two strings for equality.
 * Return ''false'' if they are.
 */

int
str_eq(const char *s1, const char *s2){
    while(*s1 == *s2){
        /*
         * At end of string return 0.
         */
        if(*s1 == 0)
            return(0);
        s1++; s2++;
    }
    /* Difference detected! */
    return(1);
}                                                    (E5.7)
```

5.4.1 Strings

Every C programmer 'knows' what a string is. It is an array of char variables, with the last character in the string followed by a null. 'But I thought a string was something in double quote marks', you cry. You are right, too. In C, a sequence like this

```
"a string"
```

is really a character array. It's the only example in C where you can declare something at the point of its use.

Be warned: in Old C, strings were stored just like any other character array, and were modifiable. Now, the Standard states that they are *not* modifiable, and are arrays of const char (which shows that they cannot be modified). The old type was array of char, which can be modified.

Whenever a string in quotes is seen, it has two effects: it provides a declaration and a substitute for a name. It makes a hidden declaration of a const char array, whose contents are initialized to the character values in the string, followed by a character whose integer value is zero. The array has no name. So, apart from the name being present and the type being const char, we have a situation like this:

```
char secret[9];
secret[0] = 'a';
secret[1] = ' ';
secret[2] = 's';
secret[3] = 't';
    .
    .
    .
secret[7] = 'g';
secret[8] = 0;
```

an array of characters, terminated by zero, with character values in it. But when it's declared using the string notation, it hasn't got a name. How can we use it?

Whenever C sees a quoted string, the presence of the string itself serves as the name of the hidden array – not only is the string an implicit sort of declaration, it is as if an array name had been given. Now, we all remember that the name of an array is equivalent to giving the address of its first element, so what is the type of this:

```
"a string"
```

It's a pointer of course: a pointer to the first element of the hidden unnamed array, which is of type const char, so the pointer is of type 'pointer to const char'. The situation is shown in Figure 5.7.

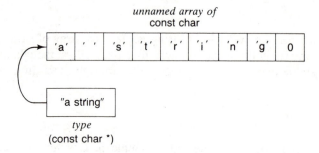

Figure 5.7   Effect of using a string

For proof of that, look at the following program:

```
#include <stdio.h>
#include <stdlib.h>
main(){
    int i;
    const char *cp;

    cp = "a string";
```

```
    while(*cp != 0){
        putchar(*cp);
        cp++;
    }
    putchar('\n');

    for(i = 0; i < 8; i++)
        putchar("a string"[i]);
    putchar('\n');
    exit(0);
}                                                       (E5.8)
```

The first loop sets a pointer to the start of the array, then walks along until it finds the zero at the end. The second one 'knows' about the length of the string and is less useful as a result. Notice how the first one is independent of the length – that is a most important point to remember. It's the way that strings are handled in C almost without exception; it's certainly the format that all of the library string manipulation functions expect. The zero at the end allows string processing routines to find out that they have reached the end of the string – look back now to the example function str_eq. The function takes two character pointers as arguments (so a string would be acceptable as one or both arguments). It compares them for equality by checking that the strings are character-for-character the same. If they are the same at any point, then it checks to make sure it hasn't reached the end of them both with if (*s1 == 0): if it has, then it returns 0 to show that they were equal. The test could just as easily have been on *s2, it wouldn't have made any difference. Otherwise a difference has been detected, so it returns 1 to indicate failure.

In the example, strcmp is called with two arguments which look quite different. One is a character array, the other is a string. In fact they're the same thing – a character array terminated by zero (the program is careful to put a zero in the first 'empty' element of in_line), and a string in quotes – which is a character array terminated by a zero. Their use as arguments to strcmp results in character pointers being passed, for the reasons explained to the point of tedium above.

5.4.2 Pointers and increment operators

I said that we'd eventually revisit expressions like

```
    (*p)++;
```

and now it's time. Pointers are used so often to walk down arrays that it just seems natural to use the ++ and -- operators on them. Here we write zeros into an array:

```
#define ARLEN 10
```

```
int ar[ARLEN], *ip;

ip = ar;
while(ip < &ar[ARLEN])
    *(ip++) = 0;
```
                                                                    (E5.9)

Ip is set to the start of the array. While it remains inside the array, the place that it points to has zero written into it, then the increment takes effect and the pointer is stepped one element along the array. The postfix form of ++ is particularly useful here.

This is very common stuff indeed. There aren't many programs where you won't find pointers and increment operators used together like that, not just once or twice, but on almost every line (or so it seems while you find them difficult). What is happening, and what combinations can we get? Well, the * means indirection, and ++ or -- mean increment; either pre- or post-increment. The combinations can be pre- or post-increment of either the pointer or the thing it points to, depending on where the brackets are put. Table 5.1 gives a list.

Table 5.1 Pointer notation

++(*p)	pre-increment thing pointed to
(*p)++	post-increment thing pointed to
*(p++)	access via pointer, post-increment pointer
*(++p)	access via pointer which has already been incremented

Read it carefully; make sure that you understand the combinations.

The expressions in the list above can usually be understood after a bit of head-scratching. Now, given that the precedence of *, ++ and -- is the same in all three cases and that they associate *right to left*, can you work out what happens if the brackets are removed? Nasty, isn't it? Table 5.2 shows that there's only one case where the brackets have to be there.

Table 5.2 More pointer notation

With parentheses	Without, if possible
++(*p)	++*p
(*p)++	(*p)++
*(p++)	*p++
*(++p)	*++p

The usual reaction to that horrible sight is to decide that you don't care that the parentheses can be removed; you will *always* use them in your code. That's all very well and good – the problem is that most C programmers have learnt the precedence rules (or at least learnt the table above) and *they* very rarely put the parentheses in. Like them, I don't – so if you want to be able to read the rest of the examples, you had better learn to read those expressions with or without parentheses. It'll be worth the effort in the end.

5.4.3 Untyped pointers

In certain cases it's essential to be able to convert pointers from one type to another. This is always done with the aid of casts, in expressions like the one below:

```
(type *) expression
```

The *expression* is converted into 'pointer to *type*', regardless of the expression's previous type. This is only supposed to be done if you're sure that you know what you're trying to do. It is not a good idea to do much of it until you have got plenty of experience. Furthermore, do *not* assume that the cast simply suppresses diagnostics of the 'mismatched pointer' sort from your compiler. On several architectures it is necessary to calculate new values when pointer types are changed.

There are some rules to do with const objects or pointers which affect this procedure slightly. Frankly, they only serve to confuse the issue just now, so they are deferred until Chapter 8. If you experiment having read only this far, and get some surprising warning messages from a compiler, it might help if you look at what is said there.

There are also some occasions when you will want to use a 'generic' pointer. The most common example is the malloc library function, which is used to allocate storage for objects that haven't been declared. It is used by telling it how much storage is wanted – enough for a float, or an array of int, or whatever. It passes back a pointer to enough storage, which it allocates in its own mysterious way from a pool of free storage (the way that it does this is its own business). That pointer is then cast into the right type – for example if a float needs 4 bytes of free store, this is the flavour of what you would write:

```
float *fp;

fp = (float *)malloc(4);
```

Malloc finds 4 bytes of store, then the address of that piece of storage is cast into pointer-to-float and assigned to the pointer.

What type should malloc be declared to have? The type must be able to represent every known value of every type of pointer; there is no guarantee that *any* of the basic types in C can hold such a value.

The solution is to use the special type, introduced for this purpose, of 'pointer to void'. This is one of the Standard's invented features: before, it was tacitly assumed that 'pointer to char' was adequate for the task. This has been a reasonably successful assumption, but was a rather untidy thing to do; the new solution is both safer and less misleading. There isn't any other use for a pointer of that type – void * can't actually point to anything – so it improves readability. Here is the last example with a declaration of malloc:

```
void *malloc();
float *fp;

fp = (float *)malloc(4);
```

The Standard points out that two pointers can be assigned to each other only if they are both of the same type, or, if one is a pointer to an object (i.e. not a pointer to a function), then the other one can be a void *. So, strictly speaking, there is no need to use a cast on the return value from malloc. None the less, this is invariably what is done in practice.

Obviously there needs to be a way to find out what value the argument to malloc should be: it will be different on different machines, so you can't just use a constant like 4. That is what the sizeof operator is for.

5.5 sizeof and storage allocation

The sizeof operator returns the size in bytes of its operand. Whether the result of sizeof is unsigned int or unsigned long is implementation defined – which is why the declaration of malloc above sidestepped the issue by omitting any parameter information; normally you would use the stdlib.h header file to declare malloc correctly. Here is the last example done portably:

```
#include <stdlib.h> /* declares malloc() */
float *fp;

fp = (float *)malloc(sizeof(float));
```

The operand of sizeof only has to be parenthesized if it's a type name. If you are using the name of an object instead, then the parentheses can be omitted, but they rarely are.

```
#include <stdlib.h>

int *ip, ar[100];
ip = (int *)malloc(sizeof ar);
```

In the last example, the array ar is an array of 100 ints, after the call to malloc (assuming that it was successful), ip will point to a region of store that can also be treated as an array of 100 ints.

The fundamental unit of storage in C is the char, and by definition

```
sizeof(char)
```

is equal to 1, so you could allocate space for an array of ten chars with

```
malloc(10)
```

while to allocate room for an array of ten ints, you would have to use

```
malloc(sizeof(int[10]))
```

If malloc can't find enough free space to satisfy a request it returns zero to indicate failure. For historical reasons, the stdio.h header file contains a defined constant called NULL which is traditionally used to check the return value from malloc and some other library functions. An explicit 0 could equally well be used.

As a first illustration of the use of malloc, here's a program which reads up to MAXSTRING strings from its input and sort them into alphabetical order using the library strcmp routine. The strings are terminated by a ' \n' character. The sort is done by keeping an array of pointers to the strings and simply exchanging the pointers until the order is correct. This saves having to copy the strings themselves, which improves the efficency somewhat.

The example is done first using fixed size arrays, then another version uses malloc and allocates space for the strings at run time. Unfortunately, the array of pointers is still fixed in size: a better solution would use a linked list or similar data structure to store the pointers and would have no fixed arrays at all. At the moment, we haven't seen how to do that.

The overall structure is this:

```
while(number of strings read < MAXSTRING
      && input still remains){

          read next string;
}
sort array of pointers;
print array of pointers;
exit;
```

A number of functions are used to implement this program:

```
char *next_string(char *destination)
```
Read a line of characters terminated by ' \n' from the program's input. The first MAXLEN-1 characters are written into the array pointed to by destination.

If the first character read is EOF, return a null pointer, otherwise return the address of the start of the string (destination). On return, destination always points to a null-terminated string.

void sort_arr(const char *p_array[])

P_array[] is an array of pointers to characters. The array can be arbitrarily long; its end is indicated by the first element containing a null pointer.

Sort_arr sorts the pointers so that the pointers point to strings which are in alphabetical order when the array is traversed in index order.

void print_arr(const char *p_array[])

Like sort_arr, but prints the strings in index order.

```c
#include <stdio.h>
#include <stdlib.h>
#include <string.h>

#define MAXSTRING    50   /* max no. of strings */
#define MAXLEN       80   /* max length. of strings */

void print_arr(const char *p_array[]);
void sort_arr(const char *p_array[]);
char *next_string(char *destination);

main(){
    /* leave room for null at end */
    char *p_array[MAXSTRING+1];

    /* storage for strings */
    char strings[MAXSTRING][MAXLEN];

    /* count of strings read */
    int nstrings;

    nstrings = 0;
    while(nstrings < MAXSTRING &&
        next_string(strings[nstrings]) != 0){

        p_array[nstrings] = strings[nstrings];
        nstrings++;
    }
    /* terminate p_array */
    p_array[nstrings] = 0;

    sort_arr(p_array);
    print_arr(p_array);
    exit(0);
}
```

```
void print_arr(const char *p_array[]){
    int index;
    for(index = 0; p_array[index] != 0; index++)
        printf("%s\n", p_array[index]);
}

void sort_arr(const char *p_array[]){
    int comp_val, low_index, hi_index;
    const char *tmp;

    for(low_index = 0;
        p_array[low_index] != 0 &&
            p_array[low_index+1] != 0;
        low_index++){

        for(hi_index = low_index+1;
            p_array[hi_index] != 0;
                hi_index++){

            comp_val=strcmp(p_array[hi_index],
                p_array[low_index]);
            if(comp_val >= 0)
                continue;
            /* swap strings */
            tmp = p_array[hi_index];
            p_array[hi_index] = p_array[low_index];
            p_array[low_index] = tmp;
        }
    }
}

char *next_string(char *destination){
    char *cp;
    int c;

    cp = destination;
    while((c = getchar()) != '\n' && c != EOF){
        if(cp-destination < MAXLEN-1)
            *cp++ = c;
    }
    *cp = 0;
    if(c == EOF && cp == destination)
        return(0);
    return(destination);
}                                         (E5.10)
```

It is no accident that `next_string` returns a pointer. We can now dispense with the `strings` array by getting `next_string` to allocate its own storage.

```c
#include <stdio.h>
#include <stdlib.h>
#include <string.h>

#define MAXSTRING    50   /* max no. of strings */
#define MAXLEN       80   /* max length. of strings */

void print_arr(const char *p_array[]);
void sort_arr(const char *p_array[]);
char *next_string(void);

main(){
    char *p_array[MAXSTRING+1];
    int nstrings;

    nstrings = 0;
    while(nstrings < MAXSTRING &&
        (p_array[nstrings] = next_string()) != 0){

        nstrings++;
    }
    /* terminate p_array */
    p_array[nstrings] = 0;

    sort_arr(p_array);
    print_arr(p_array);
    exit(0);
}

void print_arr(const char *p_array[]){
    int index;
    for(index = 0; p_array[index] != 0; index++)
        printf("%s\n", p_array[index]);
}

void sort_arr(const char *p_array[]){
    int comp_val, low_index, hi_index;
    const char *tmp;

    for(low_index = 0;
        p_array[low_index] != 0 &&
            p_array[low_index+1] != 0;
            low_index++){
```

```
        for(hi_index = low_index+1;
             p_array[hi_index] != 0;
                 hi_index++){

             comp_val=strcmp(p_array[hi_index],
                 p_array[low_index]);
             if(comp_val >= 0)
                 continue;
             /* swap strings */
             tmp = p_array[hi_index];
             p_array[hi_index] = p_array[low_index];
             p_array[low_index] = tmp;
        }
    }
}


char *next_string(void){
    char *cp, *destination;
    int c;

    destination = (char *)malloc(MAXLEN);
    if(destination != 0){
        cp = destination;
        while((c = getchar()) != '\n' && c != EOF){
            if(cp-destination < MAXLEN-1)
                *cp++ = c;
        }
        *cp = 0;
        if(c == EOF && cp == destination)
            return(0);
    }
    return(destination);
}
```
                                                        (E5.11)

Finally, for the extremely brave, here is the whole thing with even p_array allocated using malloc. Further, all the array indexing is rewritten to use pointer notation. If you are feeling queasy, skip this example. It is hard. One word of explanation: char **p means a pointer to a pointer to a character. Many C programmers find this hard to deal with.

```
#include <stdio.h>
#include <stdlib.h>
#include <string.h>

#define MAXSTRING   50  /* max no. of strings */
```

```
#define MAXLEN      80  /* max length. of strings */

void print_arr(const char **p_array);
void sort_arr(const char **p_array);
char *next_string(void);

main(){
    char **p_array;
    int nstrings;   /* count of strings read */

    p_array = (char **)malloc(
            sizeof(char *[MAXSTRING+1]));
    if(p_array == 0){
        printf("No memory\n");
        exit(1);
    }

    nstrings = 0;
    while(nstrings < MAXSTRING &&
        (p_array[nstrings] = next_string()) != 0){

        nstrings++;
    }
    /* terminate p_array */
    p_array[nstrings] = 0;

    sort_arr(p_array);
    print_arr(p_array);
    exit(0);
}

void print_arr(const char **p_array){
    while(*p_array)
        printf("%s\n", *p_array++);
}

void sort_arr(const char **p_array){
    const char **lo_p, **hi_p, *tmp;

    for(lo_p = p_array;
        *lo_p != 0 && *(lo_p+1) != 0;
                lo_p++){
        for(hi_p = lo_p+1; *hi_p != 0; hi_p++){

            if(strcmp(*hi_p, *lo_p) >= 0)
```

```
                    continue;
                    /* swap strings */
                    tmp = *hi_p;
                    *hi_p = *lo_p;
                    *lo_p = tmp;
                }
            }
        }


char *next_string(void) {
    char *cp, *destination;
    int c;

    destination = (char *)malloc(MAXLEN);
    if(destination != 0){
        cp = destination;
        while((c = getchar()) != '\n' && c != EOF){
            if(cp-destination < MAXLEN-1)
                *cp++ = c;
        }
        *cp = 0;
        if(c == EOF && cp == destination)
            return(0);
    }
    return(destination);
}
```
                                                                    (E5.12)

To further illustrate the use of malloc, another example program follows which can cope with arbitrarily long strings. It simply reads strings from its standard input, looking for a newline character to mark the end of the string, then prints the string on its standard output. It stops when it detects end-of-file. The characters are put into an array, the end of the string being indicated (as always) by a zero. The newline is not stored, but used to detect when a full line of input should be printed on the output. The program doesn't know how long the string will be, so it starts by allocating ten characters – enough for a short string.

If the string is more than ten characters long, malloc is called to allocate room for the current string plus ten more characters. The current characters are copied into the new space, the old storage previously allocated is released and the program continues using the new storage.

To release storage allocated by malloc, the library function free is used. If you don't release storage when it isn't needed any more, it just hangs around taking up space. Using free allows it to be 'given away', or at least re-used later.

The program reports errors by using fprintf, a close cousin of printf. The only difference between them is that fprintf takes an additional first argument which indicates where its output should go. There are two constants of the right type for this purpose defined in stdio.h. Using stdout indicates that the program's standard output is to be used; stderr refers to the program's standard error stream. On some systems both may be the same, but other systems do make the distinction.

```c
#include <stdio.h>
#include <stdlib.h>
#include <string.h>

#define GROW_BY 10   /* string grows by 10 chars */

main(){
    char *str_p, *next_p, *tmp_p;
    int ch, need, chars_read;

    if(GROW_BY < 2){
        fprintf(stderr,
            "Growth constant too small\n");
        exit(1);
    }

    str_p = (char *)malloc(GROW_BY);
    if(str_p == NULL){
        fprintf(stderr,"No initial store\n");
        exit(1);
    }

    next_p = str_p;
    chars_read = 0;
    while((ch = getchar()) != EOF){
        /*
         * Completely restart at each new line.
         * There will always be room for the
         * terminating zero in the string,
         * because of the check further down,
         * unless GROW_BY is less than 2,
         * and that has already been checked.
         */
        if(ch == '\n'){
            /* indicate end of line */
            *next_p = 0;
            printf("%s\n", str_p);
            free(str_p);
            chars_read = 0;
            str_p = (char *)malloc(GROW_BY);
```

```
            if(str_p == NULL){
                fprintf(stderr,"No initial store\n");
                exit(1);
            }
            next_p = str_p;
            continue;
        }
        /*
         * Have we reached the end of the current
         * allocation ?
         */
        if(chars_read == GROW_BY-1){
            *next_p = 0;      /* mark end of string */
            /*
             * use pointer subtraction
             * to find length of
             * current string.
             */
            need = next_p -  str_p +1;
            tmp_p = (char *)malloc(need+GROW_BY);
            if(tmp_p == NULL){
                fprintf(stderr,"No more store\n");
                exit(1);
            }
            /*
             * Copy the string using library.
             */
            strcpy(tmp_p, str_p);
            free(str_p);
            str_p = tmp_p;
            /*
             * and reset next_p, character count
             */
            next_p = str_p + need-1;
            chars_read = 0;
        }
        /*
         * Put character at end of current string.
         */
        *next_p++ = ch;
        chars_read++;
    }
    /*
     * EOF - but do unprinted characters exist?
     */
    if(str_p - next_p){
```

```
            *next_p = 0;
            fprintf(stderr,"Incomplete last line\n");
            printf("%s\n", str_p);
        }
        exit(0);
}                                                    (E5.13)
```

That may not be a particularly realistic example of how to handle arbitrarily long strings – for one thing, the maximum storage demand is *twice* the amount needed for the longest string – but it does actually work. It also costs rather a lot in terms of copying around.

A more sophisticated method might use a linked list, implemented with the use of **structures**, as described in the next chapter. That would have its drawbacks too though, because then the standard library routines wouldn't work for a different method of storing strings.

5.5.1 What `sizeof` can't do

One common mistake made by beginners is shown below:

```
#include <stdio.h>

const char arr[] = "hello";
const char *cp = arr;
main(){

    printf("Size of arr %lu\n", (unsigned long)
            sizeof(arr));
    printf("Size of *cp %lu\n", (unsigned long)
            sizeof(*cp));
    exit(0);
}                                                    (E5.14)
```

The numbers printed will *not* be the same. The first will, correctly, identify the size of `arr` as 6; five characters followed by a null. The second one will always, on every system, print 1. That's because the type of `*cp` is `const char`, which can only have a size of 1, whereas the type of `arr` is different: array of `const char`. The confusion arises because this is the one place that the use of an array is *not* converted into a pointer first. It is never possible, using `sizeof`, to find out how long an array a pointer points to; you *must* have a genuine array name instead.

5.5.2 The type of `sizeof`

Finally, left until last, is the question of just what this does:

```
sizeof ( sizeof (anything legal) )
```

That is to say, what type does the result of `sizeof` have? The answer is that it is implementation defined, and will be either `unsigned long` or `unsigned int`, depending on your implementation. There are two safe things to do: either always cast the return value to `unsigned long`, as the examples have done, or to use the defined type `size_t` provided in the `<stddef.h>` header file. For example:

```
#include <stddef.h>
#include <stdio.h>

main(){
    size_t sz;
    sz = sizeof(sz);
    printf("size of sizeof is %lu\n",
        (unsigned long)sz);
}
```
(E5.15)

5.6 Pointers to functions

A useful technique is the ability to have pointers to functions. Their declaration is easy: write the declaration as it would for the function, say

```
int func(int a, float b);
```

and simply put brackets around the name and a `*` in front of it: that declares the pointer. Because of precedence, if you don't parenthesize the name, you declare a function returning a pointer:

```
/* function returning pointer to int */
int *func(int a, float b);

/* pointer to function returning int */
int (*func)(int a, float b);
```

Once you've got the pointer, you can assign the address of the right sort of function just by using its name: like an array, a function name is turned into an address when it's used in an expression. You can call the function using one of two forms:

```
(*func)(1,2);
/* or */
func(1,2);
```

The second form has been newly blessed by the Standard. Here's a simple example.

```
#include <stdio.h>
```

```
    void func(int);

main(){
    void (*fp)(int);

    fp = func;

    (*fp)(1);
    fp(2);

    exit(0);
}

void
func(int arg){
    printf("%d\n", arg);
}                                                    (E5.16)
```

If you like writing finite state machines, you might like to know that you can have an array of pointers to functions, with declaration and use like this:

```
void (*fparr[])(int, float) = {
                /* initializers */
            };
/* then call one */

fparr[5](1, 3.4);                                    (E5.17)
```

But I think we'll draw a veil over it at this point!

5.7 Summary

You have been introduced to arrays, pointers and the storage allocater. The last of the topics will prove to be more useful in the next chapter, but the other two are important even as they stand.

You simply *cannot* use C properly without understanding the use of pointers. Arrays are simple and unsurprising, although the fact that, when it's used in an expression, an array name converts into a pointer to its first element often takes time to sink in.

The C approach to support for strings really is quite surprising. The null-terminated array of character model is both simple and flexible. The fact that string manipulation is not built in to the language at first glance seems to rule C out of serious contention for character-oriented work, yet that is exactly where the language scores well compared with the alternatives, at least when speed is important. All the same, it's hard work for the programmer.

Pointer arithmetic is simple, easy, and extremely convenient. It's harder for ex-assembler programmers to learn, because of the tendency to try to translate it into what you 'know' the machine is doing. However, much harder for people with very low-level experience is the idea of the non-equivalence of pointers of different types. Try hard to throw away the idea that pointers contain addresses (in the hardware sense) and it will repay the effort.

The ability, using `malloc` and the associated stuff, of obtaining arbitrary pieces of storage really is extremely important. You might wish to defer it for a while, but don't leave it for too long. An obvious feature of C programs written by inexperienced users is their dependence on fixed size arrays. `Malloc` really does give you considerably more flexibility and is worth the effort to learn about.

The examples of the use of `sizeof` will help to eliminate a few common problems, too.

Exercises

5.1   What is the valid range of indices for an array of ten objects?

5.2   What happens if you take the address of the 11th member of that array?

5.3   When is it valid to compare the values of two pointers?

5.4   What is the use of a pointer to `void`?

5.5   Write functions which:

    a)   Compare two strings for equality. If they are equal, zero is returned, otherwise the difference in value between the first two non-matching characters.

    b)   Find the first occurrence of a specific character in a given string. Return a pointer to the occurrence in the string, or zero if it is not found.

    c)   Take two strings as arguments. If the first exists in the second as a substring, return a pointer to the first occurrence, otherwise zero.

5.6   Explain the examples using `malloc` to somebody else.

CHAPTER 6

Structured Data Types

6.1 History

The development of the early computer languages went either one way or the other. COBOL concentrated on the structure of data but not on arithmetic or algorithms, FORTRAN and Algol leant the other way. Scientific users wanted to do numeric work on relatively unstructured data (although arrays were soon found to be indispensable) and commercial users needed only basic arithmetic but knew that the key issue was the structure of the data.

The ideas that have influenced C are a mixture of the two schools; it has the structured control of flow expected in a language of its age, and has also made a start on data structures. So far we have concentrated on the algorithmic aspects of the language and haven't thought hard about data storage. Whilst it's true that arrays fall into the general category of data structuring, they are so simple, and so commonly in use, that they don't deserve a chapter to themselves. Until now we have been looking at a kind of block-structured FORTRAN.

For a large class of problems in computing, it is the data and not the algorithms that are the most interesting. If the initial design gets its data structures right, the rest of the effort in putting a program together is often quite small. However, you need help from the language. If there is no support for structured data types other than arrays, writing programs becomes both less convenient and also more prone to errors. It is the job of a good language to do more than just *allow* you to do something; it must actively *help* as well.

C offers arrays, structures and unions as its contribution to data structuring. They have proved to be entirely adequate for most users' needs over the years and remain essentially unchanged by the Standard.

6.2 Structures

Arrays allow for a named collection of identical objects. This is suitable for a number of tasks, but isn't really very flexible. Most real data objects are complicated things with an inherent structure that does not fit well on to array style storage. Let's use a concrete example.

Imagine that the job is something to do with a typesetting package. In this system, the individual characters have not only their character values but also some additional attributes like font and point size. The font doesn't affect the character as such, but only the way that it is displayed: this is the normal font, *this is in italics* and **this is in bold font**. Point size is similar. It describes the size of the characters when they are printed. For example, the point size of this text increases by two now. It goes back again now. If our characters have three independent attributes, how can they be represented in a single object?

With C it's easy. First work out how to represent the individual attributes in the basic types. Let's assume that we can still store the character itself in a `char`, that the font can be encoded into a `short` (1 for regular, 2 italic, 3 bold etc.) and that the point size will also fit a `short`. These are all quite reasonable assumptions. Most systems only support a few tens of fonts even if they are very sophisticated, and point sizes are normally in the range 6 to the small hundreds. Below 6 is almost invisible, above 50 is bigger than the biggest newspaper banner headlines. So we have a `char` and two `short`s that are to be treated as a single entity. Here's how to declare it in C.

```
struct wp_char{
    char wp_cval;
    short wp_font;
    short wp_psize;
};
```

That effectively declares a new type of object which can be used in your program. The whole thing is introduced by the `struct` keyword, which is followed by an optional identifier known as the **tag**, `wp_char` in this case. The tag only serves the purpose of giving a name to this type of structure and allows us to refer to the type later on. After a declaration like the one just seen, the tag can be used like this:

```
struct wp_char x, y;
```

That defines two variables called `x` and `y` just as it would have done if the definition had been

```
int x, y;
```

but of course in the first example the variables are of type `struct wp_char`, and in the second their type is `int`. The tag is a name for the new type that we have introduced.

It's worth remembering that structure tags can safely be used as ordinary identifiers as well. They only mean something special when they are preceded by the keyword `struct`. It is quite common to see a structured object being defined with the same name as its structure tag.

```
struct wp_char wp_char;
```

That defines a variable called `wp_char` of type `struct wp_char`. This is described by saying that structure tags have their own 'name space' and cannot collide with other names. We'll investigate tags some more in the discussion of 'partial declarations'.

Variables can also be defined immediately following a structure declaration.

```
struct wp_char{
    char wp_cval;
    short wp_font;
    short wp_psize;
}v1;

struct wp_char v2;
```

We now have two variables, `v1` and `v2`. If all the necessary objects are defined at the end of the structure declaration, the way that `v1` was, then the tag becomes unnecessary (except if it is needed later for use with `sizeof` and in casts) and is often not present.

The two variables are structured objects, each containing three separate *members* called `wp_cval`, `wp_font` and `wp_psize`. To access the individual members of the structures, the 'dot' operator is used:

```
v1.wp_cval = 'x';
v1.wp_font = 1;
v1.wp_psize = 10;

v2 = v1;
```

The individual members of `v1` are initialized to suitable values, then the whole of `v1` is copied into `v2` in an assignment.

In fact the only operations permitted on whole structures are those of assignment: they can be assigned to each other, passed as arguments to functions and returned by functions. However, it is not a very efficient operation to copy structures and most programs avoid structure copying by manipulating pointers to structures instead. It is generally quicker to copy pointers around than structures. A surprising omission is the ability to compare structures for equality, but there is a good reason for this which will mentioned later.

Here is an example using an array of structures like the one before. A function is used to read characters from the program's standard input and return an appropriately initialized structure. When a newline has been read or the array is full, the structures are sorted into order depending on the character value, and then printed out.

```
#include <stdio.h>
```

```c
#include <stdlib.h>

#define ARSIZE 10

struct wp_char{
    char wp_cval;
    short wp_font;
    short wp_psize;
}ar[ARSIZE];

/*
 * type of the input function -
 * could have been declared above
 */
struct wp_char infun(void);

main(){
    int icount, lo_indx, hi_indx;
    struct wp_char wp_tmp;

    for(icount = 0; icount < ARSIZE; icount++){
        ar[icount] = infun();
        if(ar[icount].wp_cval == '\n'){
            /*
             * Leave the loop.
             * not incrementing icount means that the
             * '\n' is ignored in the sort
             */
            break;
        }
    }

    /* now a simple exchange sort */

    for(lo_indx = 0; lo_indx <= icount-2; lo_indx++)
        for(hi_indx = lo_indx+1;
            hi_indx <= icount-1;
                hi_indx++){
            if(ar[lo_indx].wp_cval >
                    ar[hi_indx].wp_cval){
                wp_tmp = ar[lo_indx];
                ar[lo_indx] = ar[hi_indx];
                ar[hi_indx] = wp_tmp;
            }
        }
```

```
                    /* now print */
                    for(lo_indx = 0; lo_indx < icount; lo_indx++){
                        printf("%c %d %d\n", ar[lo_indx].wp_cval,
                                    ar[lo_indx].wp_font,
                                    ar[lo_indx].wp_psize);
                    }
                    exit(0);
            }
            struct wp_char
            infun(void){
                    struct wp_char wp_char;

                    wp_char.wp_cval = getchar();
                    wp_char.wp_font = 2;
                    wp_char.wp_psize = 10;

                    return(wp_char);
            }                                                    (E6.1)
```

Once it is possible to declare structures it seems pretty natural to declare arrays of them, use them as members of other structures and so on. In fact the only restriction is that a structure cannot contain an example of itself as a member – in which case it would be infinitely huge – an interesting concept for philosophers to debate, but no use to a C programmer.

6.2.1 Pointers and structures

If what the last paragraph says is true – that it is more common to use pointers to structures than to use the structures directly – we need to know how to do it. Declaring pointers is easy of course:

```
        struct wp_char *wp_p;
```

gives us one straight away. But how do we access the members of the structure? One way might be to look through the pointer to get the whole structure, then select the member:

```
        /* get the structure, then select a member */
        (*wp_p).wp_cval
```

would certainly work (the parentheses are there because . has a higher precedence than *). It's not an easy notation to work with though, so C introduces a new operator to clean things up; it is usually known as the 'pointing-to' operator. Here it is being used:

```
        /* the wp_cval in the structure wp_p points to */
        wp_p->wp_cval = 'x';
```

and although it might not look a lot easier than its alternative, it pays off when the structure contains pointers, as in a linked list. The pointing-to syntax is much easier if you want to follow two or three stages down the links of a linked list. If you haven't come across linked lists before, you're going to learn a lot more than just the use of structures before this chapter finishes!

Here is the last example rewritten using pointers, and with the input function infun changed to accept a pointer to a structure rather than returning one. This is much more likely to be what would be seen in practice.

(It is fair to say that, for a really efficient implementation, even the copying of structures would probably be dropped, especially if they were large. Instead, an array of pointers would be used, and the pointers exchanged until the sorted data could be found by traversing the pointer array in index order. That would complicate things too much for a simple example.)

```
#include <stdio.h>
#include <stdlib.h>

#define ARSIZE 10

struct wp_char{
    char wp_cval;
    short wp_font;
    short wp_psize;
}ar[ARSIZE];

void infun(struct wp_char *);

main(){
    struct wp_char wp_tmp, *lo_indx, *hi_indx, *in_p;

    for(in_p = ar; in_p < &ar[ARSIZE]; in_p++){
        infun(in_p);
        if(in_p->wp_cval == '\n'){
            /*
             * Leave the loop.
             * not incrementing in_p means that the
             * '\n' is ignored in the sort
             */
            break;
        }
    }

    /* now a simple exchange sort */

    for(lo_indx = ar; lo_indx <= in_p-2; lo_indx++)
        for(hi_indx = lo_indx+1;
```

```
                    hi_indx <= in_p-1;
                        hi_indx++){
                if(lo_indx->wp_cval > hi_indx->wp_cval){
                    wp_tmp = *lo_indx;
                    *lo_indx = *hi_indx;
                    *hi_indx = wp_tmp;
                }
            }

        /* now print */
        for(lo_indx = ar; lo_indx < in_p; lo_indx++){
            printf("%c %d %d\n", lo_indx->wp_cval,
                    lo_indx->wp_font,
                    lo_indx->wp_psize);
        }
        exit(0);
}

void
infun( struct wp_char *inp){

    inp->wp_cval = getchar();
    inp->wp_font = 2;
    inp->wp_psize = 10;

    return;
}
```
(E6.2)

The next issue is to consider what a structure looks like in terms of storage layout. It's best not to worry about this too much, but it is sometimes useful if you have to use C to access record-structured data written by other programs. The last structure will be allocated storage as shown in Figure 6.1.

struct wp_char

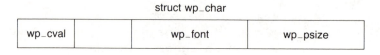

Figure 6.1   Storage layout of a structure

The diagram assumes a number of things: that a char takes 1 byte of storage; that a short needs 2 bytes; and that shorts must be aligned on even byte addresses in this architecture. As a result the structure contains an unnamed 1-byte member inserted by the compiler for architectural reasons. Such addressing restrictions are quite common and can often result in structures containing 'holes'.

The Standard makes some guarantees about the layout of structures and unions:

- Members of a structure are allocated within the structure in the order of their appearance in the declaration and have ascending addresses.
- There must not be any padding in front of the first member.
- The address of a structure is the same as the address of its first member, provided that the appropriate cast is used. Given the previous declaration of `struct wp_char`, if `item` is of type `struct wp_char`, then `(char *)item == &item.wp_cval`.
- Bitfields (see Section 6.4) don't actually have addresses, but are conceptually packed into **units** which obey the rules above.

6.2.2 Linked lists and other structures

The combination of structures and pointers opens up a lot of interesting possibilities. This is not a textbook on complex linked data structures, but it will go on to describe two very common examples of the breed: linked lists and trees. Both have a feature in common: they consist of structures containing pointers to other structures, all the structures typically being of the same type. Figure 6.2 shows a picture of a linked list.

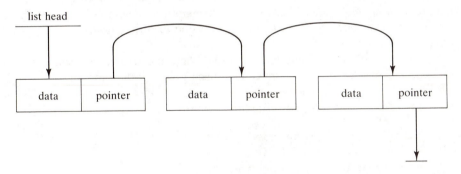

Figure 6.2   List linked by pointers

The sort of declaration needed for that is this:

```
struct list_ele{
    int data;    /* or whatever you like here */
    struct list_ele *ele_p;
};
```

Now, at first glance, it seems to contain itself – which is forbidden – but in fact it only contains a *pointer* to itself. How come the pointer declaration is allowed? Well, by the time the compiler reaches the pointer declaration it already knows that there is such a thing as a `struct list_ele` so the declaration is permitted. In fact, it is possible to make a partial declaration of a structure by saying

```
struct list_ele;
```

at some point before the full declaration. This will allow the declaration of pointers before the full declaration is seen. It is also important in the case of cross-referencing structures where each must contain a pointer to the other, as shown in the following example.

```
struct s_1; /* partial declaration */

struct s_2{
    int something;
    struct s_1 *sp;
};

struct s_1{ /* now the full declaration */
    float something;
    struct s_2 *sp;
};
```
(E6.3)

This illustrates the need for partial declaration. It also illustrates an important thing about the names of structure members: they inhabit a name-space per structure, so element names can be the same in different structures without causing any problems.

Partial declarations may only be used where the size of the structure isn't needed yet. A full declaration must have been given by the time that the size is used. The later full declaration mustn't be in an inner block because then it becomes a new declaration of a different structure.

```
struct x;    /* partial declaration */

/* valid uses of the tag */
struct x *p, func(void);

void f1(void){
    struct x{int i;};    /* redeclaration! */
}

/* full declaration now */
struct x{
    float f;
}s_x;

void f2(void){
    /* valid statements */
```

```
        p = &s_x;
        *p = func();
        s_x = func();
}

struct x
func(void){
        struct x tmp;
        tmp.f = 0;
        return (tmp);
}                                                          (E6.4)
```

There's one thing to watch out for: you get a partial declaration of a structure *simply by mentioning its name!* That means that this works:

```
struct abc{ struct xyz *p;};
        /* struct xyz now partially declared */
struct xyz{ struct abc *p;};
```

There's a horrible danger in the last example, though, as this shows:

```
struct xyz{float x;} var1;

main(){
        struct abc{ struct xyz *p;} var2;

        /* AAAGH - struct xyz REDECLARED */
        struct xyz{ struct abc *p;} var3;
}
```

The result is that `var2.p` can hold the address of `var1`, but emphatically not the address of `var3` which is of a different type! It can be fixed (assuming that it's not what you wanted) like this:

```
struct xyz{float x;} var1;

main(){
        struct xyz; /* new partial declaration of xyz */
        struct abc{ struct xyz *p;} var2;
        struct xyz{ struct abc *p;} var3;
}
```

To summarize partial declarations:

* If there is no previous reference to the tag xxx in an outer block, then *any* reference to struct xxx is a partial declaration, unless the body of the structure is also declared.

```
struct xxx *p;   /* implicit partial declaration */
struct y{
    struct xxx var; /* ditto */
};
struct xxx;        /* explicit partial declaration */
struct xxx{        /* new declaration */
    int a;
}var 1;
```

- If there *is* a previous declaration of the tag xxx in an outer block, only explicit partial declarations introduce a new meaning.

```
struct xxx *p;   /* refers to outer declaration */
struct y{
    struct xxx var; /* ditto */
};
struct xxx;        /* explicit partial declaration */
struct xxx{        /* new declaration */
    int a;
}var 1;
```

Back to the linked list. There were three elements linked into the list, which could have been built like this:

```
struct list_ele{
    int data;
    struct list_ele *pointer;
}ar[3];

main(){

    ar[0].data = 5;
    ar[0].pointer = &ar[1];
    ar[1].data = 99;
    ar[1].pointer = &ar[2];
    ar[2].data = -7;
    ar[2].pointer = 0;   /* mark end of list */
}                                                        (E6.5)
```

and the contents of the list can be printed in two ways. The array can be traversed in order of index, or the pointers can be used as in the following example.

```
#include <stdio.h>

struct list_ele{
```

```
        int data;
        struct list_ele *pointer;
}ar[3];

main(){

        struct list_ele *lp;

        ar[0].data = 5;
        ar[0].pointer = &ar[1];
        ar[1].data = 99;
        ar[1].pointer = &ar[2];
        ar[2].data = -7;
        ar[2].pointer = 0;   /* mark end of list */

        /* follow pointers */
        lp = ar;
        while(lp){
            printf("contents %d\n", lp->data);
            lp = lp->pointer;
        }
        return(0);
}
```
(E6.6)

It's the way that the pointers are followed which makes the example interesting. Notice how the pointer in each element is used to refer to the next one, until the pointer whose value is 0 is found. That value causes the while loop to stop. Of course the pointers can be arranged in any order at all, which is what makes the list such a flexible structure. Here is a function which could be included as part of the last program to sort the linked list into numeric order of its data fields. It rearranges the pointers so that the list, when traversed in pointer sequence, is found to be in order. It is important to note that the data itself is not copied. The function must return a pointer to the head of the list, because that is not necessarily at ar[0] any more.

```
struct list_ele *
sortfun( struct list_ele *list )
{

        int exchange;
        struct list_ele *nextp, *thisp, dummy;

        /*
         * Algorithm is this:
         * Repeatedly scan list.
         * If two list items are out of order,
```

```
     * link them in the other way round.
     * Stop if a full pass is made and no
     * exchanges are required.
     * The whole business is confused by
     * working one element behind the
     * first one of interest.
     * This is because of the simple mechanics of
     * linking and unlinking elements.
     */

    dummy.pointer = list;
    do{
        exchange = 0;
        thisp = &dummy;
        while( (nextp = thisp->pointer)
            && nextp->pointer){
            if(nextp->data < nextp->pointer->data){
                /* exchange */
                exchange = 1;
                thisp->pointer = nextp->pointer;
                nextp->pointer =
                    thisp->pointer->pointer;
                thisp->pointer->pointer = nextp;
            }
            thisp = thisp->pointer;
        }
    }while(exchange);

    return(dummy.pointer);
}                                               (E6.7)
```

Expressions such as thisp->pointer->pointer are commonplace in list processing. It's worth making sure that you understand it; the notation emphasizes the way that links are followed.

6.2.3 Trees

Another very popular data structure is the tree. It's actually a linked list with branches; a common type is the *binary tree* which has elements (*nodes*) looking like this:

```
struct tree_node{
    int data;
    struct tree_node *left_p, *right_p;
};
```

For historical and essentially irrelevant reasons, trees in computer science work upside down. They have their *root* node at the top and their *branches* spread out downwards. In Figure 6.3, the 'data' members of the nodes are replaced by values which will be used in the discussion that follows.

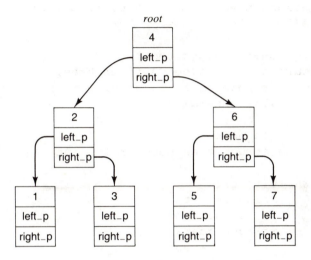

Figure 6.3   A tree

Trees may not seem very exciting if your main interest lies in routine character handling and processing, but they are extremely important to the designers of databases, compilers and other complex tools.

The advantage of a tree is that, if it is properly arranged, the layout of the data can support binary searching very simply. It is always possible to add new nodes to a tree at the appropriate place and a tree is basically a flexible and useful data structure.

Look at Figure 6.3. The tree is carefully constructed so that it can be searched to find whether a given value can be found in the data portions of the nodes. Let's say we want to find if a value *x* is already present in the tree. The algorithm is this:

Start at the root of the tree:
    if the tree is empty (no nodes)
        then return 'failure'.
    else if the data in the current node is equal to the value being searched for
        then return 'success'
    else if the data in the current node is greater than the value being searched for
        then search the tree indicated by the left pointer
    else search the tree indicated by the right pointer.

Here it is in C:

```c
#include <stdio.h>
struct tree_node{
     int data;
     struct tree_node *left_p, *right_p;
}tree[7];
/*
 * Tree search algorithm.
 * Searches for value ''v'' in tree,
 * returns pointer to first node found containing
 * the value otherwise 0.
 */
struct tree_node *
t_search(struct tree_node *root, int v){

     while(root){
          if(root->data == v)
                return(root);
          if(root->data > v)
                root = root->left_p;
          else
                root = root->right_p;
     }
     /* value not found, no tree left */
     return(0);
}

main(){
     /* construct tree by hand */
     struct tree_node *tp, *root_p;
     int i;
     for(i = 0; i < 7; i++){
          int j;
          j = i+1;

          tree[i].data = j;
          if(j == 2 || j == 6){
               tree[i].left_p = &tree[i-1];
               tree[i].right_p = &tree[i+1];
          }
     }
     /* root */
     root_p = &tree[3];
     root_p->left_p = &tree[1];
     root_p->right_p = &tree[5];
```

```
        /* try the search */
        tp = t_search(root_p, 9);
        if(tp)
            printf("found at position %d\n", tp-tree);
        else
            printf("value not found\n");
}                                                        (E6.8)
```

So that works fine. It is also interesting to note that, given a value, it can always be inserted at the appropriate point in the tree. The same search algorithm is used, but, instead of giving up when it finds that the value is not already in the tree, a new node is allocated by `malloc`, and is hung on the tree at the very place where the first null pointer was found. This is a mite more complicated to do because of the problem of handling the root pointer itself, and so a pointer to a pointer is used. Read the example carefully; it is not likely that you ever find anything more complicated than this in practice. If you can understand it, there is not much that should worry you about the vast majority of C language programs.

```
#include <stdio.h>
#include <stdlib.h>

struct tree_node{
    int data;
    struct tree_node *left_p, *right_p;
};

/*
 * Tree search algorithm.
 * Searches for value ``v'' in tree,
 * returns pointer to first node found containing
 * the value otherwise 0.
 */
struct tree_node *
t_search(struct tree_node *root, int v){

    while(root){
        printf("looking for %d, looking at %d\n",
            v, root->data);
        if(root->data == v)
            return(root);
        if(root->data > v)
            root = root->left_p;
        else
            root = root->right_p;
    }
    /* value not found, no tree left */
```

```
            return(0);
    }
    /*
     * Insert node into tree.
     * Return 0 for success,
     * 1 for value already in tree,
     * 2 for malloc error
     */
    int
    t_insert(struct tree_node **root, int v){

        while(*root){
            if((*root)->data == v)
                return(1);
            if((*root)->data > v)
                root = &((*root)->left_p);
            else
                root = &((*root)->right_p);
        }
        /* value not found, no tree left */
        if((*root = (struct tree_node *)
            malloc(sizeof (struct tree_node)))
                == 0)
            return(2);
        (*root)->data = v;
        (*root)->left_p = 0;
        (*root)->right_p = 0;
        return(0);
    }

main(){
    /* construct tree by hand */
    struct tree_node *tp, *root_p = 0;
    int i;

    t_insert(&root_p, 4);
    t_insert(&root_p, 2);
    t_insert(&root_p, 6);
    t_insert(&root_p, 1);
    t_insert(&root_p, 3);
    t_insert(&root_p, 5);
    t_insert(&root_p, 7);

    /* try the search */
    for(i = 1; i < 9; i++){
        tp = t_search(root_p, i);
```

```
            if(tp)
                printf("%d found\n", i);
            else
                printf("%d not found\n", i);
        }
        return(0);
    }
```
(E6.9)

Finally, the algorithm that allows you to walk along the tree visiting all the nodes in order is beautiful. It is the cleanest example of recursion that I have seen. Look at it and work out what it does.

```
    void
    t_walk(struct tree_node *root_p){

        if(root_p == 0)
            return;
        t_walk(root_p->left_p);
        printf("%d\n", root_p->data);
        t_walk(root_p->right_p);
    }
```
(E6.10)

6.3 Unions

Unions don't take long to explain. They are the same as structures, except that, where you would have written struct before, now you write union. Everything works the same way, but with one big exception. In a structure, the members are allocated separate consecutive chunks of storage. In a union, every member is allocated the *same* piece of storage. What would you use them for? Well, sometimes you want a structure to contain different values of different types at different times. Using a union, it's up to you to keep track of whatever type you put into it and make sure that you retrieve the right type at the right time. Here's an example:

```
    #include <stdio.h>
    #include <stdlib.h>

    main(){
        union {
            float u_f;
            int u_i;
        }var;

        var.u_f = 23.5;
        printf("value is %f\n", var.u_f);
```

```
        var.u_i = 5;
        printf("value is %d\n", var.u_i);
        exit(0);
}
```
(E6.11)

If the example had, say, put a float into the union and then extracted it as an int, a very strange value would have resulted. The two types are almost certainly not only stored differently, but of different lengths. The int retrieved would probably be the low-order bits of the machine representation of a float, and might easily be made up of part of the mantissa of the float plus a piece of the exponent.

The C compiler does no more than work out what the biggest member in a union can be and allocates enough storage (appropriately aligned if neccessary). In particular, no checking is done to make sure that the right sort of use is made of the members. That is your task, and you'll soon find out if you get it wrong. The members of a union all start at the same address – there is guaranteed to be no padding in front of any of them.

The most common way of remembering what is in a union is to embed it in a structure, with another member of the structure used to indicate the type of thing currently in the union. Here is how it might be used:

```
#include <stdio.h>
#include <stdlib.h>

/* code for types in union */
#define FLOAT_TYPE   1
#define CHAR_TYPE    2
#define INT_TYPE     3

struct var_type{
    int type_in_union;
    union{
        float   un_float;
        char    un_char;
        int un_int;
    }vt_un;
}var_type;

void
print_vt(){

    switch(var_type.type_in_union){
        default:
            printf("Unknown type in union\n");
            break;
        case FLOAT_TYPE:
            printf("%f\n", var_type.vt_un.un_float);
```

```
                    break;
              case CHAR_TYPE:
                    printf("%c\n", var_type.vt_un.un_char);
                    break;
              case INT_TYPE:
                    printf("%d\n", var_type.vt_un.un_int);
                    break;
        }
}

main(){

      var_type.type_in_union = FLOAT_TYPE;
      var_type.vt_un.un_float = 3.5;

      print_vt();

      var_type.type_in_union = CHAR_TYPE;
      var_type.vt_un.un_char = 'a';

      print_vt();
      exit(0);
}                                                   (E6.12)
```

That also demonstrates how the dot notation is used to access structures or unions inside other structures or unions. The Standard says that the full name must always be given, as shown. Some current C compilers allow you to miss bits out of the names of embedded objects provided that they are not ambiguous. In the example, such an unambiguous name would be var_type.un_int and the compiler would work out what you meant. None the less this is forbidden by the Standard.

It is because of unions that structures cannot be compared for equality. The possibility that a structure might contain a union makes it hard to compare such structures; the compiler can't tell what the union currently contains and so wouldn't know how to compare the structures. This sounds a bit hard to swallow and isn't 100% true – most structures don't contain unions – but there is also a philosophical issue at stake about just what is meant by 'equality' when applied to structures. Anyhow, the union business gives the Standard a good excuse to duck the issue by not supporting structure comparison.

6.4 Bitfields

While we're on the subject of structures, we might as well look at these things. They can only be declared inside a structure or a union, and allow you to specify some very small objects of a given number of bits in length. Their usefulness is limited and they aren't seen in many programs, but we'll deal with them anyway.

This example should help to make things clear:

```
struct {
    /* field 4 bits wide */
    unsigned field1 :4;
    /*
     * unnamed 3 bit field
     * unnamed fields allow for padding
     */
    unsigned     :3;
    /*
     * one-bit field
     *   can only be 0 or -1 in two's complement!
     */
    signed   field2 :1;
    /* align next field on a storage unit */
    unsigned    :0;
    unsigned field3 :6;
}full_of_fields;                                    (E6.13)
```

Each field is accessed and manipulated as if it were an ordinary member of a structure. The keywords signed and unsigned mean what you would expect, except that it is interesting to note that a 1-bit signed field on a two's complement machine can only take the values 0 or -1.

The main use of bitfields is either to allow tight packing of data or to be able to specify the fields within some externally produced data files. C gives no guarantee of the ordering of fields within machine words. The Standard says that fields are packed into 'storage units', which are typically machine words. The packing order, and whether or not a bitfield may cross a storage unit boundary, are implementation defined. To force alignment to a storage unit boundary, a zero width field is used before the one that you want to have aligned.

Be careful using them. It can require a surprising amount of run-time code to manipulate these things and you can end up using more space than they save.

Bit fields do not have addresses – you can't have pointers to them.

6.5 Enums

These fall into the category of 'half baked'. They aren't proper enumerated types, as in Pascal, and only really serve to help you reduce the number of #define statements in your program. They look like this:

```
enum e_tag{
    a, b, c, d=20, e, f, g=20, h
}var;
```

The `e_tag` is the tag, just like with structures and unions. The definition of the variable `var` is just like with structures, and the Standard says that its type is `int`. It is absolutely and completely indistinguishable from any other `int` and there is no special type-checking implied in its declaration.

The names inside the enumeration act as integer constants from the point of the declaration. Their values are these:

```
a == 0
b == 1
c == 2
d == 20
e == 21
f == 22
g == 20
h == 21
```

so you can see that, in the absence of anything to the contrary, the values assigned start at zero and increase. A specific value can be given if you want, when the increase will continue one at a time afterwards. It is possible for more than one of the names to have the same value.

The only use for these things is to give a better-scoped version of this:

```
#define a 0
#define b 1
/* and so on */
```

It's better scoped because the declaration of enumerations follows the standard scope rules for C, whereas `#define` statements have file scope.

All enumeration variables and members behave as `ints`. If you can find a real and compelling use for them, let me know.

6.6 Initialization

Now that we have seen all of the data types supported by C, we can look at the subject of initialization. C allows ordinary variables, structures, unions and arrays to be given initial values in their definitions. Old C had some strange rules about this, reflecting an unwillingness by compiler writers to work too hard. The Standard has rationalized this, and now it is possible to initialize things as and when you want.

There are basically two sorts of initialization: at compile time, and at run time. Which one you get depends on the *storage duration* of the thing being initialized.

Objects with **static duration** are declared either outside functions, or inside them with the keyword `extern` or `static` as part of the declaration. These can *only* be initialized at compile time.

Any other object has **automatic duration**, and can only be initialized at run time. The two categories are completely mutually exclusive.

Compile-time initialization can only be done using *constant expressions* (see Chapter 2); run-time initialization can be done using *any* expression at all. The Old C restriction, that only simple variables (not arrays, structures or unions) could be initialized at run time, has been lifted.

Here is an example using several initialized variables:

```c
#include <stdio.h>
#include <stdlib.h>

#define NMONTHS 12

int month = 0;

short month_days[] =
    {31,28,31,30,31,30,31,31,30,31,30,31};

char *mnames[] ={
    "January", "February",
    "March", "April",
    "May", "June",
    "July", "August",
    "September", "October",
    "November", "December"
};

main(){

    int day_count = month;

    for(day_count = month; day_count < NMONTHS;
        day_count++){
        printf("%d days in %s\n",
            month_days[day_count],
            mnames[day_count]);
    }
    exit(0);
}
```
(E6.14)

Initializing ordinary variables is easy: just put = expression after the variable name in a declaration, and the variable is initialized to the value of the expression. As with all objects, whether you can use any expression, or just a constant expression, depends on its storage duration.

Initializing arrays is easy for one-dimensional arrays. Just put a list of the values you want, separated by commas, inside curly brackets. The example shows how to do it. If you don't give a size for the array, then the number of initializers will determine the size. If you do give a size, then there must be at most that many initializers in the list. Too many is an error, too few will just initialize the first elements of the array.

You could build up a string like this:

```
char str[] = {'h', 'e', 'l', 'l', 'o', 0};
```

but because it is so often necessary to do that, it is also permitted to use a quoted stringliteral to initialize an array of chars:

```
char str[] = "hello";
```

In that case, the null at the end of the string will also be included if there is room, or if no size was specified. Here are examples:

```
/* no room for the null */
char str[5] = "hello";

/* room for the null */
char str[6] = "hello";
```

The example program used string literals for a different purpose: in that, they were being used to initialize an array of character pointers; a very different prospect.

For structures that have automatic duration, an expression of the right type can be used to initialize them, or else a bracketed list of constant expressions must be used:

```
#include <stdio.h>
#include <stdlib.h>

struct s{
    int a;
    char b;
    char *cp;
}ex_s = {
    1, 'a', "hello"
    };

main() {
    struct s int_s = ex_s;
    struct s int_ss = {
        2, 'b', "byebye"
        };
```

```
        exit(0);
    }                                                              (E6.15)
```

Only the first member of a union can be initialized.

For objects that contain sub-objects within them, there are two ways of writing the initializer. It can be written out with an initializer for each member:

```
struct s{
    int a;
    struct ss{
        int c;
        char d;
    }e;
}x[] = {
    1, 2, 'a',
    3, 4, 'b'
    };                                                             (E6.16)
```

which will assign 1 to x[0].a, 2 to x[0].e.c, a to x[0].e.d and 3 to x[1].a and so on.

It is *much* safer to use internal braces to show what you mean, or one missed value will cause havoc.

```
struct s{
    int a;
    struct ss{
        int c;
        char d;
    }e;
}x[] = {
    {1, {2, 'a'}},
    {3, {4, 'b'}}
    };                                                             (E6.17)
```

Always fully bracket initializers – that is much the safest thing to do.
It is the same for arrays as for structures:

```
float y[4][3] = {
    {1, 3, 5},    /* y[0][0], y[0][1], y[0][2] */
    {2, 4, 6},    /* y[1][0], y[1][1], y[1][2] */
    {3, 5, 7}     /* y[2][0], y[2][1], y[2][2] */
    };                                                             (E6.18)
```

This gives full initialization to the first three rows of y. The fourth row y[3] is uninitialized.

Unless they have an explicit initializer, all objects with static duration are given implicit initializers – the effect is as if the constant 0 had been assigned to their components. This is in fact widely used – it is an assumption made by most C programs that external objects and internal static objects start with the value zero.

Initialization of objects with automatic duration is only guaranteed if their compound statement is entered 'at the top'. Jumping into the middle of one may result in the initialization not happening – this is often undesirable and should be avoided. It isn't clear what happens with `switch` statements, since they are *designed* to be 'jumped into'. The Standard may clarify this in a later draft.

6.7 Summary

You now understand structures and unions. Bitfields and enumeration types really are not very important and you could manage quite well without them.

It is hard to emphasize how important the use of structures, pointers and `malloc` is in serious programs. If you aren't familiar with the use of structured data in the form of lists, trees and so on, get a good book now. Better still, try to enrol on a good course. Except in very specialized applications, it is usually the ability to structure data well, not the ability to write complicated algorithms, that makes it possible to construct clean, small and maintainable programs. Experienced software designers often say that once the right structure of the data has been determined, the rest is 'simple'.

Undoubtedly, one of the reasons for the popularity of C among experienced software specialists is the freedom that it gives in the structuring of data, without sacrificing speed.

Initialization should not be overlooked. Although simple in concept, it is surprising how inconvenient many other languages make this. The ludicrous extreme is to insist on the use of assignment statements; C has a practical and convenient approach. If the concept of 'fully bracketed initializers' seems a bit unpleasant, don't worry. It is rare that you have to do it in practice; all that you need is to know how to do simple initialization and to know a book that describes the more complex initialization.

Exercises

6.1 What is the declaration of an untagged structure containing two `int`s called a and b?

6.2 Why is such a declaration of limited use?

6.3 What would the structure look like with a tag of `int_struc` and two variables of the structure type being defined?

6.4   How would you declare a third variable later, with the the same type as x and y?

6.5   Assuming that p is the right type of pointer, how would you make it point to z and then set z.a to zero, using the pointer?

6.6   What are the two ways of partially declaring a structure?

6.7   What is unusual about a string `"like this"` when it's used to initialize a character array?

6.8   What if it initializes a `char *`?

6.9   Find out what a doubly linked list is. Reimplement the linked list example using one. Is it any easier to insert and delete elements in a doubly linked list?

## CHAPTER 7

The Preprocessor

7.1 Effect of the Standard

The Standard has had more effect on this poor, tired little creature than almost any other part of the language. That's because the preprocessor has long been a sort of second-class citizen; either part of C, or not part of it, depending on how you cared to view things. It was generally implemented as a separate program (hence its title) and could be used separately from C, although it rarely was in practice, and C could be used without it.

There has never been a widely accepted formal specification for the preprocessor and different versions of it have been implemented in different systems. As a result, programs using anything other than the very basic features have proved to be a problem: it's hard to port them.

Since there is no accepted standard for this thing, and since some of the less well defined features are none the less desirable, the Standard has defined a way of doing them. That it isn't compatible with previous implementations is a different issue.

At the simplest level the preprocessor is easy to use and can help a lot to make programs easy to read and maintain. Unfortunately this isn't the immediate impression that you get when you look at the specification of the preprocessor. This chapter doesn't attempt the 'executive overview' approach, hiding detail behind a partial description. This makes it hard for beginners to understand, but that may be just as well. In my experience, only the very simplest use of #define and the conditional compilation #if family are suitable for beginners. If this is your first encounter with C, read the chapter once to see what you can pick up; the exercises will test a basic understanding. Otherwise, I would suggest that at least six months experience is the minimum prerequisite for a full attack.

7.2 How the preprocessor works

Although the preprocessor (Figure 7.1) is probably going to be implemented as an integral part of an Standard C compiler, it can equally well be thought of as a separate program which transforms C source code containing preprocessor

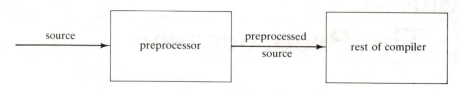

Figure 7.1 The preprocessor

directives into source code with the directives removed.

It's important to remember that the preprocessor is not working to the same rules as the rest of C. It works on a line-by-line basis, so the end of a line means something special to it. The rest of C thinks that end-of-line is little different from a space or tab character.

The preprocessor doesn't know about the scope rules of C either. As far as it is concerned, preprocessor directives like #define take effect as soon as they are seen and remain in effect until the end of the file that contains them; the program's block structure is irrelevant. This is one of the reasons why it's a good idea to make sparing use of these directives. The less you have in your program that doesn't obey the 'normal' scope rules, the less likely you are to make mistakes.

The Standard gives some complicated rules for the syntax of the preprocessor, especially with respect to 'tokens'. To understand the operation of the preprocessor you need to know a little about them. The text that is being processed is not considered to be a uniform stream of characters, but is separated into tokens *then* processed piecemeal.

For a full definition of the process, it is best to refer to the Standard, but an informal description follows. Each of the terms used to head the list below is used later in descriptions of the rules.

1. *header-name*

    - ′ <′ *almost any character* ′ >′

2. *preprocessing-token*

    - a *header-name* as above but only when the subject of # include,
    - or an *identifier* which is any C identifier or keyword,
    - or a *constant* which is any integral or floating constant,
    - or a *string-literal* which is a normal C string,
    - or an *operator* which is one of the C operators,
    - or one of [ ] ( ) { } * , : = ; ... # (punctuators)
    - or any non-white-space character not covered by the list above.

The '*almost any character*' above means any character except ′ >′ or newline.

7.3 Directives

Directives are always introduced by a line that starts with a # character, optionally preceded by white space characters, but in fact it isn't common practice to indent the #. Table 7.1 below is a list of the directives defined in the Standard.

Table 7.1 Preprocessor directives

Directive	Meaning
# include	include a source file
# define	define a macro
# undef	undefine a macro
# if	conditional compilation
# ifdef	conditional compilation
# ifndef	conditional compilation
# elif	conditional compilation
# else	conditional compilation
# endif	conditional compilation
# line	control error reporting
# error	force an error message
# pragma	used for implementation-dependent control
#	null directive; no effect

The meanings and use of these features will be described in the following sections. Make a note that the # and the following keyword, if any, are individual items. They may be separated by white space.

7.3.1 The null directive

This is simple: a plain # on a line by itself does nothing!

7.3.2 # define

There are two ways of defining macros, one of which looks like a function and one which does not. Here is an example of each:

```
#define FMAC(a,b)  a here, then b

#define NONFMAC some text here
```

Both definitions define a macro and some *replacement text*, which will be used to replace later occurrences of the macro name in the rest of the program. After those definitions, they can be used as follows, with the effect of the macro replacement shown in comments:

```
NONFMAC
/* some text here */

FMAC(first text, some more)
/* first text here, then some more */
```

For the non-function macro, its name is simply replaced by its replacement text. For the function macro, it is also replaced by its replacement text, but the replacement text is treated more carefully. Wherever the replacement text contains an identifier which is the name of one of the macro's 'formal arguments', the actual text given as the argument is used in place of the identifier in the replacement text.

For both forms of macro, leading or trailing white space around the replacement text is discarded.

The way that you distinguish between a function macro and a non-function macro whose replacement text starts with a (is simple. If there's a space in front of the (, then it can't be the definition of a function macro. The *use* of a function macro is not subject to the no white space rule.

The Standard allows either type of macro to be redefined at any time, using another # define, provided that there isn't any attempt to change the type of the macro and that the tokens making up both the original definition and the redefinition are identical in number, ordering, spelling and use of white space. In this context all white space is considered equal, so this would be correct:

```
# define XXX abc/*comment*/def hij
# define XXX abc def hij
```

because comment is a form of white space. The token sequence for both cases (*w-s* stands for a white-space token) is:

```
# w-s define w-s XXX w-s abc w-s def w-s hij w-s
```

Macro substitution

Where will occurrences of the macro name cause the replacement text to be substituted in its place? Practically anywhere in a program that the identifier is recognized as a separate token, except as the identifier following the # of a preprocessor directive. You can't do this:

```
#define define XXX

#define YYY ZZZ
```

and expect the second #define to be replaced by #XXX, causing an error.

When the identifier associated with a non-function macro is seen, it is replaced by the macro replacement tokens, then **rescanned**.

For a function macro, in an attempt to make it work more like a real function, white space around the macro name, the argument list and so on, may include the newline character:

```
#define FMAC(a, b) printf("%s %s\n", a, b)

FMAC ("hello",
    "sailor"
    );
/* results in */
printf("%s %s\n", "hello", "sailor")
```

Also, for a function macro, the 'arguments' can be absolutely any token sequence, including commas, provided the whole sequence is bracketed with (and).

```
#define ERRMAC(a, b) printf(a, b)

ERRMAC("%d %d %s\n", (1, 24, "urgh"));
/* results in */
printf("%d %d %s\n", 1, 24, "urgh");
```

When a function macro is being processed, the steps are as follows:

1. All of its arguments are identified.
2. If any of the tokens in an argument are themselves candidates for macro replacement, the replacement is done until no further replacement is possible. If this introduces commas into the argument list, there is no danger of the macro suddenly seeming to have a different number of arguments; the arguments are *only* determined in the step above.
3. In the macro replacement text, identifiers naming one of the macro formal arguments are replaced by the (by now expanded) token sequence supplied as the actual argument. The replacement is suppressed only if the identifier is preceded by one of # or ##, or followed by ##.

Stringizing

There is special treatment for places in the macro replacement text where one of the macro formal parameters is found preceded by #. The replacement text for the formal parameter will by now have expanded to one or more tokens. Any leading or trailing white space is discarded from the list of tokens, then the # and the token list are turned into a single string literal. Spaces between the tokens are treated as space characters in the string. To prevent 'unexpected' results, any " or \ characters within the new string literal are preceded by \.

This example demonstrates the feature:

```
#define MESSAGE(x) printf("Message: %s\n", #x)

MESSAGE (Text with "quotes");
```

```
/*
 * Result is
 * printf("Message: %s\n", "Text with \"quotes\"");
 */
```

Token pasting

A ## operator may occur anywhere in the replacement text for a macro except at the beginning or end. If a parameter name of a function macro occurs in the replacement text preceded or followed by one of these operators, the expanded token sequence for the corresponding macro argument is used to replace it, from step 2 above (apparently – the Standard is a bit obscure here). Then, for both function and non-function macros, the tokens surrounding the ## operator are joined together. If they don't form a sensible token, the behaviour is undefined. Then rescanning occurs.

As an example of token pasting, here is a multi-stage operation, involving the **rescanning** described below.

```
#define REPLACE some replacement text
#define JOIN(a, b) a ## b
```

```
JOIN(REP, LACE)
```
becomes, after token pasting,
```
REPLACE
```
becomes, after rescanning,
```
some replacement text
```

Rescanning

Once the processing described above has occurred, the replacement text plus the following tokens of the source file is rescanned, looking for more macro names to replace. The one exception is that, purely within macro replacement text, the name of the macro currently being replaced is not itself replaced in the replacement text. Because macro replacement is nested, it is possible for several macros to be in the process of being replaced at any one point: none of them is a candidate for further replacement in the 'inner' levels of this process. This allows redefinition of existing functions as macros:

```
#define exit(x) exit((x)+1)
```

These macro names which were not replaced now become tokens which are immune from future replacement, even if later processing might have meant that they had become available for replacement.

If I understand the Standard correctly at this point (and it does seem confusing), this prevents the danger of infinite recursion occurring in the preprocessor.

Notes

There is a subtle problem when using arguments to function macros.

```
/* warning - subtle problem in this example */
#define SQR(x)   ( x * x )
/*
 * Wherever the formal parameters occur in
 * the replacement text, they are replaced
 * by the actual parameters to the macro.
 */
printf("sqr of %d is %d\n", 2, SQR(2));
```

The formal parameter of SQR is x; the actual parameter is 2. The replacement text results in

```
printf("sqr of %d is %d\n", 2, ( 2 * 2 ));
```

The use of the parentheses should be noticed. The following example is likely to give trouble:

```
/* bad example */
#define DOUBLE(y) y+y

printf("twice %d is %d\n", 2, DOUBLE(2));
printf("six times %d is %d\n", 2, 3*DOUBLE(2));
```

The problem is that the last expression in the second printf is replaced by

```
3*2+2
```

which results in 8, not 12! The rule is that when using macros to build expressions, careful parenthesizing is necessary. Here's another example:

```
SQR(3+4)

/* expands to */

( 3+4 * 3+4 )
/* oh dear, still wrong! */
```

so, when formal parameters occur in the replacement text, you should look carefully at them too. Correct versions of SQR and DOUBLE are these:

```
#define SQR(x) ((x)*(x))
#define DOUBLE(x) ((x)+(x))
```

Macros have a last little trick to surprise you with, as this shows.

```
#include <stdio.h>
#define DOUBLE(x)  ((x)+(x))

main(){
    int a[20], *ip;

    ip = a;
    a[0] = 1;
    a[1] = 2;
    printf("%d\n", DOUBLE(*ip++));
    return(0);
}                                              (E7.1)
```

Why is this going to cause problems? Because the replacement text of the macro refers to *ip++ twice, so it gets incremented twice and we don't know whether or not the increments are saved up until the end of the expression. Macros should never be used with expressions that involve side effects, unless you check very carefully that they are safe.

Despite these warnings, they provide a very useful feature, and one which will be used a lot from now on.

7.3.3 # undef

The name of any #defined identifier can be forcibly forgotten by saying

```
#undef   NAME
```

It isn't an error to #undef a name which isn't currently defined.

This occasionally comes in handy. Chapter 9 points out that some library functions may actually be macros, not functions, but by undefing their names you are guaranteed access to a real function.

7.3.4 # include

This comes in two flavours:

```
#include <filename>
#include "filename"
```

both of which cause a new file to be read at the point where they occur. It's as if the single line containing the directive is replaced by the contents of the specified file. If that file contains erroneous statements, you can reasonably expect that the errors will be reported with a correct file name and line number. It's the compiler writer's job to get that right. The Standard specifies that at least eight nested levels of # include must be supported.

The effect of using brackets <> or quotes " " around the filename is to change the places searched to find the specified file. The brackets cause a search of a number of implementation defined places, the quotes cause a search of somewhere associated with the original source file. Your implementation notes must tell you the specific details of what is meant by 'place'. If the form using quotes can't find the file, it tries again as if you had used brackets.

In general, brackets are used when you specify standard library header files, quotes are used for private header files – often specific to one program only.

You can also write this:

```
# define NAME <stdio.h>
# include NAME
```

to get the same effect as

```
# include <stdio.h>
```

but it's a rather roundabout way of doing it, and unfortunately it's subject to implementation defined rules about how the text between < and > is treated.

It's simpler if the replacement text for NAME comes out to be a string, for example

```
#define NAME "stdio.h"

#include NAME
```

There is no problem with implementation defined behaviour here, but the paths searched are different, as explained above.

For the first case, what happens is that the token sequence which replaces NAME is (by the rules already given)

```
<
stdio
.
h
>
```

and for the second case

```
"stdio.h"
```

The second case is easy, since it's just a *string-literal* which is a legal token for a # include directive. It is implementation defined how the first case is treated, and whether or not the sequence of tokens forms a legal *header-name*.

Finally, the last character of a file which is being included must be a plain newline. Failure to include a file successfully is treated as an error.

7.3.5 Predefined names

The following names are predefined within the preprocessor:

__LINE__
> The current source file line number, a decimal integer constant.

__FILE__
> The 'name' of the current source code file, a string literal.
> The current date, a string literal. The form is

```
Nov 25 1986
```

> where the month name is as defined in asctime and the first digit of the
> date is a space if the date is less than 10.

__TIME__
> The time of the translation; again a string literal in the form produced by
> asctime ("hh:mm:ss").

__STDC__
> The integer constant 1. This is used to test if the compiler is Standard-
> conforming, the intention being that it will have different values for different
> releases of the Standard.

A common way of using these predefined names is the following:

```
#define TEST(x) if(!(x))\
    printf("test failed, line %d file %s\n",\
        __LINE__, __FILE__)

/**/

TEST(a != 23);

/**/                                                    (E7.2)
```

If the argument to TEST gives a false result, the message is printed, including the
filename and line number in the message.

There's only one minor caveat: the use of the if statement can cause
confusion in a case like this:

```
if(expression)
    TEST(expr2);
else
    statement_n;
```

The else will get associated with the hidden if generated by expanding the
TEST macro. This is most unlikely to happen in practice, but will be a thorough
pain to track down if it ever does sneak up on you. It's good style to make the
bodies of every control of flow statement compound anyway; then the problem
goes away.

None of the names `__LINE__`, `__FILE__`, `__DATE__`, `__TIME__`, `__STDC__`, or defined may be used in #define or #undef directives.

The preprocessor will reserve other names only if they start with a leading underscore. This means that the programmer is free to use names that do not start with a _ unless they conflict with predefined library identifiers and the program is being translated in a hosted environment.

7.3.6 #line

This is used to set the value of the built in names `__LINE__` and `__FILE__`. Why do this? Because a lot of tools nowadays actually generate C as their output. This directive allows them to control the current line number. It is of very limited interest to the 'ordinary' C programmer.

Its form is

>   # line *number optional-string-literal newline*

The number sets the value of `__LINE__`, the string literal, if present, sets the value of `__FILE__`.

In fact, the sequence of tokens following #line will be macro expanded. After expansion, they are expected to provide a valid directive of the right form.

7.3.7 Conditional compilation

A number of the directives control conditional compilation, which allows certain portions of a program to be selectively compiled or ignored depending upon certain conditions. The directives concerned are: #if, #ifdef, #ifndef, #elif, #else, #endif together with the preprocessor unary operator defined.

The way that they are used is like this:

```
#ifdef  NAME

/* compile these lines if NAME is defined */

#endif

#ifndef NAME

/* compile these lines if NAME is not defined */

#else

/* compile these lines if NAME is defined */

#endif
```

So, #ifdef and #endif can be used to test the definition or otherwise of a given macro name. Of course the #else can be used with #ifdef (and #if or #elif) too. These constructs can nest as deep as you like. There is no ambiguity about what a given #else binds to, because the use of #endif to delimit the scope of these directives eliminates any possible ambiguity.

These directives are most commonly used to select small fragments of C that are machine specific (when it is not possible to make the whole program completely machine independent), or sometimes to select different algorithms depending on the need to make trade-offs.

The #if and #elif constructs take a single constant expression as their arguments. A constant expression is one that involves only integral constant values, operators without side effects (i.e. not ++ or --), and none of sizeof, casts or enumeration constants. Basically, it must be capable of being worked out when the program is being compiled and before anything deep has to be understood about the program.

The token sequence that makes up the constant expression undergoes macro replacement, except that names prefixed by defined are not expanded; after this expansion the expression is evaluated. In this context, the expression defined NAME or defined (NAME) evaluates to 1 if NAME is currently defined, 0 if it is not.

The preprocessor always works as if it were using type long int or unsigned long int for the expression, as if all the integer constants had L appended to them. The usual arithmetic conversions are applied to the whole expression, which is evaluated according to the arithmetic of *the translation environment*, not the target environment. This means that it is possible to get results doing arithmetic in the preprocessor which are different from the results at run time; although presumably only if the translation and execution are done on different machines. Here's an example.

```
#include <limits.h>

#if LONG_MAX > -1
    printf("Preprocessor: LONG_MAX > -1\n");
#endif

    if(LONG_MAX > -1)
        printf("Runtime: LONG_MAX > -1\n");              (E7.3)
```

The value of LONG_MAX in <limits.h> will be appropriate for the target environment; the 'Runtime' message will always be printed. There is just a chance that the 'Preprocessor' message will not be printed if the target value of LONG_MAX has had to be promoted to unsigned long; the comparison against -1 will be very dangerous, because the negative value will have become a very large positive value when converted by the usual rules.

The situation is more obviously worse with character constants. There, they will have completely different values in the translation and the target environments unless the two environments have identical character set encodings. It is not even necessarily the case that character constants will appear to be positive in preprocessor expressions. Both these situations are implementation defined.

Identifiers not currently defined as macro names evaluate to zero.

The following skeleton example illustrates the use of such constants and also the 'conditional else', `#elif`.

```
#define NAME     100

#if ((NAME > 50) && (defined __STDC__))

/* do something */

#elif   NAME > 25

/* do something else*/

#elif   NAME > 10

/* do something else */

#else

/* last possibility */

#endif
```

A word of warning. These conditional compilation directives do not obey the same scope rules as the rest of C. They should be used sparingly, unless your program is rapidly to become unreadable. It is impossible to read C when it is laced with these things every few lines. The urge to maim the author of a piece of code becomes very strong when you suddenly come across

```
#else
      }
#endif
```

with no `#if` or whatever immediately visible above. They should be treated like chilli sauce; essential at times, but more than a tiny sprinkle is too much.

7.3.8 `#pragma`

This was the Standard Committee's way of opening the back door. It allows implementation-defined things to take place. If the implementation was not expecting what you wrote (i.e. doesn't recognize it), it is ignored. Here is a possible example:

```
#pragma target m68000
```

which could be used to tell the implementation that the program is to be compiled to run on a Motorola 68000 processor. It could, of course, mean anything else that the implementation chooses it to mean.

If your implementation doesn't have any special meaning for this, then it will have no effect. It will *not* count as an error.

It will be interesting to see the sort of things that this gets used for.

7.3.9 #error

This directive is followed by one or more tokens at the end of the line. A diagnostic message is produced by the compiler, which includes those tokens, but no further detail is given in the Standard. It might be used like this to abort a compilation on unsuitable hardware:

```
#include <limits.h>
#if CHAR_MIN > -128
#error character range smaller than required
#endif
```

which would be expected to produce some sort of meaningful compilation error and message.

7.4 Summary

To be honest, although many of the facilities provided by the preprocessor undoubtedly provide extra power and flexibility, it really is rather overcomplicated.

There are only a very few aspects that are really important.

The ability to define macros and function macros is very important, being widely used in almost every C program except the most trivial.

The conditional compilation has two important uses; one is the ability to compile with or without debugging statements included in a program, the other is to be able to select machine or application dependent statements.

Obviously, file inclusion is fundamentally important.

Having said the above, most of the rest of the features described in this chapter can be forgotten with very little loss of functionality. Perhaps each programming team should have just one preprocessor specialist who has the job of designing project-dependent macros using the arcane features such as stringizing and token pasting. Most users of C would benefit much more by putting that learning effort into other parts of the language, or, when they fully understand C, techniques of software quality control. The world would be a better place.

Exercises

These exercises are intended to test only a basic understanding of the preprocessor, suitable for a beginner. Many users will never need a more detailed understanding.

7.1 How would you arrange that the identifier MAXLEN is replaced by the value 100 throughout a program?

7.2 What is likely to cause problems in a definition of the form #define VALUE 100+MAXLEN?

7.3 Write a macro called REM which takes two integer arguments and 'returns' the remainder when the first is divided by the second.

7.4 Repeat the last example, but use casts so that any arithmetic type of argument may be used, assuming that there are no overflow problems.

7.5 What do the <> brackets around a filename in a #include directive signify?

7.6 What would " " mean in place of the <>?

7.7 How would you use the preprocessor to select implementation-specific fragments of a program?

7.8 What sort of arithmetic does the preprocessor use?

## CHAPTER 8

Specialized Areas of C

8.1 What this is all about

We've covered the fundamentals of the language in the previous chapters, but there are a few incompletely explored corners waiting to be probed. You could probably manage to write some fairly complex programs by now, with a good chance of getting them right, but some of these murky areas will yield up treasures that some programmers will find it hard to do without.

Read the following sections and make notes where you think the material is important to you; re-read them from time to time as well. What seemed uninteresting the first time round may have changed as your experience grows.

8.1.1 Declarations

Storage class

The Standard mentions five keywords in the context of this rather oddly named topic of storage class, but then it immediately points out that one of them, `typedef`, is there purely as a convenience: it makes the syntax of the language more regular to put it there, but it is separate from the other four in its use. The other four are `auto`, `extern`, `register`, and `static`.

The purpose of storage class is to describe how objects are stored in the executing program. Only one storage class specifier is permitted in a declaration – this makes sense, as there is only one way of storing things – and if you omit the storage class in a declaration, a default is chosen. For external objects the default storage class is `extern` and for internal objects it is `auto`.

To understand all this properly, there are three important concepts which must be clarified. The Standard calls them:

* scope
* linkage
* duration

and describes what they mean in a fairly readable way (for a standard). The last of the three is the easiest to deal with, so we'll look at that first.

The **duration** of an object refers to whether its storage is allocated once only, at program start-up, or if it is more transient in its nature, being allocated and freed as necessary. The classic examples of these are 'global' variables, declared outside functions and taking one fixed piece of store for the duration of the program, contrasted with 'local' variables inside functions, which are allocated when the function is entered and freed when it is left. Be careful! The terms 'global' and 'local' really have no meaning in C.

The Standard describes two types of duration of objects: static duration and automatic duration. Static duration means that the object is permanently allocated storage, automatic means that it is not. Since the only objects that can have automatic storage duration are the ones that are declared inside functions, this is not too difficult to handle: if something is declared inside a function, and the declaration does not contain the keyword static or extern, then its storage duration is automatic duration. *Anything* else has static duration.

One of the prime causes of confusion here is to assume that the word 'static' in 'static duration' is closely related to the keyword static. There is a relationship in so far that if a declaration contains static then the object being declared will also have static duration, but this is not the only way.

Internal objects, those declared inside functions, will be declared with the default storage class of auto unless some other storage class was specified. Both auto and register storage classes are permitted for internal objects only; both result in automatic duration.

The register storage class is quite interesting. It suggests to the compiler that it would be a good idea to store the object in a hardware register in the interests of speed. The compiler does not have to take any notice of this, but in case it does a further restriction on register variables is that they *do not have an address*. This is because many machines cannot take the address of a register. You should not declare register variables without taking care. Declaring too many may slow the program down, rather than speed it up, because the compiler may either have to save more registers on entrance to a function, often a slow process, or there will too few registers remaining to be used for intermediate calculations. Determining when to use registers will be a machine-specific choice and should only be taken when detailed measurements show that a particular function needs to be speeded up. Then you will have to experiment. My own opinion is that you should never declare register variables during program development. Get the program working first, then measure it, then, maybe, judicious use of registers will give a useful increase in performance. But that work will have to be repeated for every type of processor you move the program to; even within one family of processors the characteristics are different.

A final note on register variables: this is the only storage class that may be used in a function prototype or function definition. In a function prototype, the storage class is simply ignored, in a function definition it is a hint that the actual parameter should be stored in a register if possible. This example shows how it might be used:

```
#include <stdio.h>
#include <stdlib.h>

void func(register int arg1, double arg2);

main(){
    func(5, 2);
    exit(0);
}

/*
 * Function illustrating that formal parameters
 * may be declared to be of type register.
 */
void func(register int arg1, double arg2){

    /*
     * Illustrative only - nobody would do this
     * in this context.
     * Cannot take address of arg1.
     */
    double *fp = &arg2;

    while(arg1){
        printf("res = %f\n", arg1 * (*fp));
        arg1--;
    }
}                                                    (E8.1)
```

Tables 8.1 and 8.2 show the storage duration against combinations of internal and external declaration with storage class specifiers.

The major use of `static` internal variables is as counters of the number of times that a function has been called, or to monitor the depth of recursion.

Table 8.1   External declarations

Storage class	Duration
register	forbidden
auto	forbidden
static	static
extern	static

Table 8.2 Internal declarations

Storage class	Duration
register	automatic
auto	automatic
static	static
extern	static

Now we must look at the **scope** of the names of objects; this explains when and where the same name refers to the same object. The different types of scope are the following:

- function scope
- file scope
- block scope
- function prototype scope

The easiest is function scope. This only applies to labels and means that the name of a label is visible throughout the function where the label is declared. No two labels in the same function may have the same name, but because the name only has function scope, the same name can be used for labels in every function.

Any name declared outside a function has file scope, which means that the name is usable at any point from the declaration on to the end of the source code file containing the declaration. Function names themselves have file scope. It is possible for these names to be temporarily hidden by declarations within compound statements, of course.

A name declared inside a compound statement, or as a formal parameter to a function, is usable up to the end of the associated } which closes the compound statement. Any declaration of a name within a compound statement hides any outer declaration of the same name until the end of the compound statement.

A special and rather trivial example of scope is function prototype scope where a declaration of a name extends only to the end of the function prototype. That means simply that this is wrong (same name used twice):

```
void func(int i, int i);
```

and this is alright:

```
void func(int i, int j);
```

and that the names declared inside the parentheses disappear outside them.

Finally we meet **linkage**. Linkage is what is used to make the same name declared in different scopes refer to the same thing. An object only ever has one name, but in many cases we would like to be able to refer to the same object from different scopes. A typical example is the wish to be able to call `printf` from several different places in a program, even if those places are not all in the same source file.

The three different types of linkage are:

- external linkage
- internal linkage
- no linkage

In an entire program, built up perhaps from a number of source files and libraries, every instance of a given name refers to the same object if the name has external linkage. If the declarations of such an object are different in the different places, this is an error and the behaviour of the program will be undefined. This is not a good idea! It's the responsibility of the programmer to get this right, though there will probably be tools available to help you check this out.

For something which has internal linkage, it is only within a given source code file that instances of the same name will refer to the same thing.

Finally, names with no linkage refer to separate things.

How do you get the appropriate linkage for a particular name? The rules are a little complicated.

1.   For a name with file scope, if the first declaration of the name contains the keyword `static`, then the name gets internal linkage. If the `static` is missing, then it has external linkage. Notice that a name declared *inside* a function can't have file scope, so internal declarations of `static` objects do not have external linkage – in fact they will have no linkage.
2.   Identifiers declaring anything other than functions or objects ('variables') *never* have any linkage, as is the case with function parameters.
3.   Anything declared inside a function must have only one declaration in the same scope unless it is the name of a function or has the storage class `extern`.
4.   If the declaration of a function or object contains the keyword `extern`, then the identifier has internal linkage if a previous declaration with file scope has internal linkage, otherwise the identifier has external linkage.
5.   Anything declared with external linkage only needs to have a corresponding definition if it used somewhere in the program in an expression. There must be only one definition for any object with external linkage.

If this isn't very clear, there is a good reason for it. What I have written down is a paraphrase of the Standard, and if you really need to know about everything to do with linkage and scope you should read the Standard carefully. The rules are hard because they need to specify every combination of scope and linkage that can occur. Fortunately, some of the combinations are either bizarre or undesirable, and we can write down some much more easily understood combinations which will give you the effects that you are most likely to want.

The three types of accessibility that you will want of variables or functions are:

- throughout the entire program,

- restricted to one source file,
- restricted to one function (or perhaps a single compound statement).

For the three cases above, you will want external linkage, internal linkage, and no linkage respectively. The recommended practice for the first two cases is to declare all of the names in each of the relevant source files *before* you define any functions. The recommended layout of a source file would be as shown in Figure 8.1.

| external linkage declarations |
| internal linkage declarations |
| functions |

Figure 8.1   Layout of a source file

The external linkage declarations would be prefixed with extern, the internal linkage declarations with static. Here's an example.

```
/* example of a single source file layout */
#include <stdio.h>

/* Things with external linkage:
 * accessible throughout program
 */

extern int important_variable;
extern int library_func(double, int);

/*
 * Things with internal linkage:
 * only accessible inside this file.
 */

static int less_important_variable;
static int local_function(int, int);
static void lf(void);

/*
 * Finally functions within this file
 */
```

```
    /*
     * Keyword static not used, so this function
     * has external linkage and can be called
     * from anywhere in the program
     */
    void f1(int a){}

    /*
     * This function can only be called from
     * within this file.
     */
    static int local_function(int a1, int a2){
        return(a1 * a2);
    }

    /*
     * As above
     */
    static void lf(void){
        /*
         * A static variable with no linkage,
         * so usable only within this function.
         */
        static int count;

        printf("lf called for time no %d\n", ++count);
    }                                                    (E8.2)
```

8.1.2 typedef

Although typedef is thought of as being a storage class, it isn't really. It allows you to introduce synonyms for types which could have been declared some other way. The new name becomes equivalent to the type that you wanted, as this example shows.

```
    typedef int aaa, bbb, ccc;

    typedef int ar[15], arr[9][6];

    typedef char c, *cp, carr[100];

    /* now declare some objects */

    /* all ints */
    aaa int1;
    bbb int2;
```

```
ccc int3;

ar   yyy;     /* array of 15 ints */
arr  xxx;     /* 9*6 array of int */

c    ch; /* a char */
cp   pnt;     /* pointer to char */
carr     chry;     /* array of 100 char */
```

The general rule with the use of typedef is to write out a declaration as if you were declaring variables of the types that you want. Where a declaration would have introduced names with particular types, prefixing the whole thing with typedef means that, instead of getting variables declared, you declare new type names instead. Those new type names can then be used as the prefix to the declaration of variables of the new type.

The use of typedef isn't a particularly common sight in most programs; it's typically found only in header files and isn't the province of day-to-day coding.

It is sometimes found in applications requiring very high portability: there, new types will be defined for the basic variables of the program and appropriate typedefs used to tailor the program to the target machine. This can lead to hard-to-read code. The flavour of it is shown below:

```
/* file 'mytype.h' */
typedef  short    SMALLINT     /* range ±30000 */
typedef int BIGINT          /* range ± 2*10^9 */

/* program */
#include "mytype.h"

SMALLINT     i;
BIGINT       loop_count;
```

On some machines, the range of an int would not be adequate for a BIGINT which would have to be re-typedef'd to be long.

As a word of warning, typedef can only be used to declare the type of return value from a function, not the overall type of the function. The overall type includes information about the function's parameters as well as the type of its return value.

```
/*
 * Using typedef, declare 'func' to have type
 * 'function taking two int arguments, returning int'
 */
typedef int func(int, int);

/* ERROR */
```

```
func func_name{ /*....*/ }

/* Correct. Returns pointer to a type 'func' */
func *func_name(){ /*....*/ }

/*
 * Correct if functions could return functions,
 * but C can't.
 */
func func_name(){ /*....*/ }
```

If a `typedef` of a particular identifier is in scope, that identifer may not be used as the formal parameter of a function. This is because something like the following declaration causes a problem:

```
typedef int i1_t, i2_t, i3_t, i4_t;

int f(i1_t, i2_t, i3_t, i4_t)/* THIS IS POINT 'X' */
```

A compiler reading the function declaration reaches point 'X' and still doesn't know whether it is looking at a function declaration, essentially similar to

```
int f(int, int, int, int) /*...
```

or

```
int f(a, b, c, d) /*...
```

– the problem is only resolvable (in the worst case) by looking at what follows point 'X'; if it is a semicolon, then that was a declaration, if it is a { then that was a definition. The rule forbidding `typedef` names to be formal parameters means that a compiler can always tell whether it is processing a declaration or a definition by looking at the first identifier following the function name.

8.2 `const` **and** `volatile`

These are new in ANSI C, although the idea of `const` has been borrowed from C++. Now let us get one thing straight: the concepts of `const` and `volatile` are *completely independent*. It has become obvious, even at this early stage, that a common misconception is to imagine that somehow `const` is the opposite of `volatile` and vice versa. They are unrelated and you should remember the fact.

Since `const` declarations are the simpler, I'll look at them first, but only after we have seen where both of these type specifiers may be used. The complete list of type specifier keywords is

```
char     long        float    volatile
short    signed      double   void
int      unsigned    const
```

and various combinations of them are permitted:

```
char, signed char, unsigned char
int, signed int, unsigned int
short int, signed short int, unsigned short int
long int, signed long int, unsigned long int
float
double
long double
```

A few points should be noted. All declarations to do with an int will be signed anyway, so signed is redundant in that context. If *any* other type specifier is present, then the int part may be dropped, as that is the default.

The keywords const and volatile can be applied to any other declaration, including structures, unions, enumerated types or typedef names. Here are a few representative examples:

```
volatile i;

volatile int j;

const long q;

const volatile unsigned long int rt_clk;

struct{
    const long int li;
    signed char     sc;
}volatile vs;
```

Don't be put off; some of them are deliberately complicated. The point is whether or not they follow the rules: what they mean will be explained later. Remember that they could also be further complicated by introducing storage class specifications as well! In fact, the truly spectacular

```
extern const volatile unsigned long int rt_clk;
```

is a strong possibility in some real-time operating system kernels.

8.2.1 const

So let's look at what is meant when const is used. It's really quite simple: const means that something is not modifiable, so a variable, structure or whatever that is declared with const as a part of its type specification must not be assigned to in any way during the run of a program. It is very likely that the definition of the object will contain an initializer (otherwise, since you can't assign to it, how would it ever get a value?), but this is not always the case. For example, if you were accessing a hardware port at a fixed memory address and promised only to read from it, then it would be declared to be const but not initialized.

The Standard points out that expressions with type const must not be modified, and the same goes for any expression that gets converted to a type with the const attribute. This comes into effect particularly when pointers to const objects are involved, as described below.

If you take a pointer to a const type, you may assign to it the value of a pointer to a type which is not const, but it is not permitted to assign to something pointed to by the first pointer. Here is an example:

```c
#include <stdio.h>
#include <stdlib.h>

main() {
    int i;
    const int ci = 123;

    /* declare a pointer to a const.. */
    const int *cpi;

    /* ordinary pointer to a non-const */
    int *ncpi;

    cpi = &ci;
    ncpi = &i;

    /*
     * this is allowed
     */
    cpi = ncpi;

    /*
     * this needs a cast
     * because it is usually a plain error,
     * see what it permits below.
     */
    ncpi = (int *)cpi;

    /*
```

```
 * now to get undefined behaviour...
 * modify a const through a pointer
 */
*ncpi = 0;

exit(0);
}
```

(E8.3)

As the example shows, it is possible to take the address of a constant object, generate a pointer to a non-constant, then use the new pointer. This is *an error* in your program and results in undefined behaviour.

The main intention of introducing `const` objects was to allow them to be put into read-only store, and to permit compilers to do extra consistency checking in a program. Unless you defeat the intent by doing naughty things with pointers, a compiler is able to check that `const` objects are not modified explicitly by the user.

An interesting extra feature pops up now. What does this mean?

```
char c;
char *const cp = &c;
```

It's simple really; `cp` is a pointer to a `char`, which is what it would mean if the `const` weren't there. The extra `const` means that `cp` is not to be modified, although whatever it points to can be. The other way round is

```
const char *cp;
```

so now `cp` is an ordinary, modifiable pointer, but the thing that it points to must not be modified. So, depending on what you choose to do, both the pointer and the thing it points to may be modifiable or not; just choose the appropriate declaration.

8.2.2 `volatile`

After `const`, we treat `volatile`. The reason for having this type specifier is mainly to do with the problems that are encountered in real-time or embedded systems programming using C. Imagine that you are writing code that controls a hardware device. This is done by placing appropriate values in hardware registers at known absolute addresses.

Let's imagine that the device has two registers, each 16 bits long, at ascending memory addresses; the first one is the control and status register (csr) and the second is a data port. The traditional way of accessing such a device is like this:

```
/* ANSI example but without const or volatile */
/*
 * Declare the device registers.
 * Whether to use int or short
```

```
 * is implementation dependent.
 */

struct devregs{
    unsigned short  csr;    /* control & status */
    unsigned short  data;   /* data port */
};

/* bit patterns in the csr */
#define ERROR    0x1
#define READY    0x2
#define RESET    0x4

/* absolute address of the device */
#define DEVADDR ((struct devregs *)0xffff0004)

/* number of such devices in system */
#define NDEVS    4
```

```
/*
 * Busy-wait function to read a byte from device n.
 * check range of device number.
 * Wait until READY or ERROR
 * if no error, read byte, return it
 * otherwise reset error, return 0xffff
 */
unsigned int read_dev(unsigned devno){

    struct devregs *dvp = DEVADDR + devno;

    if(devno >= NDEVS)
        return(0xffff);

    while((dvp->csr & (READY | ERROR)) == 0)
        ; /* NULL - wait till done */

    if(dvp->csr & ERROR){
        dvp->csr = RESET;
        return(0xffff);
    }

    return((dvp->data) & 0xff);
}                                                   (E8.4)
```

The technique of using a structure declaration to describe the device register layout
and names is absolutely typical. Notice that there aren't actually any objects of

that type defined, so the declaration simply indicates the structure without using up any store.

To access the device registers, an appropriately cast constant is used as if it were pointing to such a structure, but of course it talks to memory addresses instead. None of that is new.

However, a major problem with previous C compilers would be in the while loop which tests the status register and waits for the ERROR or READY bit to come on. Any self-respecting optimizing compiler would notice that the loop tests the same memory address over and over again. It would almost certainly arrange to reference memory once only, and copy the value into a hardware register, thus speeding up the loop. This is, of course, exactly what we don't want; this is one of the few places where we *must* look at the place where the pointer points, every time around the loop.

Because of this problem, most C compilers have been unable to make this sort of optimization in the past. To remove the problem (and other similar ones to do with when to write to where a pointer points), the keyword volatile was introduced. It tells the compiler that the object is subject to sudden change for reasons which cannot be predicted from a study of the program itself, and forces every reference to such an object to be a genuine reference.

Here is how you would rewrite the example, with appropriate use of const and volatile.

```
/*
 * Declare the device registers
 * Whether to use int or short
 * is implementation dependent
 */

struct devregs{
    unsigned short volatile csr;
    unsigned short const volatile data;
};

/* bit patterns in the csr */
#define ERROR   0x1
#define READY   0x2
#define RESET   0x4

/* absolute address of the device */
#define DEVADDR ((struct devregs *)0xffff0004)

/* number of such devices in system */
#define NDEVS   4

/*
 * Busy-wait function to read a byte from device n.
```

```
 * check range of device number.
 * Wait until READY or ERROR
 * if no error, read byte, return it
 * otherwise reset error, return 0xffff
 */
unsigned int read_dev(unsigned devno){

    struct devregs * const dvp = DEVADDR + devno;

    if(devno >= NDEVS)
        return(0xffff);

    while((dvp->csr & (READY | ERROR)) == 0)
        ; /* NULL - wait till done */

    if(dvp->csr & ERROR){
        dvp->csr = RESET;
        return(0xffff);
    }

    return((dvp->data) & 0xff);
}
```
(E8.5)

The rules about mixing volatile and regular types goes much the way that it does for const. A pointer to a volatile object can be assigned the address of a regular object with safety, but it is dangerous (and needs a cast) to take the address of a volatile object and put it into a pointer to a regular object. Using such a derived pointer results in undefined behaviour.

If an array, union or structure is declared with const or volatile attributes, then all of the members take on that attribute too. This makes sense when you think about it – how could a member of a const structure not also be unmodifiable?

That means that an alternative rewrite of the last example would be possible. Instead of declaring the device registers to be volatile in the structure, the pointer could have been declared to point to a volatile structure instead, like this:

```
struct devregs{
    unsigned short  csr;    /* control & status */
    unsigned short  data;   /* data port */
};

volatile struct devregs *const dvp=DEVADDR+devno;
```

Since dvp points to a volatile object, it not permitted to optimize references through the pointer. My own feeling is that, although this would work, it is bad style. The `volatile` declaration belongs in the structure: it is the device registers which are `volatile` and that is where the information should be kept; it reinforces the fact for a human reader.

So, for any object likely to be subject to modification either by hardware or asynchronous interrupt service routines, the `volatile` type specifier is important.

A subtle problem to do with what is an 'atomic', that is to say uninterruptable, operation is beyond the scope of this book to solve. Be careful not to assume that any operations written in C are uninterruptable. For example,

```
extern const volatile unsigned long realtimeclock;
```

could be a counter which is updated by a clock interrupt routine. It is essential to make it `volatile` because of the asynchronous updates to it, and it is marked `const` because it should not be changed by anything other than the interrupt routine. If the program accesses it like this:

```
unsigned long int time_of_day;

time_of_day = real_time_clock;
```

there may be a major problem. What if, to copy one `long` into another, it takes several machine instructions to copy the two words making up `real_time_clock` and `time_of_day`? It is possible that an interrupt will occur in the middle of the assignment and that in the worst case, when the low-order word of `real_time_clock` is `0xffff` and the high-order word is `0x0000`, then the low-order word of `time_of_day` will receive `0xffff`. The interrupt arrives and increments the low-order word of `real_time_clock` to `0x0` and then the high-order word to `0x1`, then returns. The rest of the assignment then completes, with `time_of_day` ending up containing `0x0001ffff` and `real_time_clock` containing the correct value, `0x00010000`.

This whole class of problem is what is known as a **critical region**, and is well understood by those who regularly work in asynchronous environments. It should be understood that ANSI C takes no special precautions to avoid these problems, and that the usual techniques should be employed.

The header `<signal.h>` declares a type called `sig_atomic_t` which is guaranteed to be modifiable safely in the presence of asynchronous events. This means only that it can be modified by assigning a value to it; incrementing or decrementing it, or anything else which produces a new value depending on its previous value, is not safe.

8.3 Sequence points

Associated with, but distinct from, the problems of real-time programming are **sequence points**. These are the Standard's attempt to define when certain sorts of optimization may and may not be permitted to be in effect. For example, look at this program:

```
#include <stdio.h>
#include <stdlib.h>

int i_var;
void func(void);

main(){
    while(i_var != 10000){
        func();
        i_var++;
    }
    exit(0);
}

void
func(void){
    printf("in func, i_var is %d\n", i_var);
}                                                              (E8.6)
```

The compiler might want to optimize the loop so that i_var can be stored in a machine register for speed. However, the function needs to have access to the correct value of i_var so that it can print the right value. This means that the register must be stored back into i_var at each function call (at least). When and where these conditions must occur are described by the Standard. At each sequence point, the side effects of all previous expressions will be completed. This is why you cannot rely on expressions such as:

```
a[i] = i++;
```

because you don't know when the effect of the increment on i occurs.

The sequence points laid down in the Standard are the following:

- The point of calling a function, after evaluating its arguments.
- The unary + operator.
- The && operator.
- The || operator.
- The peculiar conditional operator in ? :.
- The comma operator.
- Completing the evaluation of a full expression. They are the following:

  - Evaluating the initializer of an auto object.
  - The expression in an 'ordinary' statement – an expression followed by semicolon.
  - The controlling expressions in do, while, if, switch or for statements.
  - The expression in a return statement.

8.4 Summary

This is a chapter describing specialized areas of the language.

Undoubtedly, the issues of scope, linkage and duration are important. If you find the whole topic too much to digest, just learn the simple rules. The problem is that the Standard tries to be complete and unambiguous, so it has to lay down lots of rules. It's much easier if you just stick to the easy way of doing things and don't try to get too clever. Use Example 8.2 as a model if in doubt.

Whether or not `typedef` is considered useful seems to be user-dependent. When I learnt C, it wasn't even in the language, so I tend not to use it. Some people find this astonishing, others quite natural.

The use of `const` will be widespread in many programs, once it has gained familiarity. The idea of a pointer to something which is not modifiable is well and truly emphasized in the library function prototypes.

Only specialized applications will use `volatile`. If you work in the field of real-time programming, or embedded systems, this will matter to you. Otherwise it probably won't. The same goes for sequence points.

## CHAPTER 9

Libraries

9.1 Introduction

There is no doubt that the Standard Committee's decision to define a set of library routines will prove to be a huge benefit to users of C. Previously there were *no* standard, accepted, definitions of library routines to provide support for the language. As a result, portability suffered seriously.

However, the library routines do not have to be present; they will only be present in a *hosted* environment – typically the case for applications programmers. Writers of embedded systems, and the writers of the hosted environment libraries, will not have the libraries present. They are using 'raw' C, in a *freestanding* environment, and this chapter will not be of much interest to them.

The descriptions (except for this introduction) are not meant to be read as a whole chapter, but as individual pieces. The material included here is meant more for information and convenient reference than as a full tutorial introduction. It would take a full book to do real justice to the libraries.

9.1.1 Headers and standard types

A number of types and macros are used widely by the library functions. Where necessary, they are defined in the appropriate `#include` file for that function. The header will also declare appropriate types and prototypes for the library functions. Some important points should be noted here:

- All external identifiers declared in any of the library headers are reserved. They must not be used, or redefined, for any other purpose. In some cases they may be 'magic' – their names may be known to the compiler and cause it to use special methods to implement them.
- All external names and macro names that begin with an underscore also fit the category described above. They too are reserved.
- Headers may be included in any order, and more than once, but must be included *before* any use of functions or macros defined inside.
- Giving a 'bad value' to a function – say a null pointer, or a value outside the range of values expected by the function – results in undefined behaviour unless otherwise stated.

The Standard headers are:

```
<assert.h>    <math.h>      <stdio.h>
<ctype.h>     <setjmp.h>    <stdlib.h>
<float.h>     <signal.h>    <string.h>
<limits.h>    <stdarg.h>    <time.h>
<locale.h>    <stddef.h>
```

There are also a small number of types and macros, found in stddef.h, which are widely used in other headers. They are described in the following paragraphs.

Subtracting one pointer from another gives a result whose type differs between different implementations. To allow safe use of the difference, the type is defined in stddef.h to be ptrdiff_t. Similarly, you can use size_t to store the result of sizeof.

For reasons which still escape me, there is an 'implementation defined null pointer constant' defined in stddef.h called NULL. Since the language explicitly defines the integer constant 0 to be the value which can be assigned to, and compared with, a null pointer, this would seem to be unnecessary. However, it is *very* common practice among experienced C programmers to write this sort of thing:

```
#include <stdio.h>
#include <stddef.h>

FILE *fp;

if((fp = fopen("somefile", "r")) != NULL){
    /* and so on */
```

There is also a macro called offsetof which can be used to find the offset, in bytes, of a structure member. The offset is the distance between the member and the start of the structure. It would be used like this:

```
#include <stdio.h>
#include <stdlib.h>
#include <stddef.h>

main(){
    size_t distance;
    struct x{
        int a, b, c;
    }s_tr;
```

```
        distance = offsetof(s_tr, c);
        printf("Offset of x.c is %lu bytes\n",
            (unsigned long)distance);

        exit(0);
}                                                          (E9.1)
```

Note very carefully the way that a size_t has to be cast to the longest possible unsigned type to ensure that not only is the argument to printf of the type that it expects (%lu is the format string for unsigned long), but also no precision is lost. This is all because the type of size_t is not known to the programmer.

Finally, we come to errno, which is used to tell you when library functions have detected an error. This is not, as it used to be, necessarily an external variable. It is now a 'modifiable volatile int' expression.

Errno is set to zero at program start-up, but from then on never reset unless explicitly assigned to; in particular, the library routines never reset it. If an error occurs in a library routine, errno is set to a particular value to indicate just what went wrong. The usual use is like this:

```
#include <stdio.h>
#include <stddef.h>

errno = 0;
some_library_function(arguments);
if(errno){
    /* error processing code... */
```

The implementation of errno is not known to the programmer, so don't try to do anything other than reset it or inspect its value. It isn't guaranteed to have an address, for example.

What's more, you should only check errno if the particular library function in use documents its effect on errno. Other library functions are free to set it to arbitrary values after a call unless their description explicitly states what they do with it.

A last general point is that many of the library routines may be implemented as macros, provided that it can safely be done that way. The Standard guarantees that, if a function *is* normally implemented as a macro, there will also be a true function provided to do the same job. To use the real function, simply undefine the macro name with #undef.

9.1.2 Character set and cultural dependencies

The Committee has introduced features that attempt to cater for the use of C in environments which are not based on the character set of US ASCII and where there are cultural dependencies such as the use of comma or full stop to indicate the decimal point. Facilities have been provided (see Section 9.4) for setting a program's idea of its **locale**, which is used to control the behaviour of the library functions.

Providing full support for different native languages and customs is a difficult and poorly understood task; the facilities provided by the C library are only a first step on the road to a full solution.

In several places the C locale is referred to. This is the only locale defined by the Standard and effectively provides support for the way that Old C worked. Other locale settings may provide different behaviour in implementation-defined ways.

9.2 Diagnostics

While you are debugging programs, it is often useful to check that the value of an expression is the one that you expected. The assert function provides such a diagnostic aid.

In order to use assert you must first include the header file assert.h. The function is defined as

```
#include <assert.h>

void assert(int expression)
```

If the expression evaluates to zero (i.e. false) then assert will write a message about the failing expression, including the name of the source file, the line at which the assertion was made and the expression itself. After this, the abort function is called, which will halt the program.

```
assert(1 == 2);

/* Might result in */

Assertion failed: 1 == 2, file silly.c, line 15
```

Assert is actually defined as a macro, not as a real function. In order to disable assertions when a program is found to work satisfactorily, defining the name NDEBUG *before* including assert.h will disable assertions totally. You should beware of side effects that the expression may have: when assertions are turned off with NDEBUG, the expression is *not* evaluated. Thus the following example will behave unexpectedly when debugging is turned off with the #define NDEBUG.

```
#define NDEBUG
#include <assert.h>
```

```
    void
    func(void)
    {
        int c;
        assert((c = getchar()) != EOF);
        putchar(c);
    }                                                    (E9.2)
```

9.3 Character handling

There are a variety of functions provided for testing and mapping characters. The testing functions allow you to test if a character is of a particular type, such as alphabetic, upper or lower case, numeric, a control character, a punctuation mark, printable or not and so on. Each of them takes an integer argument, which should either be an unsigned char or the integer constant EOF, as returned from functions such as getchar(). Each returns an integer, either zero if the character supplied is not of the category specified, or non-zero if it was.

In order to make use of these functions, the header file ctype.h must be included.

These functions are not dependent on the underlying character set. However, if the 7-bit ASCII character set is used, the printing characters are those that lie between space (0x20) and tilde (0x7e), the control characters are those between NUL (0x0) and US (0x1f), and the character DEL (0x7f).

These functions depend on the program's locale setting. The terms 'printing character' and 'control character' are implementation defined.

The following is a summary of all the character testing functions.

isalnum(int c)
  True if c is alphabetic or a digit; specifically
  (isalpha(c)||isdigit(c)).
isalpha(int c)
  True if (isupper(c)||islower(c)).
    Also true for an implementation-defined set of characters which do not
    return true results from any of iscntrl, isdigit, ispunct or
    isspace. In the C locale, this extra set of characters is empty.
iscntrl(int c)
  True if c is a control character.
isdigit(int c)
  True if c is a decimal digit.
isgraph(int c)
  True if c is any printing character except space.
islower(int c)
  True if c is a lower case alphabetic letter.

Also true for an implementation defined set of characters which do not return true results from any of `iscntrl`, `isdigit`, `ispunct` or `isspace`. In the C locale, this extra set of characters is empty.

`isprint(int c)`
True if c is a printing character (including space).

`ispunct(int c)`
True if c is any printing character except for space or which returns true from `isalnum`.

`isspace(int c)`
True if c is a white space character: `' '` `'\f'` `'\n'` `'\r'` `'\t'` `'\v'`.

`isupper(int c)`
True if c is an upper case alphabetic character.

Also true for an implementation-defined set of characters which do not return true results from any of `iscntrl`, `isdigit`, `ispunct` or `isspace`. In the C locale, this extra set of characters is empty.

`isxdigit(int c)`
True if c is a valid hexadecimal digit.

Two additional functions map characters from one set into another. The function `tolower` will, if given a upper case character as its argument, return the lower case equivalent. For example,

```
tolower('A') == 'a'
```

If `tolower` is given any character other than an upper case letter, it will return that character.

The converse function `toupper` maps lower case alphabetic letters onto their upper case equivalent.

For each, the conversion is only performed if there *is* a corresponding character in the alternate case. In some locales, not all upper case characters have lower case equivalents, and vice versa.

9.4 Localization

This is where the program's idea of its current locale can be controlled. The header file `locale.h` declares the `setlocale` function and a number of macros:

```
LC_ALL
LC_COLLATE
LC_CTYPE
LC_NUMERIC
LC_TIME
```

all of which expand to integral constant expressions and are used as values of the `category` argument to `setlocale`. Other names may also be defined: they will all start with `LC_X` where `X` is an upper case letter.

9.4.1 The `setlocale` function

```
#include <locale.h>

char *setlocale(int category, const char *locale);
```

This function allows the program's idea of its locale to be set. All or parts of the locale can be set by providing values for `category` as follows:

`LC_ALL`
> Set entire locale.

`LC_COLLATE`
> Modify behaviour of `strcoll`.

`LC_CTYPE`
> Modify behaviour of character-handling functions.

`LC_NUMERIC`
> Modify decimal-point character for formatted I/O and string conversion routines.

`LC_TIME`
> Modify behaviour of `strftime`.

The values for locale can be:

`"C"`   Select the minimal environment for C translation.

`""`   Select the implementation-defined 'native environment'.

implementation defined
> Select other environments.

When the program starts, it has an environment as if

```
setlocale(LC_ALL, "C");
```

has been executed.

If a non-null (`char *`) is given as the value for `locale`, and the selection can be performed, the string associated with the specified `category` for the new locale is returned. If the selection cannot be performed, a null pointer is returned and the locale is not changed.

The current string associated with a given category can be queried by passing a null pointer as the value for `locale`. An enquiry may fail only if `category` is `LC_ALL` and the most recent successful call which changed the locale did not use a category of `LC_ALL`.

9.5 Limits

Two header files float.h and limits.h define several implementation specific limits.

9.5.1 limits.h

Table 9.1 gives the names declared, the allowable values, and a comment on what they mean. For example, the description of SHRT_MIN shows that in a given implementation the value must be less than or equal to −32767: this means that for maximum portability a program cannot rely on short variables being able to hold values more negative than −32767. Implementations may choose to support values which are more negative but must provide support for at least −32767.

Table 9.1 <limits.h>

Name	Allowable value	Comment
CHAR_BIT	(≥8)	bits in a char
CHAR_MAX	(≥127)	max value of a char
CHAR_MIN	(≤0	min value of a char
INT_MAX	(≥+32767)	max value of an int
INT_MIN	(≤−32767)	min value of an int
LONG_MAX	(≥+2147483647)	max value of a long
LONG_MIN	(≤−2147483647)	min value of a long
SCHAR_MAX	(≥+127)	max value of a signed char
SCHAR_MIN	(≤−127)	min value of a signed char
SHRT_MAX	(≥+32767)	max value of a short
SHRT_MIN	(≤−32767)	min value of a short
UCHAR_MAX	(≥255U)	max value of an unsigned char
UINT_MAX	(≥65535U)	max value of an unsigned int
ULONG_MAX	(≥4294967295U)	max value of an unsigned long
USHRT_MAX	(≥65535U)	max value of an unsigned short

9.5.2 float.h

For floating point numbers, the file float.h contains a similar set of minimum values. (It is assumed that where no minimum value is specified, there is either no minimum, or the value depends on another value.)

I do not pretend to understand the subtleties of some of the values described here, so in Table 9.2 I have not indicated the direction in which the values may be varied, as in Table 9.1.

Table 9.2 `<float.h>`

Name	Allowable value	Comment
FLT_RADIX	(2)	the radix of exponent representation
DBL_DIG	(6)	the number of digits of precision in a double
DBL_EPSILON	(1e-5)	minimum positive number such that $1.0+x \neq 1.0$
DBL_MANT_DIG	(-)	the number of base FLT_RADIX digits in the mantissa part of a double
DBL_MAX	(1E+37)	max value of a double
DBL_MAX_10_EXP	(37)	max value of exponent (base 10) of a double
DBL_MAX_EXP	(-)	max value of exponent (base FLT_RADIX)) of a double
DBL_MIN	(1E-37)	min value of a double
DBL_MIN_10_EXP	(-37)	minimum value of exponent (base 10) of a double
DBL_MIN_EXP	(-)	min value of exponent part of a double (base FLT_RADIX)
FLT_DIG	(6)	the number of digits of precision in a float
FLT_EPSILON	(1e-5)	minimum positive number such that $1.0+x \neq 1.0$
FLT_MANT_DIG	(-)	the number of base FLT_RADIX digits in the mantissa of a float
FLT_MAX	(1E+37)	max value of a float
FLT_MAX_10_EXP	(+37)	max value (base 10) of exponent part of a float
FLT_MAX_EXP	(-)	max value (base FLT_RADIX) of exponent part of a float
FLT_MIN	(1E-37)	min value of a float
FLT_MIN_10_EXP	(-37)	min value (base 10) of exponent part of a float

FLT_MIN_EXP	(-)	min value (base FLT_RADIX) of exponent part of a float
FLT_ROUNDS	(0)	addition of floating point numbers round (1), chop (0), or are indeterminate with regard to rounding (-1)
LDBL_DIG	(6)	the number of digits of precision in a long double
LDBL_EPSILON	(1e-5)	minimum positive number such that $1.0+x \neq 1.0$
LDBL_MANT_DIG	(-)	the number of base FLT_RADIX digits in the mantissa part of a long double
LDBL_MAX	(1E+37)	max value of a long double
LDBL_MAX_10_EXP	(37)	max value of exponent (base 10) of a long double
LDBL_MAX_EXP	(-)	max value of exponent (base FLT_RADIX) of a long double
LDBL_MIN	(1E-37)	minimum value of a long double
LDBL_MIN_10_EXP	(-37)	min value of exponent part (base 10) of a long double
LDBL_MIN_EXP	(-)	min value of exponent part of a long double (base FLT_RADIX)

9.6 Mathematical functions

If you are writing mathematical programs, involving floating point calculations and so on, then you will undoubtedly require access to the mathematics library. This set of functions all take double arguments, and return a double result. The functions and associated macros are defined in the include file math.h.

For all the functions, a *domain error* occurs if an input argument is outside the domain over which the function is defined. An example might be attempting to take the square root of a negative number. If this occurs, errno is set to the constant EDOM, and the function returns an implementation defined value.

Similarly, a *range error* occurs if the result of the function cannot be represented as a double value. If the magnitude of the result is too large to represent, the functions return ±HUGE_VAL (the sign will be correct) and errno is set to ERANGE. If the result is too small, 0.0 is returned and the value of errno is implementation defined.

The following list describes briefly each of the functions available:

```
double acos(double x);
```
    Principal value of the arc cosine of x.
    Errors: EDOM if x is not in the range −1..1.

```
double asin(double x);
```
    Principal value of the arc sine of x.
    Errors: EDOM if x is not in the range −1..1.

```
double atan(double x);
```
    Principal value of the arc tangent of x.

```
double atan2(double y, double x);
```
    Principal value of the arc tangent of y/x, using the signs of both arguments
    to determine the quadrant of the return value.
    Errors: EDOM occurs if both x and y are zero.

```
double cos(double x);
```
    Cosine of x (in radians).
    Errors: A large magnitude argument may yield a result with little or no
    significance.

```
double sin(double x);
```
    Sine of x (in radians).
    Errors: A large magnitude argument may yield a result with little or no
    significance.

```
double tan(double x);
```
    Tangent of x (in radians).
    Errors: A large magnitude argument may yield a result with little or no
    significance.

```
double cosh(double x);
```
    Hyperbolic cosine of x.
    Errors: ERANGE occurs if the magnitude of x is too large.

```
double sinh(double x);
```
    Hyperbolic sine of x.
    Errors: ERANGE occurs if the magnitude of x is too large.

```
double tanh(double x);
```
    Hyperbolic tangent of x.

```
double exp(double x);
```
    Exponential function of x.
    Errors: ERANGE occurs if the magnitude of x is too large.

```
double frexp(double value, int *exp);
```
    Break a floating point number into a normalized fraction and an integral
    power of two. This integer is stored in the object pointed to by exp.

```
double ldexp(double x, int exp);
```
    Multiply x by 2 to the power exp.
    Errors: ERANGE may occur.

```
double log(double x);
```
    Natural logarithm of x.
    Errors: EDOM occurs if x is negative. ERANGE occurs if x is zero.

```
double log10(double x);
```
   Base-ten logarithm of x.
   Errors: EDOM occurs if x is negative. ERANGE occurs if x is zero.
```
double modf(double value, double *iptr);
```
   Break the argument value into integral and fractional parts, each of which
   has the same sign as the argument. It stores the integral part as a double in
   the object pointed to by iptr, and returns the fractional part.
```
double pow(double x, double y);
```
   Compute x to the power y.
   Errors: EDOM occurs if x is 0, and y is ≤0.   ERANGE may also occur.
```
double sqrt(double x);
```
   Compute the square root of x.
   Errors: EDOM occurs if x is negative.
```
double ceil(double x);
```
   Smallest integer not less than x.
```
double fabs(double x);
```
   Absolute value of x.
```
double floor(double x);
```
   Largest integer not greater than x.
```
double fmod(double x, double y);
```
   Floating point remainder of x/y.
   Errors: If the quotient of x/y cannot be represented the behaviour is
   undefined.

9.7 Non-local jumps

Provision is made for you to perform what is, in effect, a goto from one function
to another. It isn't possible to do this by means of a goto and a label, since the
label has only *function scope*. However, the two functions setjmp and longjmp
provide an alternative, known as a *non-local goto*, or a *non-local jump*.

   The file setjmp.h declares something called a jmp_buf, which is used
by the two cooperating functions to store the information necessary to make the
jump. The declarations of the functions are as follows:

```
#include <setjmp.h>

int setjmp(jmp_buf env);
void longjmp(jmp_buf env, int val);
```

   The setjmp function is used to initialize the jmp_buf and returns zero on
its initial call. The bizarre thing is that it returns *again*, later, with a non-zero
value, when the corresponding longjmp call is made! The non-zero value is
whatever value was supplied to the call of longjmp. This is easier to demonstrate
than to explain, so look at the example:

```
#include <stdio.h>
#include <stdlib.h>
#include <setjmp.h>

void func(void);
jmp_buf place;

main(){
    int retval;

    /*
     * First call returns 0,
     * a later longjmp will return non-zero.
     */
    if((retval = setjmp(place)) != 0){
        printf("Returned %d using longjmp\n",retval);
        exit(0);
    }

    /*
     * This call will never return - it
     * ``jumps'' back above.
     */
    func();
    printf("What! func returned!\n");
}

void
func(void){
    /*
     * Return to main.
     * Looks like a second return from setjmp,
     * returning 4!
     */
    longjmp(place, 4);
    printf("What! longjmp returned!\n");
}
```
(E9.3)

The val argument to longjmp is the value seen in the second and subsequent 'returns' from setjmp. It should normally be something other than 0; if you attempt to return 0 via longjmp, it will be changed to 1. It is therefore possible to tell whether the setjmp was called directly, or whether it was reached by calling longjmp.

If there has been no call to setjmp before calling longjmp, the effect of longjmp is undefined, almost certainly causing the program to crash. The longjmp function is never expected to return, in the normal sense, to the instructions immediately following the call. All accessible objects on 'return' from setjmp have values as of the time longjmp was called, except that the values of objects of automatic storage class that do not have volatile type and have been changed between the setjmp and longjmp calls are indeterminate.

As it bypasses the normal call and return mechanisms, the longjmp function executes correctly in the contexts of interrupts, signals and any of their associated functions. However, if longjmp is invoked from a nested signal handler (a function called as a result of a signal arriving while handling another signal), the behaviour is undefined.

It's a serious error to longjmp to a setjmp in a function which is no longer active (has already returned).

For maximum portability, it is only safe to use setjmp as part of a comparison to an integral constant in an if statement, or as the only operand in the controlling expression of a switch statement. Any other use is implementation defined.

9.8 Signal handling

Two functions allow for asynchronous event handling to be provided. A *signal* is a condition that may be reported during program execution, and can be ignored, handled specially, or, as is the default, used to terminate the program. One function allows for sending signals, another determines how a signal will be processed. Many of the signals may be generated by the underlying hardware or operating system as well as by means of the signal-sending function raise.

The signals are defined in the include file signal.h.

SIGABRT
> Abnormal termination, such as instigated by the abort function. (Abort.)

SIGFPE
> Erroneous arithmetic operation, such as divide by 0 or overflow. (Floating point exception.)

SIGILL
> An invalid object program has been detected. This usually means that there is an illegal instruction in the program. (Illegal instruction.)

SIGINT
> Interactive attention signal; on interactive systems this is usually generated by typing some 'break-in' key at the terminal. (Interrupt.)

SIGSEGV
> Invalid storage access; most frequently caused by attempting to store some value in an object pointed to by a bad pointer. (Segment violation.)

SIGTERM
> Termination request made to the program. (Terminate.)

Some implementations may have additional signals available, over and above this standard set. They will be given names that start SIG, and will have unique values, apart from the set above.

The function `signal` allows you to specify the action taken on receipt of a signal. Associated with each signal condition above, there is a pointer to a function provided to handle this signal. The `signal` function changes this pointer, and returns the original value. Thus the function is defined as

```
#include <signal.h>
void (*signal (int sig, void (*func)(int)))(int);
```

That is to say, `signal` is a function that returns a pointer to another function. This second function takes a single `int` argument and returns `void`. The second argument to `signal` is similarly a pointer to a function returning `void` which takes an `int` argument.

Two special values may be used as the `func` argument (the signal-handling function), `SIG_DFL`, the initial, default, signal handler; and `SIG_IGN`, which is used to ignore a signal.

If the call to `signal` succeeds, the previous value of `func` for the specified signal is returned. Otherwise, `SIG_ERR` is returned and `errno` is set.

When a signal event happens, if the associated `func` is a pointer to a function, first the equivalent of `signal(sig, SIG_DFL)` is executed. This resets the signal handler to the default action: terminate the program. If the signal was `SIGILL` then this resetting is implementation defined.

Next, a call is made to the signal-handling function. If that function returns normally, then under most circumstances the program will resume at the point where the event occurred. However, if the value of `sig` was `SIGFPE` (a floating point exception), or any implementation defined computational exception, then the behaviour is undefined. The most usual thing to happen in this case is to call one of the functions `abort`, `exit`, or `longjmp`.

The following program fragment shows the use of `signal` to perform a tidy exit to a program on receipt of the interrupt or 'interactive attention' signal.

```
#include <stdio.h>
#include <stdlib.h>
#include <signal.h>


FILE *temp_file;
void leave(int sig);

main() {
    (void) signal(SIGINT,leave);
    temp_file = fopen("tmp","w");
    for(;;) {
        /*
        * Do things....
        */
        printf("Ready...\n");
```

```
        (void)getchar();
    }
    /* can't get here ... */
    exit(0);
}

/* on receipt of SIGINT, close tmp file */

void
leave(int sig) {
    fprintf(temp_file,"\nInterrupted..\n");
    fclose(temp_file);
    exit(sig);
}                                                    (E9.4)
```

It is possible for a program to send signals to itself by means of the raise function. This is defined as follows

```
#include <signal.h>
int raise (int sig);
```

The signal sig is sent to the program.

Raise returns zero if successful, non-zero otherwise. The abort library function is essentially implementable as follows:

```
#include <signal.h>

void
abort(void) {
    raise(SIGABRT);
}
```

If a signal occurs for any reason other than calling abort or raise, the signal-handling function may only call signal or assign a value to a volatile static object of type sig_atomic_t. The type sig_atomic_t is declared in signal.h. It is the only type of object that can safely be modified as an atomic entity, even in the presence of asynchronous interrupts. This is a very onerous restriction imposed by the Standard, which, for example, invalidates the leave function in the example program above; although the function would work correctly in some environments, it does not follow the strict rules of the Standard.

9.9 Variable numbers of arguments

It is often required to implement a function where the number of arguments is not known, or is not constant, when the function is written. Such a function is `printf`, dealt with in Section 9.11. The following example shows the declaration of such a function.

```
int f(int, ... );

int f(int, ... ) {
        .
        .
        .
}

int g() {
    f(1,2,3);
}
```
(E9.5)

In order to access the arguments within the called function, the functions declared in the `stdarg.h` header file must be included. This introduces a new type, called a `va_list`, and three functions that operate on objects of this type, called `va_start`, `va_arg`, and `va_end`.

Before any attempt can be made to access a variable argument list, `va_start` *must* be called. It is defined as

```
#include <stdarg.h>
void va_start(va_list ap, int parmN);
```

The `va_start` macro initializes `ap` for subsequent use by the functions `va_arg` and `va_end`. The second argument to `va_start` is the identifier naming the rightmost parameter in the variable parameter list in the function definition (the one just before the `, ... `).

Once initialized, the arguments supplied can be accessed sequentially by means of the `va_arg` macro. This is peculiar because the type returned is determined by an argument to the macro. Note that this is impossible to implement as a true function, only as a macro. It is defined as

```
#include <stdarg.h>
type va_arg(va_list ap, type);
```

Each call to this macro will extract the next argument from the argument list as a value of the specified type. The `va_list` argument must be the one initialized by `va_start`. If the next argument is not of the specified type, the behaviour is undefined. Take care here to avoid problems which could be caused by the arithmetic conversions. Use of `char` or `short` as the second argument to `va_arg` is invariably an error: these types always promote up to one of `signed int` or `unsigned int`, and `float` converts to `double`. Note that it is implementation defined whether objects declared to have the types `char`, `unsigned char`, `unsigned short` and unsigned bitfields will promote to unsigned int, rather complicating the use of va_arg. This may be an area where some unexpected subtleties arise; only time will tell.

The behaviour is also undefined if var_arg is called when there were no further arguments.

The *type* argument must be a type name which can be converted into a pointer to such an object simply by appending a * to it (this is so the macro can work). Simple types such as char are fine (because char * is a pointer to a character) but array of char won't work (char [] does not turn into 'pointer to array of char' by appending a *). Fortunately, arrays can easily be processed by remembering that an array name used as an actual argument to a function call is converted into a pointer. The correct *type* for an argument of type 'array of char' would be char *.

When all the arguments have been processed, the va_end function should be called. This will prevent the va_list supplied from being used any further. If va_end is not used, the behaviour is undefined.

The entire argument list can be re-traversed by calling va_start again, after calling va_end. The va_end function is declared as

```
#include <stdarg.h>
void va_end(va_list ap);
```

The following example shows the use of va_start, va_arg, and va_end to implement a function that returns the biggest of its integer arguments.

```
/* WARNING - NOT TESTED BY COMPILER */
#include <limits.h>
#include <stdlib.h>
#include <stdarg.h>

int maxof(int, ...) ;
void f(void);

main(){
    f();
    exit(0);
}

int maxof(int n_args, ...){
    register int i;
    int max, a;
    va_list ap;

    va_start(ap, n_args);
    max = va_arg(ap, int);
    for(i = 2; i <= n_args; i++) {
        if((a = va_arg(ap, int)) > max)
```

```
                    max = a;
            }
        va_end(ap);
        return max;
    }

    f() {
        int i;
        int j[256];
        printf("%d\n",maxof(3, i, j[42], 0));
    }
```
                                                                    (E9.6)

9.10 Input and output

9.10.1 Introduction

One of the reasons that has prevented many programming languages from becoming widely used for 'real programming' is their poor support for I/O, a subject which has never seemed to excite language designers. C has avoided this problem, oddly enough, by having no I/O at all! The C language approach has always been to do I/O using library functions, which ensures that system designers can provide tailored I/O instead of being forced to change the language itself.

As C has evolved, a library package known as the 'Standard I/O Library' or **stdio**, has evolved with it and has proved to be both flexible and portable. This package has now become part of the Standard.

However, the old stdio package relied heavily on the UNIX model of file access, in particular the assumption that there is no distinction between unstructured binary files and files containing readable text. Many operating systems do maintain a distinction between the two, and to ensure that C programs can be written portably to run on both types of file model, the stdio package has been modified. There are changes in this area which affect many existing programs, although strenuous efforts were taken to limit the amount of damage.

Old C programs should still be able work unmodified in a UNIX environment.

9.10.2 The I/O model

The I/O model does not distinguish between the types of physical devices supporting the I/O. Each source or sink of data (file) is treated in the same way, and is viewed as a **stream** of bytes. Since the smallest object that can be represented in C is the character, access to a file is permitted at any character boundary. Any number of characters can be read or written from a movable point, known as the **file position indicator**. The characters will be read, or written, in sequence from this point, and the position indicator moved accordingly. The position indicator is initially set to the beginning of a file, but can be also moved by means of positioning requests. (Where random access is not possible, the file position indicator is ignored.)

The overall effect is to provide sequential reads or writes unless the stream was opened in append mode, or the file position indicator is explicitly moved.

There are two types of file, *text files* and *binary files*, which, within a program, are manipulated as *text streams* and *binary streams* once they have been opened for I/O. The stdio package does not permit operations on the contents of files 'directly', but only by viewing them as streams.

Text streams

A **text stream** is an ordered sequence of characters composed into **lines**. A line is zero or more characters and a terminating newline character. At a low level, invisible to the user of the stream, characters may have to be added, altered, or deleted on input and output to conform to differing conventions for representing text in the host environment. There need not to be a one-to-one correspondence between the characters in a stream and those in the external file. For example, if a system insists that externally all text lines end with the two-character sequence \r\n, writing simply a \n to a text stream will map into the two-character sequence in the file; reading this sequence will map back on to the one-character newline in a text stream.

Data read in from a text stream is only guaranteed to compare equal to the data that was earlier written out to the file if the data consists only of complete lines of printable characters and the control characters horizontal-tab, newline, vertical-tab, and form-feed.

It is guaranteed that, if the last character written to a text file is a newline, it will read back as the same.

It is implementation defined whether the last line written to a text file must terminate with a newline character; this is because on some implementations text files and binary files are the same.

Some implementations will strip the leading space from lines consisting only of a space followed by a newline!

An implementation must support text files with lines containing at least 254 characters, including the terminating newline.

Binary streams

A binary stream is an ordered sequence of characters that can transparently record a program's internal data, for example the contents of structures or arrays in binary form. Data read in from a binary stream will always compare equal to data written out earlier to the same stream, under the same implementation. In some circumstances, an implementation-defined number of NUL characters may be appended to a binary stream.

The contents of binary files are exceedingly machine specific, and not, in general, portable.

Other streams

Other stream types may exist, but are implementation defined.

9.10.3 The `stdio.h` header file

To provide support for streams of the various kinds, a number of functions and macros exist. The `stdio.h` header file contains the various declarations necessary for the functions, together with the following macro and type declarations:

FILE

> The type of an object used to contain stream control information. Users of stdio never need to know the contents of these objects, but simply manipulate pointers to them. It is not safe to copy these objects within the program; sometimes their addresses may be 'magic'.

fpos_t

> A type of object that can be used to record unique values of a stream's file position indicator.

_IOFBF _IOLBF _IONBF

> Values used to control the buffering of a stream in conjunction with the `setvbuf` function.

BUFSIZ

> The size of the buffer used by the `setbuf` function. At least 256.

EOF

> A negative integral constant expression, indicating the end-of-file condition on a stream.

L_tmpnam

> The maximum length of the string generated by `tmpnam`.

OPEN_MAX

> The maximum number of files that a program may hold open concurrently; at least eight are guaranteed. Note that three predefined streams exist and may need to be closed if a program needs to open more than five files explicitly.

SEEK_CUR SEEK_END SEEK_SET

> Integral constant expressions used to control the actions of `fseek`.

TMP_MAX

> The minimum number of unique filenames generated by `tmpnam`; at least 25.

stdin stdout stderr

> Predefined objects of type `(FILE *)` referring to the standard input, output and error streams respectively. These streams are automatically open when a program starts execution.

9.10.4 Opening, closing and buffering of streams

Opening

A stream is connected to a file by means of the `fopen`, `freopen` or `tmpfile` functions. These functions will, if successful, return a pointer to a `FILE` object.

Three streams are available without any special action; they are normally all connected to the physical device associated with the executing program: usually your terminal. They are referred to by the names **stdin**, the *standard input*, **stdout**, the *standard output*, and **stderr**, the *standard error* streams. Normal keyboard input is from `stdin`, normal terminal output is to `stdout`, and error messages are directed to `stderr`. The separation of error messages from normal output messages allows the `stdout` stream to be connected to something other than the terminal device, and still to have error messages appear on the screen in front of you, rather than to be redirected to this file. These files are only fully buffered if they do not refer to interactive devices.

As mentioned earlier, the file position indicator may or may not be movable, depending on the underlying device. It is not possible, for example, to move the file position indicator on `stdin` if that is connected to a terminal, as it usually is.

All non-temporary files must have a *filename*, which is a string. The rules for composing valid filenames are implementation defined. Whether a file can be simultaneously open multiple times is also implementation defined.

Closing

Files are closed by explicitly calling `fclose`, `exit` or by returning from `main`. Any buffered data is flushed. If a program stops for some other reason, the status of files which it had open is undefined.

Buffering

There are three types of buffering:

- *Unbuffered*
  Minimum internal storage is used by stdio in an attempt to send or receive data as soon as possible.
- *Line buffered*
  Characters are processed on a line-by-line basis. This is commonly used in interactive environments, and internal buffers are flushed only when full or when a newline is processed.
- *Fully buffered*
  Internal buffers are only flushed when full.

The buffering associated with a stream can always be flushed by using `fflush` explicitly. Support for the various types of buffering is implementation defined, and can be controlled within these limits using `setbuf` and `setvbuf`.

9.10.5 Direct file manipulation

A number of functions exist to operate on files directly.

```
#include <stdio.h>

int remove(const char *filename);
int rename(const char *old, const char *new);
```

```
char *tmpnam(char *s);
FILE *tmpfile(void);
```

remove

Causes a file to be removed. Subsequent attempts to open the file will fail, unless it is created anew. If the file is already open, the operation of remove is implementation defined. The return value is zero for success, any other value for failure.

rename

Changes the name of the file identified by old to new. Subsequent attempts to open the original name will fail, unless another file is created with the old name. As with remove, rename returns zero for a successful operation, any other value indicating a failure.

If a file with the new name exists prior to calling rename, the behaviour is implementation defined.

If rename fails for any reason, the original file is unaffected.

tmpnam

Generates a string that may be used as a filename and is guaranteed to be different from any existing filename. It may be called repeatedly, each time generating a new name. The constant TMP_MAX is used to specify how many times tmpnam may be called before it can no longer find a unique name. TMP_MAX will be at least 25. If tmpnam is called more than this number of times, its behaviour is undefined.

If the argument s is set to NULL, then tmpnam uses an internal buffer to build the name, and returns a pointer to that. Subsequent calls may alter the same internal buffer. The argument may instead point to an array of at least L_tmpnam characters, in which case the name will be filled into the supplied buffer. Such a filename may then be created, and used as a temporary file. Since the name is generated by the function, it is unlikely to be very useful in any other context. Temporary files of this nature are not removed, except by direct calls to the remove function. They are most often used to pass temporary data between two separate programs.

tmpfile

Creates a temporary binary file, opened for update, and returns a pointer to the stream of that file. The file will be removed when the stream is closed. If no file could be opened, tmpfile returns a null pointer.

9.10.6 Opening named files

Named files are opened by a call to the fopen function, whose declaration is this:

```
#include <stdio.h>
FILE *fopen(const char *pathname, const char *mode);
```

The `pathname` argument is the name of the file to open, such as that returned from `tmpnam`, or some program-specific filename.

Files can be opened in a variety of **modes**, such as *read* mode for reading data, *write* mode for writing data, and so on.

Note that if you only want to write data to a file, `fopen` will *create* the file if it does not already exist, or truncate it to zero length (losing its previous contents) if it did exist.

The Standard list of modes is shown in Table 9.3, although implementations may permit extra modes by appending extra characters at the end of the modes.

Table 9.3   File opening modes

Mode	Type of file	Read	Write	Truncate/create	Append
`"r"`	text	yes	no	no	no
`"rb"`	binary	yes	no	no	no
`"r+"`	text	yes	yes	no	no
`"r+b"`	binary	yes	yes	no	no
`"rb+"`	binary	yes	yes	no	no
`"w"`	text	no	yes	yes	no
`"wb"`	binary	no	yes	yes	no
`"w+"`	text	yes	yes	yes	no
`"w+b"`	binary	yes	yes	yes	no
`"wb+"`	binary	yes	yes	yes	no
`"a"`	text	no	yes	yes	yes
`"ab"`	binary	no	yes	yes	yes
`"a+"`	text	no	yes	yes	yes
`"a+b"`	binary	no	yes	yes	yes
`"ab+"`	binary	no	yes	yes	yes

Beware that some implementations of binary files may pad the last record with NULL characters, so opening them with modes ab, ab+ or a+b could position the file pointer beyond the last data written.

If a file is opened in append mode, *all* writes will occur at the end of the file, regardless of attempts to move the file position indicator with `fseek`.

Attempts to open a file in read mode, indicated by an `'r'` as the first character in the mode string, will fail if the file does not already exist or can't be read.

Files opened for update may be both read and written, but a read may not immediately follow a write, or a write follow a read, without an intervening call of one (or more) of `fflush`, `fseek`, `fsetpos` or `rewind`. The only exception is that a write may immediately follow a read if EOF was read.

It may also be possible in some implementations to omit the b in the binary modes, using the same modes for text and binary files.

Streams opened by `fopen` are fully buffered only if they are not connected to an interactive device; this ensures that prompts and responses are handled properly.

If `fopen` fails to open a file, it returns a null pointer; otherwise, it returns a pointer to the object controlling the stream.

9.10.7 `freopen`

The `freopen` function is used to take an existing stream pointer, and associate it with another named file:

```
#include <stdio.h>
FILE *freopen(const char *pathname,
        const char *mode, FILE *stream);
```

The `mode` argument is just as for `fopen`. The `stream` is closed first, and any errors from the close are ignored. On error, `NULL` is returned, otherwise the new value for `stream` is returned.

9.10.8 Closing files

An open file is closed using `fclose`.

```
#include <stdio.h>

int fclose(FILE *stream);
```

Any unwritten data buffered for `stream` is flushed out and any unread data is thrown away. If a buffer had been automatically allocated for the stream, it is freed. The file is then closed.

Zero is returned on success, non-zero if errors occur or the stream was not open.

9.10.9 `setbuf`, `setvbuf`

These two functions are used to change the buffering strategy for an open `stream`:

```
#include <stdio.h>

int setvbuf(FILE *stream, char *buf,
        int type, size_t size);
void setbuf(FILE *stream, char *buf);
```

They must both be used *before* the file is either read from or written to. The `type` argument defines how the `stream` will be buffered (see Table 9.4).

Table 9.4 Type of buffering

Value	Effect
_IONBF	Do not buffer I/O
_IOFBF	Fully buffer I/O
_IOLBF	Line buffer: flush buffer when full, when newline is written or when a read is requested.

The buf argument can be a null pointer, in which case an array is automatically allocated to hold the buffered data. Otherwise, the user can provide a buffer, but should ensure that its lifetime is at least as long as that of the stream: a common mistake is to use automatic storage allocated inside a compound statement; in correct usage it is usual to obtain the storage from malloc instead. The size of the buffer is specified by the size argument.

A call on setbuf is exactly the same as a call on setvbuf with _IOFBF for the type argument, and BUFSIZ for the size argument. If buf is a null pointer, the value _IONBF is used for type instead.

No value is returned by setbuf, setvbuf returns zero on success, non-zero if invalid values are provided for type or size, or the request cannot be complied with.

9.10.10 fflush

```
#include <stdio.h>

int fflush(FILE *stream);
```

If stream refers to a file opened for output or update, any unwritten data is 'written' out. Exactly what that means is a function of the host environment, and C cannot guarantee, for example, that data immediately reaches the surface of a disk which might be supporting the file. If the stream is associated with a file opened for input or update, any preceding ungetc operation is forgotten.

9.11 Formatted I/O

There are a number of related functions used for formatted I/O, each one determining the format of the I/O from a **format string**. For output, the format string consists of plain text, which is output unchanged, and embedded *format specifications* which call for some special processing of one of the remaining arguments to the function. On input, the plain text must match what is seen in the input stream; the format specifications again specify what the meaning of remaining arguments is.

Each format specification is introduced by a % character, followed by the rest of the specification.

9.11.1 Output: the printf family

For those functions performing output, the format specification takes the following form, with optional parts enclosed in brackets:

%<flags><field width><precision>conversion<length>

The meaning of *flags*, *field width*, *precision*, *length*, and *conversion* are given below, although tersely. For more detail, it is worth looking at what the Standard says.

flags

Zero or more of the following:

−   Left justify the conversion within its field.

+   A signed conversion will always start with a plus or minus sign.

space

If the first character of a signed conversion is not a sign, insert a space. Overridden by + if present.

Forces an alternative form of output. The first digit of an octal conversion will always be a 0; inserts 0X in front of a non-zero hexadecimal conversion; forces a decimal point in all floating point conversions even if one is not necessary; does not remove trailing zeros from g and G conversions.

field width

A decimal integer specifying the minimum output field width. This will be exceeded if necessary. If an asterisk is used here, the next argument is converted to an integer and used for the value of the field width; if the value is negative it is treated as a − flag followed by a positive field width. Output that would be less than the field width is padded with spaces (zeros if the *field width* integer starts with a zero) to fit. The padding is on the left unless the left-adjustment flag is specified.

precision

This starts with a period '.'. It specifies the minimum number of digits for d, i, o, u, x, or X conversions; the number of digits after the decimal point for e, E, f conversions; the maximum number of digits for g and G conversions; the number of characters to be printed from a string for s conversion. The amount of padding overrides the *field width*. If an asterisk is used here, the next argument is converted to an integer and used for the value of the field width. If the value is negative, it is treated as if it were missing.

length

h following a specifier to print an integral type causes it to be treated as if it were a short. (Note that the various sorts of short are always promoted

Table 9.5   Conversions

Specifier	Effect	Default precision
d	signed decimal	1
i	signed decimal	1
u	unsigned decimal	1
o	unsigned octal	1
x	unsigned hexadecimal (0-f)	1
X	unsigned hexadecimal (0-F)	1
	Precision specifies minimum number of digits, expanded with leading zeros if necessary. Printing a value of zero with zero precision outputs no characters.	
f	Print a double with *precision* digits (rounded) after the decimal point. To suppress the decimal point use a *precision* of explicitly zero. Otherwise, at least one digit appears in front of the point.	6
e,E	Print a double in exponential format, rounded, with one digit before the decimal point, *precision* after it. A *precision* of zero suppresses the decimal point. There will be at least two digits in the exponent, which is printed as 1.23e15 in e format, or 1.23E15 in E format.	6
g,G	Use style f, or e (E with G) depending on the exponent. If the exponent is less than –4 or greater than the *precision*, f is not used. Trailing zeros are suppressed, a decimal point is only printed if there is a following digit.	unspecified
c	The int argument is converted to an unsigned char and printed as a character.	
s	Print a string up to *precision* digits long.	infinite
p	Display the value of a (void *) pointer in a system-dependent way.	
n	The argument must be a pointer to an integer. The number of characters output so far by this call will be written into the integer.	
%	A %	—

to one of the flavours of int when passed as an argument.) l works like h but applies to a long integral argument. L is used to indicate that a long double argument is to be printed, and only applies to the floating-point specifiers. These are ignored if they follow the 'wrong' type of *conversion*.

conversion

See Table 9.5.

The functions that use these formats are described in Table 9.6. All need the inclusion of stdio.h. Their declarations are as shown.

```
#include <stdio.h>

int fprintf(FILE *stream, const char *format, ...);
int printf(const char *format, ...);
int sprintf(char *s, const char *format, ...);

#include <stdarg.h> /* as well as stdio.h */
int vfprintf(FILE *stream, const char *format,
            va_list arg);
int vprintf(const char *format, va_list arg);
int vsprintf(char *s, const char *format,
            va_list arg);
```

Table 9.6 Functions performing formatted output

Name	Purpose
fprintf	General formatted output as described. Output is written to the file indicated by stream.
printf	Identical to fprintf with a first argument equal to stdout.
sprintf	Identical to fprintf except that the output is not written to a file, but written into the character array pointed to by s.
vfprintf	Formatted output as for fprintf, but with the variable argument list replaced by arg which must have been initialized by va_start. va_end is not called by this function.
vprintf	Identical to vfprintf with a first argument equal to stdout.
vsprintf	Formatted output as for sprintf, but with the variable argument list replaced by arg which must have been initialized by va_start. va_end is not called by this function.

All of the above functions return the number of characters output, or a negative value on error. The trailing null is *not* counted by sprintf and vsprintf.

Implementations must permit at least 509 characters to be produced by any single conversion.

9.11.2 Input: the `scanf` family

A number of functions exist analogous to the `printf` family, but for the purposes of input instead. The most immediate difference between the two families is that the `scanf` group needs to be passed *pointers* to their arguments, so that the values read can be assigned to the proper destinations. Forgetting to pass a pointer is a very common error, and one which the compiler cannot detect – the variable argument list prevents it.

The format string is used to control interpretation of a stream of input data, which generally contains values to be assigned to the objects pointed to by the remaining arguments to `scanf`. The contents of the format string may contain:

white space
> This causes the input stream to be read up to the next non-white-space character.

ordinary character
> Anything except white-space or % characters. The next character in the input stream *must* match this character.

conversion specification
> This is a % character, followed by an optional * character (which suppresses the conversion), followed by an optional decimal integer specifying the maximum field width, an optional h, l or L to control the length of the conversion and finally a non-optional conversion specifier. Note that use of h, l, or L will affect the type of pointer which must be used.

Except for the specifiers c, n and [, a field of input is a sequence of non-space characters starting at the first non-space character in the input. It terminates at the first conflicting character or when the input field width is reached.

The result is put into wherever the corresponding argument points, unless the assignment is suppresed using the * mentioned already. The following conversion specifiers may be used:

d i o u x
> Convert a signed integer, a signed integer in the form of a C constant, an octal integer, an unsigned integer and a hexadecimal integer respectively.

e f g
> Convert a float (*not* a double).

s
> Read a string, and add a null at the end. The string is terminated by whitespace on input (which is not read as part of the string).

[
> Read a string, but do not stop on white space. Instead, a list of characters is given which may terminate the string. For example, %[abcd] means a string terminated by one of abcd. The] delimits the list. If the first character in the list is a circumflex ^, then the input string is delimited by any character *not* in the list. If the initial sequence is [^] or [], the] is not

a delimiter, but part of the list – another] will be needed to end the list. If there is a minus sign (–) in the list, it must be either the first or the last character; otherwise the meaning is implementation defined.

c Read a single character; white space is significant here. To read the first non-white-space character, use %1s. A field width indicates that an array of characters is to be read.

p Read a (void *) pointer previously written out using the %p of one of the printfs.

% A % is expected in the input, no assignment is made.

n Return as an integer the number of characters read by this call so far.

The size specifiers have the effect shown in Table 9.7.

Table 9.7 Size specifiers

Specifier	Modifies	Converts
l	d i o u x	long int
h	d i o u x	short int
l	e f	double
L	e f	long double

The functions are described below, and have the following declarations:

```
#include <stdio.h>

int fscanf(FILE *stream, const char *format, ...);
int sscanf(const char *s, const char *format, ...);
int scanf(const char *format, ...);
```

Fscanf takes its input from the designated stream, scanf is identical to fscanf with a first argument of stdin, and sscanf takes its input from the designated character array.

If an input failure occurs before any conversion, EOF is returned. Otherwise, the number of successful conversions is returned: this may be zero if no conversions are performed.

An input failure is caused by reading EOF or reaching the end of the input string (as appropriate). A conversion failure is caused by a failure to match the proper pattern for a particular conversion.

9.12 Character I/O

A number of functions provide for character oriented I/O. Their declarations are:

```
#include <stdio.h>
```

```
/* character input */
int fgetc(FILE *stream);
int getc(FILE *stream);
int getchar(void);
int ungetc(int c, FILE *stream);

/* character output */
int fputc(int c, FILE *stream);
int putc(int c, FILE *stream);
int putchar(int c);

/* string input */
char *fgets(char *s, int n, FILE *stream);
char *gets(char *s);

/* string output */
int fputs(const char *s, FILE *stream);
int puts(const char *s);
```

Their descriptions are as follows.

Character input
These read an unsigned char from the input stream where specified, or otherwise stdin. In each case, the next character is obtained from the input stream. It is treated as an unsigned char and converted to an int, which is the return value. On End of File, the constant EOF is returned, and the end-of-file indicator is set for the associated stream. On error, EOF is returned, and the error indicator is set for the associated stream. Successive calls will obtain characters sequentially. Only one of the three is guaranteed not to be a macro: fgetc. The others may be, and may evaluate their stream argument more than once, so do not use side effects here.

There is also the supporting ungetc routine, which is used to push back a character on to a stream, causing it to become the next character to be read. This is not an output operation and can never cause the external contents of a file to be changed. A fflush, fseek, or rewind operation on the stream between the pushback and the read will cause the pushback to be forgotten. Only one character of pushback is guaranteed, and attempts to pushback EOF are ignored. In every case, pushing back a number of characters then reading or discarding them leaves the file position indicator unchanged. The file position indicator is decremented by every successful call to ungetc for a binary stream, but unspecified for a text stream, or a binary stream which is positioned at the beginning of the file.

Character output
These are identical in description to the input functions already described, except performing output. They return the character written, or EOF on error. There is no equivalent to End of File for an output file.

String output

These write strings to the output file; stream where specified, otherwise stdout. The terminating null is not written. Non-zero is returned on error, zero otherwise. *Beware*: puts appends a newline to the string output; fputs does not!

String input

Fgets reads a string into the array pointed to by s from the stream stream. It stops on either EOF or the first newline (which it reads), and appends a null character. At most n-1 characters are read (leaving room for the null).

Gets works similarly for the stream stdin, but discards the newline!

Both return s if successful, or a null pointer otherwise. In each case, if EOF is encountered before any characters have been read, the array is unchanged and a null pointer is returned. A read error in the middle of a string leaves the array contents undefined and a null pointer is returned.

9.13 Unformatted I/O

This is simple: only two functions provide this facility, one for reading and one for writing:

```
#include <stdio.h>

size_t fread(void *ptr, size_t size,
        size_t nelem, FILE *stream);
size_t fwrite(const void *ptr, size_t size,
        size_t nelem, FILE *stream);
```

In each case, the appropriate read or write is performed on the data pointed to by ptr. Up to nelem elements, of size size, are transferred. Failure to transfer the full number is an error only when writing; End of File can prevent the full number on input. The number of elements actually transferred is returned. To distinguish between End of File on input, or an error, use feof or ferror.

If size or nelem is zero, fread does nothing except to return zero.

An example may help.

```
#include <stdio.h>
#include <stdlib.h>

struct xx{
    int xx_int;
    float xx_float;
}ar[20];

main(){
```

```
FILE *fp = fopen("testfile", "w");

if(fwrite((const void *)ar,
    sizeof(ar[0]), 5, fp) != 5){

    fprintf(stderr,"Error writing\n");
    exit(1);
}

rewind(fp);

if(fread((void *)&ar[10],
    sizeof(ar[0]), 5, fp) != 5){

    if(ferror(fp)){
        fprintf(stderr,"Error writing\n");
        exit(1);
    }
    if(feof(fp)){
        fprintf(stderr,"End of File\n");
        exit(1);
    }
}
exit(0);
}                                          (E9.7)
```

9.14 Random access functions

The file I/O routines all work in the same way; unless the user takes explicit steps to change the file position indicator, files will be read and written sequentially. A read followed by a write followed by a read (if the file was opened in a mode to permit that) will cause the second read to start immediately following the end of the data just written. (Remember that stdio insists on the user inserting a buffer-flushing operation between each element of a read-write-read cycle.) To control this, the Random Access functions allow control over the implied read/write position in the file. The file position indicator is moved by a read or a write, and indicates the byte to be the subject of the next operation on the file.

Three functions exist which allow the file position indicator to be examined or changed. Their declarations and descriptions follow.

```
#include <stdio.h>

/* return file position indicator */
long ftell(FILE *stream);
int fgetpos(FILE *stream, fpos_t *pos);
```

```
/* set file position indicator to zero */
void rewind(FILE *stream);

/* set file position indicator */
int fseek(FILE *stream, long offset, int ptrname);
int fsetpos(FILE *stream, const fpos_t *pos);
```

Ftell returns the current value (measured in bytes) of the file position indicator if stream refers to a binary file. For a text file, a 'magic' number is returned, which may only be used on a subsequent call to fseek to reposition to the current file position indicator. On failure, −1L is returned and errno is set.

Rewind sets the current file position indicator to the start of the file indicated by stream. The file's error indicator is reset by a call of rewind. No value is returned.

Fseek allows the file position indicator for stream to be set to an arbitrary value (for binary files), or for text files, only to a position obtained from ftell.

In the general case, the file position indicator is set to offset bytes (characters) from a point in the file determined by the value of ptrname. Offset may be negative. The values of ptrname may be SEEK_SET, which sets the file position indicator relative to the beginning of the file, SEEK_CUR, which sets the file position indicator relative to its current value, and SEEK_END, which sets the file position indicator relative to the end of the file. The latter is not necessarily guaranteed to work properly on binary streams.

For text files, offset must either be zero or a value returned from a previous call to ftell for the same stream, and the value of ptrname must be SEEK_SET.

Fseek clears the end of file indicator for the given stream and erases the memory of any ungetc. It works for both input and output.

Zero is returned for success, non-zero for a forbidden request.

Note that for ftell and fseek it must be possible to encode the value of the file position indicator into a long. This may not work for very long files, so the Standard introduces fgetpos and fsetpos which have been specified in a way that removes the problem.

Fgetpos stores the current file position indicator for stream in the object pointed to by pos. The value stored is 'magic' and only used to return to the specified position for the same stream using fsetpos.

Fsetpos works as described above, also clearing the stream's end-of-file indicator and forgetting the effects of any ungetc operations.

For both functions, on success, zero is returned; on failure, non-zero is returned and errno is set.

9.14.1 Error handling

The standard I/O functions maintain two indicators with each open stream to show the end-of-file and error status of the stream. These can be interrogated and set by the following functions:

```
#include <stdio.h>

void clearerr(FILE *stream);

int feof(FILE *stream);

int ferror(FILE *stream);

void perror(const char *s);
```

Clearerr clears the error and EOF indicators for the stream.

Feof returns non-zero if the stream's EOF indicator is set, zero otherwise.

Ferror returns non-zero if the stream's error indicator is set, zero otherwise.

Perror prints a single-line error message on the program's standard output, prefixed by the string pointed to by s, with a colon and a space appended. The error message is determined by the value of errno and is intended to give some explanation of the condition causing the error. For example, this program produces the error message shown:

```
#include <stdio.h>
#include <stdlib.h>

main() {

    fclose(stdout);
    if(fgetc(stdout) >= 0) {
        fprintf(stderr, "What - no error!\n");
        exit(1);
    }
    perror("fgetc");
    exit(0);
}

/* Result */

fgetc: Bad file number                                    (E9.8)
```

Well, I didn't say that the message had to be very meaningful!

9.15 General utilities

These all involve the use of the header stdlib.h, which declares a number of types and macros and several functions of general use. The types and macros are as follows:

`div_t`
>   This is the type of the structure returned by `div`.

`ldiv_t`
>   This is the type of the structure returned by `ldiv`.

`ERANGE`
`HUGE_VAL`
>   These are values described among the mathematical functions.

`RAND_MAX`
>   This is the maximum value returned by the `rand` function.

9.15.1 String conversion functions

Three functions take a string as an argument and convert it to a number of the type shown below:

```
#include <stdlib.h>

double atof(const char *nptr);
long atol(const char *nptr);
int atoi(const char *nptr);
```

For each of the functions, the number is converted and the result returned. None of them guarantees to set `errno` (although they may do in some implementations), and the results of a conversion which overflows or cannot be represented is undefined.

More sophisticated functions are:

```
#include <stdlib.h>

double strtod(const char *nptr, char **endptr);
long strtol(const char *nptr, char **endptr,
                  int base);
unsigned long strtoul(const char *nptr,
         char **endptr, int base);
```

All three functions work in a similar way. Leading white space is skipped, then a *subject sequence*, resembling an appropriate constant, is found, followed by a sequence of unrecognized characters. The trailing null at the end of a string is always unrecognized. The subject sequence can be empty. The subject sequences are determined as follows:

`strtod`
>   Optional + or –, followed by a digit sequence containing an optional decimal point character, followed by an optional exponent. No floating suffix will be recognized. If there is no decimal point present, it is assumed to follow the digit sequence.

strtol

> Optional + or −, followed by a digit sequence. The digits are taken from the decimal digits or an upper or lower case letter in the range a–z of the English alphabet; the letters are given the values 10–35 respectively. The base argument determines which values are permitted, and may be zero, or otherwise 2–36. Only 'digits' with a value less than that of base are recognized. A base of 16 permits the characters 0x or 0X to follow the optional sign. A base of zero permits the input of characters in the form of a C integer constant. No integer suffix will be recognized.

strtoul

> Identical to strtol but with no sign permitted.

If endptr is non-null, the address of the first unrecognized character is stored in the object that it points to. If the subject sequence is empty or has the wrong form, this is the value of nptr.

If a conversion can be performed, the functions convert the number and return its value, taking into account a leading sign where permitted. Otherwise they return zero. On overflow or error the action is as follows:

strtod

> On overflow, returns ±HUGE_VAL according to the sign of the result; on underflow, returns zero. In either case, errno is set to ERANGE.

strtol

> On overflow, LONG_MAX or LONG_MIN is returned according to the sign of the result, errno is set to ERANGE.

strtoul

> On overflow, ULONG_MAX is returned, errno is set to ERANGE.

9.15.2 Random number generation

Provision for pseudo-random number generation is made by the following functions.

```
#include <stdlib.h>

int rand(void);
void srand(unsigned int seed);
```

Rand returns a pseudo-random number in the range 0 to RAND_MAX, which has a value of at least 32767.

Srand allows a given starting point in the sequence to be chosen according to the value of seed. If srand is not called before rand, the value of the seed is taken to be 1. The same sequence of values will always be returned from rand for a given value of seed.

The Standard specifies the algorithm to be used for rand and srand, thus guaranteeing repeatable behaviour.

9.15.3 Memory allocation

These functions are used to allocate and free storage. The storage so obtained is only guaranteed to be large enough to store an object of the specified type and aligned appropriately so as not to cause addressing exceptions. No further assumptions can be made.

```
#include <stdlib.h>

void *malloc(size_t size);
void *calloc(size_t nmemb, size_t size);
void *realloc(void *ptr, size_t size);

void *free(void *ptr);
```

All of the memory allocation functions return a pointer to allocated storage of size `size` bytes. If there is no free storage, they return a null pointer. The differences between them are that `calloc` takes an argument `nmemb` which specifies the number of elements in an array, each of whose members is `size` bytes, and so allocates a larger piece of store (in general) than `malloc`. Also, the store allocated by `malloc` is not initialized, whereas `calloc` sets all bits in the storage to zero. This is not necessarily the equivalent representation of floating-point zero, or the null pointer.

`Realloc` is used to change the size of the thing pointed to by `ptr`, which may require some copying to be done and the old storage freed. The contents of the object pointed to by `ptr` is unchanged up to the smaller of the old and the new sizes. If `ptr` is null, the behaviour is identical to `malloc` with the appropriate size.

`Free` is used to free space previously obtained with one of the allocation routines. It is permissible to give `free` a null pointer as the argument, in which case nothing is done.

It is an error to attempt to free store which was never allocated, or has already been freed.

9.15.4 Communication with the environment

A miscellany of functions is found here.

```
#include <stdlib.h>

void abort(void);
int atexit(void (*func)(void));
void exit(int status);
char *getenv(const char *name);
int system(const char *string);
```

abort

Causes abnormal program termination to occur, by raising the SIGABRT signal. Abnormal termination is only prevented if the signal is being caught, and the signal handler does not return. Otherwise, output files may be flushed and temporary files may be removed according to implementation definition, and an 'unsuccessful termination' status returned to the host environment. This function cannot return.

atexit

The argument `func` becomes a function to be called, without arguments, when the program terminates. Up to at least 32 such functions may be registered, and are called on program termination in reverse order of their registration. Zero is returned for success, non-zero for failure.

exit

Normal program termination occurs when this is called. First, all of the functions registered using `atexit` are called, but beware – by now, `main` is considered to have returned and *no* objects with automatic storage duration may safely be used. Then, all the open output streams are flushed, then closed, and all temporary files created by `tmpfile` are removed. Finally, the program returns control to the host environment, returning an implementation-defined form of successful or unsuccessful termination status depending on whether the argument to `exit` was zero or non-zero, respectively. `Exit` *cannot* return.

getenv

The implementation-defined *environment list* is searched to find an item which corresponds to the string pointed to by `name`. A pointer to the item is returned – it points to an array which must not be modified by the program, but may be overwritten by a subsequent call to `getenv`. A null pointer is returned if no item matches.

The purpose and implementation of the environment list depends on the host environment.

system

An implementation-defined *command processor* is passed the string `string`. A null pointer will cause a return of zero if no command processor exists, non-zero otherwise. A non-null pointer causes the command to be processed. The effect of the command and the value returned are implementation defined.

9.15.5 Searching and sorting

Two functions exist in this category: one for searching an already sorted list, the other for sorting an unsorted list. They are completely general, handling arrays of arbitrary size with elements of arbitrary size.

To enable them to compare two elements, the user provides a comparison function, which is called with pointers to two of the elements as its arguments. It returns a value less than, equal to or greater than zero depending on whether the first pointer points to an element considered to be less than, equal to or greater than the object pointed to by the second pointer, respectively.

```
#include <stdlib.h>

void *bsearch(const void *key, const void *base,
    size_t nmemb, size_t size,
    int (*compar)(const void *, const void *));

void *qsort(const void *base, size_t nmemb,
    size_t size,
    int (*compar)(const void *, const void *));
```

For both functions, nmemb is the number of elements in the array, size is the size in bytes of an array element and compar is the function to be called to compare them. Base is a pointer to the base of the array.

Qsort will sort the array into ascending order.

Bsearch assumes that the array is already sorted and returns a pointer to the first element it finds that compares equal to the object pointed to by key. A null pointer is returned if no match is found.

9.15.6 Integer arithmetic functions

These provide ways of finding the absolute value of an integral argument and the quotient and remainder of a division, for both int and long types.

```
#include <stdlib.h>

int abs(int j);
long labs(long j);

div_t div(int numerator, int denominator);
ldiv_t ldiv(long numerator, long denominator);
```

abs
labs

> These return the absolute value of their argument – choose the appropriate one for your needs. The behaviour is undefined if the value cannot be represented – this can happen in two's complement systems where the most negative number has no positive equivalent.

div
ldiv

> These divide the numerator by the denominator and return a structure of the indicated type. In each case the structure will contain a member called quot which contains the quotient of the division, and a member called rem which will contain the remainder. The type of each member is int for div and long for ldiv.

9.16 String handling

Numerous functions exist to handle strings. In C, a string is an array of characters terminated by a null. In all cases, the functions expect a pointer to the first character in the string. The header string.h declares these functions.

9.16.1 Copying

The functions for this purpose are:

```
#include <string.h>

void *memcpy(void *s1, const void *s2, size_t n);
void *memmove (void *s1, const void *s2, size_t n);
char *strcpy(char *s1, const char *s2);
char *strncpy(char *s1, const char *s2, size_t n);
char *strcat(char *s1, const char *s2);
char *strncat(char *s1, const char *s2, size_t n);
```

memcpy
> This copies n bytes from the place pointed to by s2 to the place pointed to by s1. If the objects overlap, the result is undefined. The value of s1 is returned.

memmove
> Identical to memcpy, but works even for overlapping objects. It may be marginally slower, though.

strcpy
strncpy
> Both of these copy the string pointed to by s2 into the string pointed to by s1, including the trailing null. Strncpy will copy at most n characters, and pad with trailing nulls if s2 is shorter than n characters. If the strings overlap, the behaviour is undefined. They return s1.

strcat
strncat
> Both append the string in s2 to s1, overwriting the null at the end of s1. A final null is always written. At most n characters are copied from s2 by strncat, which means that for safety the destination string should have room for its original length (not counting the null) plus n + 1 characters. They return s1.

9.16.2 String and byte comparison

These comparison functions are used to compare arrays of bytes. This obviously includes the traditional C strings, which are an array of char (bytes) with a terminating null. All of these functions work by comparing a byte at a time, and stopping either when two bytes differ (in which case they return the sign of the difference between the two bytes), or the arrays are considered to be equal: no differences were found, and the length of the arrays was equal to the specified amount, or the null was found at the end of a string comparison.

The sign of the result is implementation defined if one of the bytes being compared has its most significant bit set. This has profound implications to the writer of C programs – in most environments, with 8-bit bytes, programs that try to use the extended alphabets now in common use are not necessarily portable. This is because the extended alphabets often use the top bit of the byte.

Be warned that they all return *zero* for equality!

```c
#include <string.h>

int memcmp(const void *s1, const void *s2, size_t n);
int strcmp(const char *s1, const char *s2);
int strncmp(const char *s1, const char *s2, size_t n);
size_t strxfrm(char *to, const char *from,
               size_t maxsize);
int strcoll(const char *s1, const char *s2);
```

memcmp

> Compares the first n characters in the objects pointed to by s1 and s2. It is very dodgy to compare structures in this way, because unions or 'holes' caused by alignment padding can contain junk.

strcmp

> Compares the two strings. This is one of the most commonly used of the string-handling functions.

strncmp

> As for strcmp, but compares at most n characters.

strxfrm

> This is one of the more recent inventions to help deal with natural language processing. The string in from is converted (by some magic), and placed wherever to points. At most maxsize characters (including the trailing null) are written into the destination. The magic guarantees that two such transformed strings will give the same comparison with each other for the user's current locale when using strcmp, as when strcoll is applied to the original two strings.
>
> In all cases, the length of the resulting string (not counting its terminating null) is returned. If the value is equal to or greater than maxsize, the contents of *to is undefined.

strcoll

> This function compares the two strings according to the collating sequence specified by the current locale, as if both strings had been transformed by strxfrm and then compared by strcmp.

9.16.3 Character and string searching functions

```
#include <string.h>

void *memchr(const void *s, int c, size_t n);
char *strchr(const char *s, int c);
size_t strcspn(const char *s1, const char *s2);
char *strpbrk(const char *s1, const char *s2);
char *strrchr(const char *s, int c);
size_t strspn(const char *s1, const char *s2);
char *strstr(const char *s1, const char *s2);
char *strtok(const char *s1, const char *s2);
```

memchr

Returns a pointer to the first occurrence in the initial n characters of *s of the (unsigned char) c. Returns null if there is no such occurrence.

strchr

Returns a pointer to the first occurrence of (char) c in *s, including the null in the search. Returns null if there is no such occurrence.

strcspn

Returns the length of the initial part of the string s1 which contains no characters from s2. The terminating null is not considered to be part of s2.

strpbrk

Returns a pointer to the first character in s1 which is any of the characters in s2, or null if there is none.

strrchr

Returns a pointer to the last occurrence in s1 of (char) c counting the null as part of s1, or null if there is none.

strspn

Returns the length of the initial part of s1 consisting entirely of characters from s1.

strstr

Returns a pointer to the first occurrence in s1 of the string s2, or null if there is none.

strtok

Breaks the string in s1 into 'tokens', each delimited by one of the characters from s2 and returns a pointer the first token, or null if there is none. Subsequent calls with (char *) 0 as the value of s1 return the next token in sequence, with the extra fun that s2 (and hence the delimiters) may differ on each subsequent call. A null pointer is returned if no tokens remain.

9.16.4 Miscellaneous functions

```
#include <string.h>

void *memset(void *s, int c, size_t n);
char *strerror(int errnum);
size_t strlen(const char *s);
```

memset
> Sets the n bytes pointed to by s to the value of (unsigned char)c. Returns s.

strlen
> Returns the length of the string s not counting the terminating null. This is a very widely used function.

strerror
> Returns a pointer to a string describing the error number errnum. This string may be changed by subsequent calls to strerror. Useful for finding out what the values in errno mean.

9.17 Date and time

These functions deal with either 'elapsed' or 'calendar' time. They share the time.h header, which declares the functions as necessary and also the following:

CLK_TCK
> This is the number of 'ticks' per second returned by the clock function.

clock_t
time_t
> These are arithmetic types used to represent different forms of time.

struct tm
> This structure is used to hold the values representing a calendar time. It contains the following members, with the meanings as shown.

```
int tm_sec      /* seconds after minute [0-59] */
int tm_min      /* minutes after hour [0-59] */
int tm_hour     /* hours after midnight [0-23] */
int tm_mday     /* day of the month [1-31] */
int tm_mon      /* month of year [0-11] */
int tm_year     /* current year-1900 */
int tm_wday     /* days since Sunday [0-6] */
int tm_yday     /* days since January 1st [0-365] */
int tm_isdst    /* daylight savings indicator */
```

The tm_isdst member is positive if daylight saving time is in effect, zero if not and negative if that information is not available.

The time manipulation functions are the following:

```
#include <time.h>

clock_t clock(void);
double difftime(time_t time1, time_t time2);
time_t mktime(struct tm *timeptr);
time_t time(time_t *timer);
char *asctime(const struct tm *timeptr);
char *ctime(const time_t *timer);
struct tm *gmtime(const time_t *timer);
struct tm *localtime(const time_t *timer);
size_t strftime(char *s, size_t maxsize,
     const char *format,
     const struct tm *timeptr);
```

The functions asctime, ctime, gmtime, localtime, and strftime all share static data structures, either of type struct tm or char [], and calls to one of them may overwrite the data stored by a previous call to one of the others. If this is likely to cause problems, their users should take care to copy any values needed.

clock

Returns the best available approximation to the time used by the current invocation of the program, in 'ticks'. (clock_t) -1 is returned if no value is available. To find the actual time used by a run of a program, it is necessary to find the difference between the value at the start of the run and the time of interest – there is an implementation-defined constant factor which biases the value returned from clock.

difftime

This returns the difference in seconds between two calendar times.

mktime

This returns the calendar time corresponding to the values in a structure pointed to by timeptr, or (time_t) -1 if the value cannot be represented.

The tm_wday and tm_yday members of the structure are ignored, the other members are not restricted to their usual values. On successful conversion, the members of the structure are all set to appropriate values within their normal ranges. This function is useful to find out what value of a time_t corresponds to a known date and time.

time

Returns the best approximation to the current calendar time in an unspecified encoding. (time_t) -1 is returned if the time is not available.

asctime

Converts the time in the structure pointed to by timeptr into a string of the form

```
Sun Sep 16 01:03:52 1973\n\0
```

the example being taken from the Standard. The Standard defines the algorithm used, but the important point to notice is that all the fields within that string are of constant width and relevant to most English-speaking communities. The string is stored in a static structure which may be overwritten by a subsequent call to one of the other time-manipulation functions (see above).

ctime

Equivalent to asctime(localtime(timer));. See asctime for the return value.

gmtime

Returns a pointer to a struct tm set to represent the calendar time pointed to by timer. The time is expressed in terms of Greenwich Mean Time. A null pointer is returned if GMT is not available.

localtime

Converts the time pointed to by timer into local time and puts the results into a struct tm, returning a pointer to that structure.

strftime

Fills the character array pointed to by s with at most maxsize characters. The format string is used to format the time represented in the structure pointed to timeptr. Characters in the format string (including the terminating null) are copied unchanged into the array, unless one of the following format directives is found – then the value specified below is copied into the destination, *as appropriate to the locale*.

%a   abbreviated weekday name
%A   full weekday name
%b   abbreviated month name
%B   full month name
%c   date and time representation
%d   decimal day of month number 0–31
%H   hour 0–23
%I   hour 0–12
%j   day of year 1–366
%m   month 1–12
%M   minute 01–59
%p   local equivalent of 'AM' or 'PM'
%S   second 0–59
%U   week number in year 0–52 (Sunday is first day of week)
%w   weekday 0–6 (Sunday is 0)
%W   week number in year 0–52 (Monday is first day of week)
%x   local date representation
%X   local time representation
%y   year without century prefix 0–99

%Y   year with century prefix

%Z   timezone name, or no characters if no timezone exists

%%   a % character

Any unrecognized character following a % format indicator gives undefined behaviour.

The total number of characters copied into *s is returned, excluding the null. If there was not room (as determined by maxsize) for the trailing null, zero is returned.

9.18 Arguments to main

The use of arguments to main is a key feature of many hosted C programs. The Standard has enshrined the practice established long ago when C was only used with UNIX, and the declaration of main looks like this:

```
int main(int argc, char *argv[]);
```

The declaration of argv normally scares the wits out of people. It means that argv is an array of pointers to characters. By the normal rules about arguments whose type is *array* of anything, what actually gets passed to main is the address of the first element of the array. As a result, an equivalent (and widely used) declaration is

```
int main(int argc, char **argv);
```

When the program starts, the following conditions hold true:

- Argc is greater than zero.
- Argv[argc] is a null pointer.
- Argv[0] through to argv[argc-1] are pointers to strings with implementation defined meanings.
- Argv[0] is a string which contains the program's name, or is an empty string if the name isn't available. Remaining members of argv are the program's arguments. These are, of course, highly implementation specific. If there is only support for single-case characters, the contents of these strings will all be in lower case.

Program arguments are typically passed from an operating system's command interpreter or job control language.

The example below is a program which echoes its arguments to the standard output file.

```
#include <stdio.h>
#include <stdlib.h>

main(int argc, char **argv){
```

```
    while(argc--){
        printf("%s\n", *argv++);
    }
    exit(0);
}
```
                                                                    (E9.9)

If the program name is show_args and it has the arguments abcde text hello when it is run, the state of the arguments and the value of argv will be as shown in Figure 9.1.

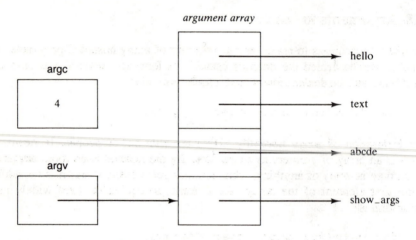

Figure 9.1   Arguments to a program

Each time that argv is incremented, it is stepped one item further along the array of arguments (see Figure 9.2). And so on.

On the system where this program was tested, a program is run by typing first its name, then the arguments, all separated by spaces, as a single line to the command processor. This is what happened (the $ symbol is a prompt):

```
$ show_args abcde text hello
show_args
abcde
text
hello
$
```

A more ambitious program follows, intended to illustrate at least a few of the library functions.

The program takes at least one argument, a string of text which we will call the **target**. If there are other arguments, they are taken to be the names of text files to be used in sequence as the **input**. If there are no such arguments, the program's

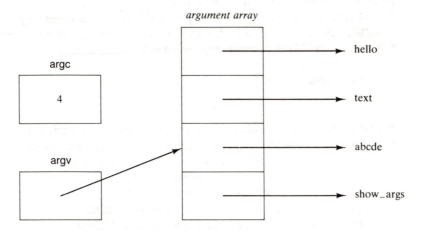

Figure 9.2   Arguments after incrementing `argv`

standard input is used instead.

The program reads the input one line at a time, with considerable effort spent on ensuring that arbitrarily long lines are handled as well as possible. Each line of input is inspected to see if it contains the target as a substring. If it does, the entire line is written to the program's standard output. If there is more than one input file, each line written out is preceded by its filename with a colon and a space appended to it.

The program exits with the following status values:

0   a match was found
1   no match was found
2   an error occurred

An error is defined to be one of the following:

- failure to open an input file
- error reading an input file
- error writing to the ouput
- missing target string (too few arguments)
- out of memory (extremely long input line)

An error message is written to the standard error stream if one of the error conditions is detected.

```
#include <stdio.h>
#include <stdlib.h>
#include <string.h>

/*
```

```
 * The input line can be very long,
 * malloc is used to allocate store as necessary.
 * LINE is the intial length allocated, and the amount
 * that the line grows by on each increment.
 */
#define LINE    50

/*
 * External variables. These are used to communicate
 * between main() and the function process() which
 * does the bulk of the work. This would be
 * an undesirable way of comunicating in a large
 * program; arguments would be tidier.
 * Note that variables (like these) with
 * static duration are always initialised to
 * zero at program start-up.
 */

char *infilename;      /* name of current input file */
char *target;          /* target string */
int matchfound;        /* true if any match in input */
int showname;          /* filename printed on a match */

/*
 * Declare functions (only one!)
 */
void process(FILE *fp);


int
main(int argc, char **argv){

    /* is target string present? */
    if(argc < 2){
        fprintf(stderr,"No target string\n");
        exit(2);
    }

    target = argv[1];

    /* Any filenames given? */
    if(argc == 2){
        infilename = "stdin";
        process(stdin);
    }
    else{
```

```
            /* process a file at a time */
            FILE *fp;
            int argcounter;

            /* more than one input filename? */
            showname = (argc > 3);
            /* index of first filename in argv */
            argcounter = 2;

            /*
             * while there are names left to process,
             * process them!
             */
            while(argv[argcounter]){
                infilename = argv[argcounter];
                if((fp = fopen(infilename, "r"))
                    == NULL){
                    perror(infilename);
                    exit(2);
                }
                process(fp);
                fclose(fp);
                argcounter++;
            }
        }
    if(matchfound)
        exit(0);
    exit(1);
}

void
process(FILE *fp){
    /* longest line so far */
    static int lineleng;

    /* address of line start */
    static char *line_p;

    /* space left in line */
    static int room;

    /* indicates a full line was read */
    int full_line;

    /* place to read in input line */
    char *readpoint;
```

```
        do{
            /*
             * If necessary, grow the line storage.
             * The statics initialise to zero, remember.
             */
            if(room < LINE){
                line_p = realloc(line_p, lineleng+LINE);
                /* this addition could overflow */
                lineleng += LINE;
                room += LINE;
                if(line_p == NULL){
                    fprintf(stderr,
                        "Input line too long\n");
                    exit(2);
                }
            }
            /*
             * Find place for data,
             * continue reading input.
             */
            readpoint = line_p+lineleng-room;
            if(fgets(readpoint, room, fp) == NULL){
                /* error or EOF */
                if(feof(fp)){
                    full_line = 1;
                }
                else{
                    perror(infilename);
                    exit(2);
                }
            }
            else{
                /* was end of line read? */
                while(*readpoint){
                    if(*readpoint == '\n'){
                        full_line = 1;
                        break;
                    }
                    readpoint++;
                    /* note less space left */
                    room--;
                }
            }
            if(full_line){
                if(strstr(line_p, target)){
                    matchfound = 1;
```

```
        if(showname)
            printf("%s: ", infilename);
        fputs(line_p, stdout);
        if(ferror(stdout)){
            perror("stdout");
            exit(2);
        }
    }
    full_line = 0;
    room = lineleng;
    /*
     * treat EOF the same as end of line.
     * If the last line in the file matched,
     * it would be printed again on EOF.
     * Put in a null.
     */
    *line_p = 0;
    }
}while(!feof(fp));
}
```
(E9.10)

9.19 Summary

It will almost certainly be the standardization of the run-time library that has the most effect on the portability of C programs. Prospective users of C really should read through this chapter carefully and familiarize themselves with its contents. The lack of a widely implemented, portable library has been the biggest single barrier to portability so far.

If you are writing programs for embedded systems, bad luck! The library is not defined for stand-alone applications, but in practice we can expect suppliers to produce a stand-alone library package too. It will probably come without the file handling, but there is no reason why, say, the string-handling functions should not work just as well in hosted and unhosted environments.

Answers to Exercises

Chapter 1

Exercise 1.2

```c
#include <stdio.h>

main(){
    int this_number, divisor, not_prime;
    int last_prime;

    this_number = 3;
    last_prime = 3;

    printf("1, 3 is a prime pair\n");

    while(this_number < 10000){
        divisor = this_number / 2;
        not_prime = 0;
        while(divisor > 1){
            if(this_number % divisor == 0){
                not_prime = 1;
                divisor = 0;
            }
            else
                divisor = divisor-1;
        }

        if(not_prime == 0){
            if(this_number == last_prime+2)
                printf("%d, %d is a prime pair\n",
                    last_prime, this_number);
            last_prime = this_number;
```

```
            }
            this_number = this_number + 1;
        }
        return(0);
    }
```

Exercise 1.3

```
    #include <stdio.h>

    main(){
        printf("Type in a string: ");
        printf("The value was: %d\n", getnum());
    }

    getnum(){
        int c, value;;

        value = 0;
        c = getchar();
        while(c != '\n'){
            value = 10*value + c - '0';
            c = getchar();
        }
        return (value);
    }
```

Exercise 1.4

```
    #include <stdio.h>

    /* array size */
    #define NUMBER   10

    main(){
        int arr[NUMBER], count, lo, hi;

        count = 0;
        while(count < NUMBER){
            printf("Type in a string: ");
            arr[count] = getnum();
            count = count+1;
        }
        lo = 0;
        while(lo < NUMBER-1){
```

```
            hi = lo+1;
            while(hi < NUMBER){
                int tmp;
                if(arr[lo] > arr[hi]){
                    tmp = arr[lo];
                    arr[lo] = arr[hi];
                    arr[hi] = tmp;
                }
                hi = hi + 1;
            }
            lo = lo + 1;
        }
        /* now print them */
        count = 0;
        while(count < NUMBER){
            printf("%d\n", arr[count]);
            count = count+1;
        }
        exit(0);
    }

getnum(){
    int c, value;;

    value = 0;
    c = getchar();
    while(c != '\n'){
        value = 10*value + c - '0';
        c = getchar();
    }
    return (value);
}
```

Exercise 1.5

```
#include <stdio.h>

/*
 * To print an int in binary, hex, decimal,
 * we build an array of characters and print it out
 * in order.
 * The values are found least significant digit first,
 * and printed most significant digit first.
 */
#define NDIG    32  /* assume max no. of digits */
```

```
int getnum(void);

main(){
     int val, i, count;
     char chars[NDIG];

     i = getnum();

     /* print in binary */
     val = i;
     count = 0;
     do{
          chars[count] = val % 2;
          val = val / 2;
          count = count + 1;
     }while(val);
     count = count - 1; /* just incremented above */

     while(count >= 0){
          printf("%d", chars[count]);
          count = count - 1;
     }
     printf("\n");

     /* print in decimal */
     val = i;
     count = 0;
     do{
          chars[count] = val % 10;
          val = val / 10;
          count = count + 1;
     }while(val);
     count = count - 1; /* just incremented above */

     while(count >= 0){
          printf("%d", chars[count]);
          count = count - 1;
     }
     printf("\n");

     /* print in hex */
     val = i;
     count = 0;
     do{
          chars[count] = val % 16;
          val = val / 16;
```

```
                count = count + 1;
        }while(val);
        count = count - 1; /* just incremented above */

        while(count >= 0){
            if(chars[count] < 10)
                printf("%d", chars[count]);
            else{
                /* assume 'A' - 'F' consecutive */
                chars[count] = chars[count]-10+'A';
                printf("%c", chars[count]);
            }
            count = count - 1;
        }
        printf("\n");
        exit(0);
}

getnum(){
        int c, value;;

        value = 0;
        c = getchar();
        while(c != '\n'){
            value = 10*value + c - '0';
            c = getchar();
        }
        return (value);
}
```

Chapter 2

Exercise 2.1

Trigraphs are used when the input device used, or the host system's native character set, do not support enough distinct characters for the full C language.

Exercise 2.2

Trigraphs would not be used in a system that has enough distinct characters to allocate a separate one to each of the C language symbols. For maximum portability, one might see a trigraph representation of a C program being distributed, on the grounds that most systems which do not use ASCII will be able to read ASCII coded data and translate it into their native codeset. A Standard C compiler could then compile such a program directly.

Exercise 2.3

White space characters are not equivalent to each other inside strings and character constants. Newline is special to the preprocessor.

Exercise 2.4

To continue a long line. Especially in systems that have an upper limit on physical line length.

Exercise 2.5

They become joined.

Exercise 2.6

Because the `*/` which apparently terminates the inner comment actually terminates the outer comment.

Exercise 2.7

31 characters for internal variables, six for external variables. The six character names must not rely on distinction between upper and lower case, either.

Exercise 2.8

A declaration introduces a name and a type for something. It does not necessarily reserve any storage.

Exercise 2.9

A definition is a declaration that also reserves storage.

Exercise 2.10

It is always the case that the largest range of values can be held in a `long double`, although it may not actually be any different from one of the smaller floating point types.

Exercise 2.11

The same answer holds true for the type with the greatest precision: `long double`. C does not permit the language implementor to use the same number of bits for, say, `double` and `long double`, then to allocate more bits for precision in one type and more for range in the other.

Exercise 2.12

There can never be problems assigning a shorter floating point type to a longer one.

Exercise 2.13

Assigning a longer floating type to a shorter one can result in overflow and undefined behaviour.

Exercise 2.14

Undefined behaviour is completely unpredictable. *Anything* may happen. Often, nothing seems to happen except that erroneous arithmetic values are produced.

Exercise 2.15

Signed int (by the integral promotions).

Exercise 2.16

This cannot be predicted without knowing about the implementation. If an int can hold all of the values of an unsigned char the result will be int, again by the integral promotions. Otherwise, it will have to be unsigned int.

Exercise 2.17

Unsigned int.

Exercise 2.18

Long.

Exercise 2.19

Long.

Exercise 2.20

Float.

Exercise 2.21

Float.

Exercise 2.22

Long double.

Exercise 2.23

```
i1 % i2
```

Exercise 2.24

```
i1 % (int)f1
```

Exercise 2.25

If either operand is negative, the sign is implementation defined, otherwise it is positive. This means that, even if both operands are negative, you can't predict the sign.

Exercise 2.26

Two – unary negate, binary subtract.

Exercise 2.27

```
i1 &= 0xf;
```

Exercise 2.28

```
i1 |= 0xf;
```

Exercise 2.29

```
i1 &= ~0xf;
```

Exercise 2.30

```
i1 = ((i2 >> 4) & 0xf) | ((i2 & 0xf) << 4);
```

Exercise 2.31

The result is unpredictable. You must never use the same variable more than once in an expression if the expression changes its value.

Exercise 2.32

```
(c = (( u * f) + 2.6L);
(int = ((float) + long double);
(int = (long double));
(int);
```

Note: the integral promotion of char to int might be to unsigned int, depending on the implementation.

Exercise 2.33

```
(u += (((--f) / u) % 3));
(unsigned += ((float / unsigned) % int));
(unsigned += (float % int));
(unsigned += float);
(unsigned);
```

Exercise 2.34

```
(i <<= (u * (- (++f))));
(int <<= (unsigned * (- float)));
(int <<= (unsigned * float));
(int <<= float);
(int);
```

The rules for the shift operators state the right-hand operand is always converted to int. However, this does not affect the result, whose type is always determined by the type of the left-hand operand. This is doubly so for the current example, since an assignment operator is being used.

Exercise 2.35

```
(u = (((i + 3) + 4) + 3.1));
```

The rules state that the subexpressions involving + can be arbitrarily regrouped, as long as no type changes would be introduced. The types are:

```
(unsigned = (((int + int) + int) + double))
```

so the leftmost two additions can be regrouped. Working from the left:

```
(unsigned = ((int + int) + double));
(unsigned = (int + double));
(unsigned = double);
(unsigned);
```

Exercise 2.36

```
(u = (((3.1 + i) + 3 ) + 4));
```

See the comments above on regrouping.

```
(unsigned = (((double + int) + int) + int));
```

The two rightmost additions can be regrouped.

```
(unsigned = ((double + int) + int));
(unsigned = (double + int));
(unsigned = double);
(unsigned);
```

Exercise 2.37

```
(c = ((i << (- (--f))) & 0xf));
(char = ((int <<  (- (--float))) & int ));
(char = ((int << (- float)) & int ));
(char = ((int << float) & int));
(char = (int & int));
(char);
```

Chapter 3

Exercise 3.1

They all give an int result with a value of 1 for true and 0 for false.

Exercise 3.2

They all give an int result with a value of 1 for true and 0 for false.

Exercise 3.3

They guarantee an order of evaluation: left to right, and stop as soon as the overall result can be determined.

Exercise 3.4

Break can be used to turn a switch statement into a set of exclusive choices of action.

Exercise 3.5

Continue has no special meaning in a switch statement, but only to an outer do, while or for statement.

Exercise 3.6

Inside a while statement, the use of continue may cause the update of the loop control variable to be missed. It is, of course, the responsibility of the programmer to get this right.

Exercise 3.7

Because the scope of a label doesn't extend outside the function that it lives in, you can't use goto to jump from one function to another. Using the longjmp library routine, described in Chapter 9, a form of function-to-function jump is supported, but not a completely general one.

Chapter 4

Exercise 4.1

```
#include <stdio.h>
#include <stdlib.h>

main(){
    int i, abs_val(int);;

    for(i = -10; i <= 10; i++)
        printf("abs of %d is %d\n", i, abs_val(i));
}

int
abs_val(int x){

    if(x < 0)
        return(-x);
    return(x);
}
```

Exercise 4.2

There are two files that form the answer to this exercise. This is the first.

```
#include <stdio.h>
#include <stdlib.h>

int curr_line(void), curr_col(void);
void output(char);
```

```
main () {
    printf ("line %d\n", curr_line ());
    printf ("column %d\n", curr_col ());

    output ('a');
    printf ("column %d\n", curr_col ());

    output ('\n');
    printf ("line %d\n", curr_line ());
    printf ("column %d\n", curr_col ());
    exit (0);
}
```

The second file contains the functions and static variables.

```
#include <stdio.h>

int curr_line (void), curr_col (void);
void output (char);

static int lineno=1, colno=1;

int
curr_line (void) {
    return (lineno);
}

int
curr_col (void) {
    return (colno);
}

void
output (char a) {
    putchar (a);
    colno++;
    if (a == '\n') {
        colno = 1;
        lineno++;
    }
}
```

Exercise 4.3

The recursive function:

```
#include <stdio.h>
#include <stdlib.h>

void recur(void);

main(){
    recur();
    exit(0);
}

void
recur(void){
    static ntimes;

    ntimes++;
    if(ntimes < 100)
        recur();
    printf("%d\n", ntimes);
    ntimes--;
}
```

Exercise 4.4

And finally, the largest of all of the answers.

```
#include <stdio.h>
#include <stdlib.h>

#define PI 3.141592
#define INCREMENT (PI/20)
#define DELTA .0001

double sine(double), cosine(double);
static unsigned int fact(unsigned int n);
static double pow(double x, unsigned int n);

main(){
    double arg = 0;

    for(arg = 0; arg <= PI; arg += INCREMENT){
        printf("value %f\tsine %f\tcosine %f\n", arg,
            sine(arg), cosine(arg));
    }
    exit(0);
}
```

```
static unsigned int
fact(unsigned int n){
    unsigned int answer;

    answer = 1;
    while(n > 1)
        answer *= n--;

    return(answer);
}

static double
pow(double x, unsigned int n){
    double answer;

    answer = 1;
    while(n){
        answer *= x;
        n--;
    }
    return(answer);
}

double
sine(double x){
    double difference, thisval, lastval;
    unsigned int term;
    int sign;

    sign = -1;
    term = 3;

    thisval = x;
    do{
        lastval = thisval;
        thisval = lastval + pow(x, term)/fact(term)
            * sign;
        term += 2;
        sign = -sign;
        difference = thisval - lastval;
        if(difference < 0)
            difference = -difference;
    }while(difference >  DELTA && term < 16);

    return(thisval);
}
```

```
double
cosine (double x) {
      double difference, thisval, lastval;
      unsigned int term;
      int sign;

      sign = -1;
      term = 2;

      thisval = 1;
      do {
            lastval = thisval;
            thisval = lastval + pow(x, term)/fact(term)
                  * sign;
            term += 2;
            sign = -sign;
            difference = thisval - lastval;
            if (difference < 0)
                  difference = -difference;
      } while (difference >  DELTA && term < 16);

      return (thisval);
}
```

Chapter 5

Exercise 5.1

0-9.

Exercise 5.2

Nothing. It is guaranteed to be a valid address and can be used to check a pointer against the end of the array.

Exercise 5.3

Only when they point into the same array, or to the same object.

Exercise 5.4

It can safely be used to hold the value of a pointer to any sort of object.

a)
```
      int
      st_eq(const char *s1, const char * s2) {
```

```
        while(*s1 && *s2 && (*s1 == *s2)){
            s1++; s2++;
        }

        return(*s1-*s2);
    }
```

b)
```
    const char *
    find_c(char c, const char *cp){

        while(*cp && *cp != c)
            cp++;
        if(*cp)
            return(cp);

        return(0);
    }
```

c)
```
    const char *
    sub_st(const char *target, const char *sample){

        /*
         * Try for a substring starting with
         * each character in sample.
         */
        while(*sample){
            const char *targ_p, *sample_p;

            targ_p = target;
            sample_p = sample;
            /* string compare */
            while(*targ_p && *sample_p
                && (*targ_p == *sample_p)){
                targ_p++; sample_p++;
            }
            /*
             * If at end of target, have substring!
             */
            if(*targ_p == 0)
                return(sample);
            /* otherwise try next place */
            sample++;
        }
        return(0);   /* no match */
    }
```

Exercise 5.5

No answer can be given.

Chapter 6

Exercise 6.1

```
struct {
    int a,b;
};
```

Exercise 6.2

Without a tag or any variables defined, the structure declaration is of little use. It cannot be referred to later.

Exercise 6.3

```
struct int_struc{
    int a,b;
}x,y;
```

Exercise 6.4

```
struct int_struc z;
```

Exercise 6.5

```
p = &z;
p->a = 0;
```

Exercise 6.6

Explicitly, for example

```
struct x;
```

or implicitly,

```
struct x *p;
```

when no outer declaration exists.

Exercise 6.7

It is not treated as a pointer, but as a short-hand way of initializing the individual array elements.

Exercise 6.8

Nothing unusual at all, the string is treated as a literal constant of type `const char *`.

Exercise 6.9

Yes. It is easier!

Chapter 7

Exercise 7.1

```
#define MAXLEN 100
```

Exercise 7.2

In expressions, there may be precedence problems. A safer definition would be `#define VALUE (100+MAXLEN)`.

Exercise 7.3

```
#define REM(a,b)  ((a)%(b))
```

Exercise 7.4

```
#define REM(a,b)  ((long)(a)%(long)(b))
```

Exercise 7.5

It generally signifies a library header file.

Exercise 7.6

It generally signifies a private header file.

Exercise 7.7

By using the conditional compilation directives. Examples are shown in the text.

Exercise 7.8

Long int or unsigned long int, using the arithmetic environment provided
by the translator, not the target.

Index